Journal of Semitic Studies Supplement 18

MULLĀ ṢADRĀ SHĪRĀZĪ: HIS LIFE AND WORKS AND THE SOURCES FOR SAFAVID PHILOSOPHY

by

Sajjad H. Rizvi

Published by Oxford University Press
on behalf of the University of Manchester
2007

OXFORD JOURNALS
OXFORD UNIVERSITY PRESS

Great Clarendon Street, Oxford OX2 6DP

Oxford University Press is a department of the University of Oxford.
It furthers the University's objective of excellence in research, scholarship,
and education by publishing worldwide in

Oxford New York

Athens Auckland Bangkok Bogotá Buenos Aires Cape Town
Chennai Dar es Salaam Delhi Florence Hong Kong Istanbul Karachi
Kolkata Kuala Lumpur Madrid Melbourne Mexico City Mumbai Nairobi
Paris São Paulo Shanghai Singapore Taipei Tokyo Toronto Warsaw

with associated companies in Berlin Ibadan

Published in the United Kingdom
by Oxford University Press, Oxford

First published 2007

A catalogue for this book is available from the British Library

Library of Congress Cataloguing in Publication Data
(Data available)

ISSN 0022-4480
ISBN 0-19-929742-8
ISBN 978-0-19-929742-9

Subscription information for the *Journal of Semitic Studies* is available at the journal website:
jss.oupjournals.org

Printed in Great Britain by Bell & Bain Ltd, Glasgow

Contents

Preface iv

Abbreviations v

Figures vii

Chapter 1
Mullā Ṣadrā – a 'Life' in Progress 1
Appendix I
The Harrassment of Mullā Ṣadrā 31
Appendix II
Mullā Ṣadrā and the Akhbāriyya – some notes 37
Appendix III
Commentaries on *al-Kāfī* of al-Kulaynī in the Safavid Period 47

Chapter 2
An Annotated Bibliography of the Works of Mullā Ṣadrā 51
Appendix IV
The Personal Library of Mullā Ṣadrā 117

Chapter 3 Sources on Safavid Intellectual History 137

Guide to Further Reading on Mullā Ṣadrā 177

Index of Qur'ānic Citations 181
Index of Ḥadīth Citations 182
Index of Persons, Groups and Places 183

Preface

The present work is designed to act as a research aid for those interested in the intellectual history of the Safavid period, in particular the thought associated with the most eminent philosopher of the reign of Shah ʿAbbās I, namely Mullā Ṣadrā Shīrāzī. It is not a study of the complete cultural and intellectual content of the Safavid period nor indeed of the thought of its most illustrious exponent; for the latter, I would direct readers to my forthcoming work *Mullā Ṣadrā: Philosopher of Mystics* (Cambridge 2008). In Chapter 1, I construct an intellectual biography of Mullā Ṣadrā based on a wide range of sources on the Safavid period that were at my disposal, including works in manuscript. Chapter 2 is a complete descriptive bibliography of his works including details of the most important manuscripts especially for those works that are still in search of an editor to produce a critical text. Chapter 3 is an examination of the sources for the intellectual history of the Safavid period prefaced by some comments on methodology and the conception of philosophical traditions. In this chapter, I consider in more detail the sources that I have used in Chapter 1 to demonstrate their efficacy as witnesses to the intellectual contexts and history of the time.

I would like to thank Dr Andreas Christmann for his encouragement and for recommending this work for publication, and the editorial committee of the *Journal of Semitic Studies* for accepting it for their supplement series. I do not have the words to express my gratitude to my wife Sarwat for her patience; a special thanks is due to Qaisar Iskander for his assistance for the formatting.

Common place-names are not fully transliterated but others are, e.g. Tehran, Isfahan, Shiraz, Mashhad, but Kirmān, Zanjān, Qazwīn. Some common anglicised words are not fully transliterated, such as Shah, Shiʿi, Imam, mujtahid, Shariʿa.

Waʾl-tawfīq min Allāh,

Sajjad Hayder Rizvi
London

Abbreviations

AA	Al-Ḥurr al-ʿĀmilī, *Amal al-āmil*, ed. S. A. al-Ḥusaynī (2 vols, Najaf 1966).
Al-Dharīʿa	Āqā Buzurg al-Ṭihrānī, *al-Dharīʿa ilā taṣānīf al-Shīʿa* (26 vols, Najaf 1939–87).
Aʿyān	Muḥsin al-Amīn, *Aʿyān al-Shīʿa*, ed. Ḥ. al-Amīn (10 vols, Beirut 1986).
Barakat	Muḥammad Barakat, *Kitābshināsī-yi falsafī-yi Maktab-i Shīrāz* (Shiraz 1382 Sh/2003).
Biḥār	Muḥammad Bāqir Majlisī, *Biḥār al-anwār* (111 vols, Beirut 1983).
BSOAS	*Bulletin of the School of Oriental and African Studies.*
EI^2	*Encyclopaedia of Islam* (Second edition), gen. eds. H. A. R. Gibb et al (11 vols, Leiden 1954–2004).
EIr	*Encyclopaedia Iranica*, gen. ed. E. Yarshater (New York 1979–).
GAL	C. Brockelmann, *Geschichte der arabischen Literatur* (2 vols, and 3 suppl, Leiden 1937–42, 1943–9).
H	Hijrī qamarī (Anno Hegirae lunar).
IBM	Iskandar Beg Munshī, *Tārīkh-i ʿĀlam-ārāʾ-yi ʿAbbāsī*, ed. Īraj Afshār (2 vols, Tehran 1350 Sh/1971).
IJMES	*International Journal of Middle East Studies.*
Iran	*Iran: the Journal of the British Institute of Persian Studies.*
IS	*Iranian Studies.*
JAOS	*Journal of the American Oriental Society.*
JIS	*Journal of Islamic Studies.*
JNES	*Journal of Near Eastern Studies.*
JRAS	*Journal of the Royal Asiatic Society (London)*, 3rd series.
Kashf	Ḥājjī Khalīfa, *Kashf al-ẓunūn ʿan asāmī al-kutub waʾl-funūn*, ed. G. Flügel (2 vols, London 1858).
KH	Muḥammad Khāminihī, *Mullā Ṣadrā: zindagī, shakhṣiyyat va*

	maktab-i Ṣadr al-muta'allihīn (Tehran 1379 Sh/2000).
LB	Yūsuf al-Baḥrānī, *Lu'lu'at al-Baḥrayn*, ed. M. Ṣ. Āl Baḥr al-ʿUlūm (Najaf 1966).
Mahdavi	Yaḥyā Mahdavī, *Fihrist-i nuskha-hā-yi muṣannafāt-i Ibn Sīnā* (Tehran 1954).
MAS	*Modern Asian Studies.*
MM	Mīrāth-i Maktūb, a major publishing house based in Tehran.
MT	Hossein Modarressi Tabataba'i, *An Introduction to Shīʿī Law* (London 1984).
QU	Muḥammad Tunikābunī, *Qiṣaṣ al-ʿulamā'* (Tehran lithograph 1888).
RU	ʿAbd Allāh Afandī, *Riyāḍ al-ʿulamā' wa-ḥiyāḍ al-fuḍalā'*, ed. S. A. al-Ḥusaynī (6 vols, Qum 1981).
Rawḍāt	Muḥammad Bāqir Khwānsārī, *Rawḍāt al-jannāt fī aḥwāl al-ʿulamā' wa'l-sādāt* (8 vols, Beirut 1991).
rpt	Reprint
SA	Sayyid ʿAlī-Khān Ibn Maʿṣūm Madanī Shīrāzī, *Sulāfat al-ʿaṣr fī maḥāsin al-shuʿarā' bi-kulli miṣr* (Cairo 1324/1906).
Ṣadrā	*Khiradnāma-yi Ṣadrā*, the journal of the Bunyād-i Ḥikmat-i Islāmī-yi Ṣadrā (Tehran).
SI	*Studia Islamica.*
SIr	*Studia Iranica.*
SIPRIn	Sadra Islamic Philosophy Research Institute/ Bunyād-i Ḥikmat-i Islāmī-yi Ṣadrā (Tehran).
Sh	Hijrī Shamsī (Anno Hegirae solar).
ZDMG	*Zeitschrift der deutschen morgenländischen Gesellschaft.*

Figures

Figure 1. The School of Mullā Ṣadrā 20

Figure 2. The School of Isfahan 139

Figure 3. The Dashtakī family of philosophers 141

Figure 4.1 The School of Shiraz 143

Figure 4.2. The School of Shiraz 144

Chapter 1
Mullā Ṣadrā – a 'Life' in Progress

Muḥammad b. Ibrāhīm b. Yaḥyā al-Qawāmī al-Shīrāzī [1] known as *Ṣadr al-muta'allihīn* (Master of the theosists) [2] and popularly known as Mullā Ṣadrā still remains relatively unknown in Islamic intellectual history. [3] Arguably the most important Islamic philosopher after Avicenna and the 'greatest philosopher of modern times in Persia' according to Edward Browne, [4] his ideas have yet to find an appropriate exposition in academic works and an engaged and critical audience. He became famous as the thinker who revolutionised the doctrine of existence in Islamic metaphysics and extended the shift from Aristotelian substance metaphysics to Neoplatonic process metaphysics of change. A keen thinker who wrote works in

---

[1] In his various works he describes himself as follows [for bibliographical details of the works, see Chapter 2]:

Muḥammad known as Ṣadr al-Dīn al-Shīrāzī – *Asfār*, I, 1; *al-Shawāhid*, 4; *al-Mashā'ir*, 2; *al-Tashakhkhuṣ*, 120; *Mutashābihāt*, 75; *Tafsīr Sūrat al-wāqi'a*, 131; *Tafsīr Sūrat al-Ṭāriq*, 145.

Muḥammad b. Ibrāhīm known as Ṣadr al-Dīn al-Shīrāzī – *Sharḥ al-hidāya*, 1.

Muḥammad b. Ibrāhīm b. Yaḥyā known as Ṣadr-i al-Shīrāzī – *Sih Aṣl* (Nasr), 1.

Muḥammad known as Ṣadr al-Dīn b. Ibrāhīm al-Qawāmī – *Tafsīr Sūrat al-Jum'a*, VII, 136.

[2] This title is first attested in a marginal note in a manuscript dated 1039/1630 of *al-Shawāhid al-rubūbiyya* on the issue of the unity of the subject and object of intellection; see Muḥaqqiq Dāmād, 'Fawā'id dar masā'il va mafāhīm-i ḥikmiyya', *Ṣadrā* 5 and 6 (1376 Sh/1997), 61. The term *ta'alluh* (from which *muta'allih* is derived) denotes an Arabic naturalisation of the Hellenic notion of *theosis*, the Platonic goal of philosophy as the attempt to become like God that is rooted in commentaries and understandings of the famous passage in *Theætetus* 176 on 'becoming god as far as possible' (*homoiōsis theōi kata to dunaton=al-tashabbuh bi'l-Bāri' ḥasab al-ṭāqa al-bashariyya*). See David Sedley, 'The idea of godlikeness', in Gail Fine (ed.), *Plato 2: Ethics, Politics, Religion and the Soul* (Oxford 1999), 309–28; Julia Annas, *Platonic Ethics, Old and New* (Ithaca, NY 1999), Ch. 3; J. Dürlinger, 'Ethics and the divine life in Plato's philosophy', *Journal of Religious Ethics* 13 (1985), 312–31; John M. Armstrong, 'After the ascent: Plato on becoming like God', *Oxford Studies in Ancient Philosophy* 26 (2004), 171–83.

[3] For short introductions to his life and thought, see Sajjad Rizvi, 'Mollā Ṣadrā', *EIr* forthcoming [available at http://www.iranica.com]; John Cooper, 'Mulla Sadra', *Routledge Encyclopaedia of Philosophy* 6: 595–9; S. H. Nasr, 'Mullā Ṣadrā: his teachings', in S. H. Nasr and O. Leaman (eds), *History of Islamic Philosophy* (London 1996), I, 643–62.

[4] E. G. Browne, *A History of Persian Literature IV* (Cambridge 1924), 408.

philosophy, theology, mysticism and scriptural exegesis, he attempted a wide-ranging synthesis of approaches to Islamic thought and argued for the necessity of the method of understanding reality through a mixture of logical reasoning, spiritual inspiration and a deep meditation upon the key scriptural sources of the Twelver Shiʿi tradition.[5] A key figure of a group of thinkers whom Seyyed Hossein Nasr and Henry Corbin [d. 1978] dubbed the 'school of Isfahan',[6] he played a major role in the intellectual life of the Safavid renaissance under Shah ʿAbbās I [d. 1039/1629] and later in life was the most important teacher at the Madrasa-yi Khān in his home town of Shiraz. In the Safavid period he was also one of the foremost proponents of a revival of Neoplatonic concerns in intellectual inquiry. Given his significance (which Nasr signalled with characteristic exaggeration by noting that Mullā Ṣadrā is 'a household name in Persia, Afghanistan and India'),[7] it is perhaps therefore ironic that we know so little about his life, family, social intercourse and historical context. This is a familiar state of affairs to those engaged in the study of Islamic intellectual history. Pre-modern intellectuals did not live in the glare of media attention; nor did scholarship and antiquarian interest produce a scrutiny of the minute trivia of lives.

The standard biographical and historiographical sources reveal very little about his life.[8] Modern biographies have similarly failed to add much to what we

---

[5] It has recently been argued that his synthesis was preceded by two other important Shiʿi thinkers: Ṣāʾin al-Dīn Ibn Turka Iṣfahānī [d. ca. 835/1432] – see Hossein Ziai, 'Recent trends in Arabic and Persian philosophy', in P. Adamson and R. Taylor (eds), *The Cambridge Companion to Arabic Philosophy* (Cambridge 2005), 413–5, and the major work of Ibn Turka, *Tamhīd al-qawāʿid*, ed. S. J. Āshtiyānī (Tehran 1977); and Ibn Abī Jumhūr al-Aḥsāʾī [d. 906/1501] – see Sabine Schmidtke, *Theologie, Philosophie und Mystik im zwölferschiitischen Islam des 9./15. Jahrhunderts: Die Gedankenwelt des Ibn Abī Ǧumhūr al-Aḥsāʾī* (Islamic Philosophy, Theology and Science Texts and Studies vol. XXXIX, Leiden 2000), and his major work *al-Mujlī mirʾāt al-munjī fiʾl-kalām waʾl-ḥikmatayn waʾl-taṣawwuf*, ed. Sayyid Aḥmad Shīrāzī (Tehran 1329/1911).

[6] See the beginning of Chapter 3.

[7] Seyyed Hossein Nasr, *Sadr al-Din al-Shirazi and his Transcendent Theosophy* (Tehran 1977), 12.

[8] I have consulted the following sources (in rough chronological order):

Al-Ḥurr al-ʿĀmilī [d. 1693], *Amal al-āmil*, ed. S. A. al-Ḥusaynī (Najaf 1966), I, 233.

Al-Majlisī [d. 1699], *Biḥār al-anwār*, CVI, 130–1: 'the most learned of his time in philosophy and proficient in the other disciplines'.

Sayyid ʿAlī-Khān Ibn Maʿṣūm Madanī Shīrāzī [d. ca. 1707], *Sulāfat al-ʿaṣr fī maḥāsin al-shuʿarāʾ bi-kulli miṣr* (Cairo 1324/1906), 499.

ʿAbd Allāh Afandī [d. ca. 1717–8], *Riyāḍ al-ʿulamāʾ wa-ḥiyāḍ al-fuḍalāʾ*, ed. S. A. al-Ḥusaynī (Qum 1981), V, 15.

Yūsuf al-Baḥrānī [d. 1772], *Luʾluʾat al-Baḥrayn*, ed. M. Ṣ. Āl Baḥr al-ʿUlūm (Najaf 1966), 131–2.

Riḍā-qulī-Khān Hidāyat [d. 1871], *Tadhkira-yi Riyāḍ al-ʿārifīn* (Tehran 1937), 375–6.

Muḥammad Kashmīrī Lakhnawī [d. 1892], *Nujūm al-samāʾ* (Lucknow lithograph 1303/1885–6), 82.

Muḥammad Tunikābunī [d. ca. 1892], *Qiṣaṣ al-ʿulamāʾ* (Tehran lithograph 1888), 109.

already know.[9] No doubt the construction of a discursive and coherent life is not always of prime importance to the compilers of biographical dictionaries: details of his life were thus less important than his lived presence that gave authority to his ideas and legacy. As Hayden White once said, 'no-one and nothing lives a story', so we ought to beware of neatly packaged lives if we find them.[10] The attempt made in this chapter to present a life of Mullā Ṣadrā should thus been seen as a work in progress, a picture that emerges hazily from the sketchy connections made between points that themselves are at times rather speculative.[11] Manuscript evidence, letters, notes in little-known codices and evidence from his own works will be adduced to give form to the picture and flesh to the character. An examination of his life may contribute to our understanding of the linguistic and intellectual context in which his work was composed, and give us insights into the character and thought of a theosist sage (*ḥakīm muta'allih*), as he called himself.[12] The lived experience of a thinker cannot be divorced from his thought and his writing, although one hesitates to say that it may determine them.[13] Rather, it may be said that for a philosopher, his work is his

---

Muḥammad Bāqir Khwānsārī [d. 1895], *Rawḍāt al-jannāt fī aḥwāl al-ʿulamāʾ waʾl-sādāt* (Beirut 1991), IV, 117–9.

Mīrzā Ḥasan Fasāʾī [d. 1898], *Fārsnāma-yi Nāṣirī*, ed. M. Rustigār (Tehran 1367 Sh/1988), II, 1144–5.

Maʿṣūm-ʿAlī-Shāh Shīrāzī [d. 1926], *Ṭarāʾiq al-ḥaqāʾiq*, ed. M. J. Maḥjūb (Tehran 1339 Sh/1960), I, 181–3.

ʿAbbās Qummī [d. 1941], *al-Fawāʾid al-Raḍawiyya fī aḥwāl ʿulamāʾ madhhab al-Jaʿfariyya* (Qum 1980), 378–81.

Muḥsin al-Amīn [d. 1952], *Aʿyān al-Shīʿa*, ed. Ḥ. al-Amīn (Beirut 1986), IX, 321–30.

Mudarris Tabrīzī [d. 1954], *Rayḥānat al-adab* (Tehran 1326–33 Sh/1947–54), III, 417–20.

Āqā Buzurg Ṭihrānī [d. 1970], *Ṭabaqāt aʿlām al-Shīʿa* (Qum 1372 Sh/1993), VI, 378–81.

ʿAbd Allāh Niʿma, *Falāsifat al-Shīʿa* (Beirut 1965), 346–66.

[9] The notable exception is KH, a creative and thoughtful account. My reliance upon it is quite clear.

[10] Hayden White, *Tropics of Discourse* (Baltimore, MD 1978), 111.

[11] My previous attempt has some mistakes and represents an earlier stage of my thought on his life – 'Reconsidering the life of Mullā Ṣadrā Shīrāzī', *Iran* 40 (2002), 181–201.

[12] *Tafsīr sūrat al-Baqara* in *Tafsīr*, II, 29.

[13] I am thus a soft contextualist and resistant to the determinism implicit in the hard contextualism of Quentin Skinner expressed in a number of works since the 1960s and summarised in his statements 'a rational agent will be someone who … believes what he or she ought to believe', and 'the understanding of texts presupposes the grasp of what they were intended to mean and how that meaning was intended to be taken' in *Visions of Politics I* (Cambridge 2002), 31, 86. For an alternative approach that eschews conventionalism and contextualism for a holistic approach to coherence, see Mark Bevir, *The Logic of the History of Ideas* (Cambridge 1999), especially 125: 'Historians should justify their theories by comparing them with their rivals by reference to criteria of accuracy, comprehensiveness, consistency, progressiveness, fruitfulness and openness'; idem, 'Mind and method in the history of ideas', *History and Theory* 36 (1997), 167–89; idem, 'Meaning and intention: a defence of procedural individualism', *New Literary History* 31 (2000), 385–403.

life (and for one with Neoplatonic tastes arguably the life of an ensouled body has no significance). Porphyry [d. 309] reported, with some hyperbole indicative of the Neoplatonic disdain for the body, that his famous teacher Plotinus [d. 270]

> seemed ashamed of being in the body. So deeply rooted was this feeling that he could never be induced to tell of his ancestry, his parentage, or his birthplace. He showed, too, an unconquerable reluctance to sit to a painter or a sculptor and when Amelius persisted in urging him to allow of a portrait being made he asked him, "Is it not enough to carry about this image in which nature has enclosed us? Do you really think I must also consent to leave, as a desirable spectacle to posterity, an image of this image?"[14]

Despite this obstacle, I hope to demonstrate that one can successfully read his works to deduce evidence for his life beyond the text. Although I have indicated some avenues for further investigation, I hope that I have not indulged in unsubstantiated speculation but rather answered some queries and raised further ones that may form the basis for future research. This present work is yet a further step along the way to producing a complete and far more satisfactory intellectual biography which can only be constructed once we have much more of his work available to study, know more about his life and the sources that mention or allude to it, and once we have at hand a sophisticated and feasible hermeneutics for the study of early modern Islamic texts.[15] In attempting to provide a narrative structure to his life, to start 'his-story' at the beginning, we begin with his birth.

---

[14] Porphyry, *Life of Plotinus* 1.2–5 in Plotinus, *Enneads*, tr. S. MacKenna (London 1991), cii. As ironies go, Porphyry reports in the next section the intestinal ailments from which Plotinus suffered! For a discussion of Neoplatonic disdain for the body, see Stephen R. L. Clark, 'Plotinus: Body and soul', in L. P. Gerson (ed.), *The Cambridge Companion to Plotinus* (Cambridge 1996), 288–91.

[15] This is not to say that attempts have not been made to produce such a hermeneutics; see Henry Corbin, *The Concept of Comparative Philosophy*, tr. P. Russell (Ipswich 1981); idem, 'De Heidegger à Sohravardī', in C. Jambet (ed.), *Cahiers de l'Herne: Henry Corbin* (Paris 1981), 23–56; Todd Lawson, 'Hermeneutics', *EIr* XII, 235–9. For a method that proposes an 'esoteric' reading of medieval philosophical texts suggesting that the apparent meaning hides the author's intent due to his fear of persecution, see Leo Strauss, *Persecution and the Art of Writing* (New York 1952), and its critique in Oliver Leaman, *An Introduction to Medieval Islamic Philosophy* (Cambridge 1985), 182–201. For a good survey of various approaches to the study of Islamic philosophical texts, see Dimitri Gutas, 'The study of Arabic philosophy in the twentieth century', *British Journal of Middle East Studies* 29 (2002), 5–25.

I Early Life

A sole son and heir, Mullā Ṣadrā was born into a noble family of Shiraz in 979/1571–2. This date is deduced from evidence in his works. In his commentary on *ḥadīth* 239 of the *kitāb al-tawḥīd* of the *Uṣūl* section of *al-Kāfī*, the pre-eminent early Twelver Shiʿi *ḥadīth* collection, he states that he came to an understanding of the issue late in life when he was sixty-five years old.[16] We know that his commentary (at least as much as he completed) was composed by the year 1044/1634–5,[17] so we can deduce that he was born sixty-five lunar years before that, i.e. in 979/1571–2. Similarly, in his commentary on *Sūrat al-Ṭāriq* verse 14 (Qurʾān 86:14), he addresses himself:

> O [my] soul, abandon your caprice and travel the paths of your Lord with guidance. Has not your time come now? You are no longer young so why have you not yet become aware? You have reached the age of fifty but have not yet stepped from your threshold towards the stations of the sanctified ones.[18]

At the end of the commentary on this chapter, he tells us that he completed it on the last Friday of Rajab 1030 (which would have fallen on 27 Rajab/18 June 1621).[19] This yields a birth date late in the lunar year 979 or early 980. A marginal completion date on his autograph of *al-Mashāʿir* (MS Tehran University Central Library 7698) attests that he completed it 'on Friday afternoon 7 Jumāda I 1037/14 January 1628, when this writer has completed fifty-eight years of his life'. This also yields the lunar year 979.[20]

His father, Ibrāhīm b. Yaḥyā Qawāmī, was a court official. A modern biographer Khājavī claims without any evidence that he was the governor of Shiraz but an examination of the historiographical sources will show this to be without foundation.[21] The governor of the province of Fārs in the sixteenth century was usually a Safavid prince and at the time of the birth of Mullā Ṣadrā, was Muḥammad

---

[16] *Sharḥ Uṣūl al-Kāfī*, III, 101.

[17] *Sharḥ Uṣūl al-Kāfī*, II, 386.

[18] *Tafsīr*, VII, 354.

[19] *Tafsīr*, VII, 359.

[20] The first person in modern times to arrive at this date based on the manuscript evidence was the late philosopher Sayyid Muḥammad Ḥusayn Ṭabāṭabāʾī [d. 1981] as cited by Henry Corbin in his Introduction to *al-Mashāʿir*, 2.

[21] Muḥammad Khājavī, *Lavāmiʿ al-ʿārifīn* (Tehran 1367 Sh/1988), 27.

Khudābanda, the younger son of Shah Ṭahmāsp [d. 984/1576].[22] The governor of the city of Shiraz was a notable from an established local family of repute, Abū Isḥāq Injū, and one local source suggests that Ibrāhīm was his vizier.[23] Roger Savory incorrectly assumes that he was actually the vizier of the Queen of Shah Muḥammad Khudābanda [d. 995/1587], Khayr al-Nisā᾽ Begum, known as Mahd-i ʿUlyā, the real power-broker from the death of Shah Ṭahmāsp to her own assassination in Jumāda I 987/July 1579.[24] However, it seems that Savory has mistaken Ibrāhīm Qawāmī for Mīr Qawām al-Dīn Shīrāzī, the financial controller of the province and a significant member of the entourage of the Queen, an odd mistake given that their names are barely similar.[25] The actual vizier of the Queen was Mīrzā Salmān Jābirī [d. 991/1583],[26] the father-in-law of the prince Sulṭān Ḥamza [d. 994/1586].[27]

As an only child of an influential personage, Mullā Ṣadrā was no doubt indulged. It is a familiar trope of historical writing that the birth and circumstances surrounding a great individual are often auspicious, a divine boon after disappointments and frustrations. One nineteenth century account given by the philosopher ʿAlī Zunūzī [d. 1307/1889–90] presents the legend thus:

> His [Mullā Ṣadrā] father was an important vizier but he had no male heir. So he made a vow to distribute a large part of his wealth in the way of God if God would bestow upon him a righteous and monotheist male child. God accepted his prayer and granted him this brilliant, righteous and monotheist son.[28]

---

[22] In practice, real authority often lay elsewhere; in the sixteenth century it resided with the Turkmen Dhu᾽l-Qadr tribe – see Ann Lambton, 'Fārs', *EIr* IX, 340.

[23] Raḥmat Allāh Mihrāz, *Buzurgān-i Shīrāz* (Tehran 1348 Sh/1969), 325.

[24] R. M. Savory, *Iran under the Safavids* (Cambridge 1980), 218. She was the daughter of ʿAbd Allāh Khān II, a Qawāmī Marʿashī *sayyid* and governor of Māzandarān, as well as the mother of the future Shah ʿAbbās I [b. 979/1571] – see M. Szuppe, 'The Jewels of Wonder. Learned ladies and princess politicians in the provinces of early Safavid Iran', in G. Hambly (ed.), *Women in the Medieval Islamic World* (London 1998), 332–4; J. Calmard, 'Marʿashīs', *EI²* VI, 515; Iskandar Beg Munshī, *ʿĀlam-ārā᾽-yi ʿAbbāsī*, tr. R. M. Savory as *The History of Shah ʿAbbas* (Boulder, CO 1977), I, 208.

[25] Savory, *The History of Shah ʿAbbas*, I, 371.

[26] Roger Savory, 'The significance of the political murder of Mīrzā Salmān', in Savory, *Studies in the History of Safawid Iran* (London 1987), XV.

[27] Maria Szuppe, 'La participation des femmes de la famille royale au pouvoir', *SIr* 23 (1994), 232; R. Quiring-Zoche, *Isfahan im 15. und 16. Jahrhundert* (Freiburg 1980), 237–40.

[28] Zunūzī, *Tārīkh-i ḥukamā᾽*, in *Muṣannafāt-i Ḥakīm ʿAlī Zunūzī*, ed. M. Kadīvar (Tehran 1378 Sh/1999), III, 140.

Encouraged by his father, he began his studies in his home town at an early age and was captivated by philosophy in a town that had had a reputation for more than a century of being a centre of philosophical learning. In the introduction to his major philosophical work commonly known as *al-Asfār*, he indicated his early interest in philosophy and philosophical theology: 'I devoted my capabilities for many years from my earliest childhood and youth to philosophy'.[29] But he never indicated who his teachers may have been at this stage and there is little evidence that the philosophical school of Shiraz remained flourishing at this time. The students of Mīr Ghiyāth al-Dīn Manṣūr Dashtakī [d. 1542] had dispersed and there is no conclusive evidence of any philosophical education in the seminaries of the city. It is likely, therefore, that at this stage he became an autodidact, like his great philosophical predecessor Avicenna [d. 428/1037], and studied the books of the philosophers, in particular the works of his immediate predecessors in Shiraz.[30] He became confident of his understanding and believed that he had achieved something as a philosopher. He discussed this in the introduction to his commentary on *Sūrat al-Wāqiʿa* where he wrote that he realised true knowledge was beyond the discursive philosophy of the Peripatetics (*mashshāʾiyyūn*, 'Aristotelians') and the Illuminationists (*Ishrāqiyyūn*, 'Platonists') as expressed in the thought of philosophers of Shiraz:

> I exerted great effort and devotion consistently and carefully to study the books of the rational philosophers (*al-ḥukamāʾ al-nuẓẓār*) until I began to think that I was something. But when my [spiritual] insight opened up a little and I looked at my state, I saw myself ... far removed from the knowledge of reality and true visible realities, which can only be perceived by experience and ecstasy and are reported in the Scripture and the Sunna concerning the knowledge of God, His attributes, His names, His scriptures, His prophets, and knowledge of the soul and its states from the grave to the resurrection ... which one can only know from divine teachings and which can only be revealed by the light of prophecy and sainthood (*bi-nūr al-nubūwa waʾl-walāya*).[31]

---

[29] *Al-Asfār*, I, 4.

[30] On Avicenna's education, see Dimitri Gutas, *Avicenna and the Aristotelian Tradition* (Islamic Philosophy, Theology and Science Texts and Studies vol. IV, Leiden 1988), 149–98.

[31] *Tafsīr*, VII, 10.

Thus as a young man having turned twenty and mastered discursive philosophy, he realised that he needed to seek out a spiritual master, someone who could train him in a higher philosophy that would incorporate spiritual intuition and mystical experience, and a master who would initiate him into a proper understanding of the Scripture and the sayings of the Imams and their teachings. Such a quest for a guide in philosophy and spiritual training was entirely characteristic of the Illuminationist (*ishrāqī*) philosophical tradition that combined Neoplatonic taste with Pythagorean piety;[32] its founder the philosopher-martyr (*maqtūl*) Shihāb al-Dīn Yaḥyā Suhrawardī [d. 586/1191] advised at the end of his magnum opus *Ḥikmat al-ishrāq*:

> I exhort you, my brethren, to keep God's commandments … I exhort you to preserve this book … Give it to one well versed in the method of the Peripatetics … Let him meditate for forty days, abstaining from meat, taking little food, concentrating upon the contemplation of the light of God … and upon that which he who holds the authority to teach the book shall command.[33]

Mullā Ṣadrā decided to seek out the one who acts as a master based on his authority to teach (*qayyim al-kitāb*). Unable to find such a person in Shiraz, it is thus no surprise that he decided to leave his home town and seek out such teachers.

II Teachers

Between 1000/1590–1 and 1003/1595 (and in 995/1587 Shah ʿAbbās his exact contemporary had ascended the throne), as a young man of wealth and knowledge, he moved to the capital Qazwīn to pursue his studies with two major figures of the court of Shah ʿAbbās I, Shaykh Bahāʾ al-Dīn al-ʿĀmilī [d. 1030/1620–1] and Mīr Muḥammad Bāqir Dāmād Astarābādī [d. 1040/1631]. Their fame as spiritual figures,

---

[32] For a (historically speculative) discussion of the neo-Pythagorean Neoplatonism of Illuminationism, see John Walbridge, *The Leaven of the Ancients: Suhrawardī and the Heritage of the Greeks* (SUNY Series in Islam, Albany, NY 2000).

[33] Suhrawardī, *Ḥikmat al-Ishrāq [The Philosophy of Illumination]*, eds. H. Ziai and J. Walbridge (Islamic Translations Series, Provo, UH 1999), 162. On the founder of Illuminationism, see Hossein Ziai, 'al-Suhrawardī', *EI*[2] IX, 782–4; idem, 'Illuminationism', *EIr* XII, 670–2, XIII, 1–2; Henry Corbin, *En Islam iranien*, vol. II; John Walbridge, 'Suhrawardī and Illuminationism', in P. Adamson and R. Taylor (eds), *The Cambridge Companion to Arabic Philosophy*, 201–23; Hermann Landolt, *Suhrawardī* (Makers of the Muslim World, Oxford 2008).

jurists and polymaths at the heart of the culture of the Safavid court no doubt attracted him.

The former, known as Shaykh Bahāʾī, was a jurist, poet and scientist and a close confidant of the king, serving as Shaykh al-Islām of Isfahan. Bahāʾ al-Dīn Muḥammad b. al-Ḥusayn b. ʿAbd al-Ṣamad al-ʿĀmilī was born in Baʿlbakk in 953/1547.[34] Part of the community of Shiʿi scholars from Jabal ʿĀmil in modern-day Lebanon who migrated to the new Shiʿi Safavid Empire in search of security and patronage,[35] he arrived in Iran with his father, al-Shaykh ʿIzz al-Dīn al-Ḥusayn b. ʿAbd al-Ṣamad [d. 984/1576], a student of the famous Shiʿi jurist-martyr Zayn al-Dīn al-ʿĀmilī known as al-Shahīd II [exec. 965/1558], by 960/1553 and initially settled in Mashhad.[36] His father later became the first Shaykh al-Islām of the capital Qazwīn in 963/1556, a post he held until 970/1563 when he was removed from office and replaced by al-Sayyid al-Ḥusayn b. al-Ḥasan al-Karakī [d. 1001/1592–3].[37] He was compensated with the post of Shaykh al-Islām of Mashhad and then Herat on the frontier. He died after his pilgrimage in 984/1576. Shaykh Bahāʾī studied law, *ḥadīth* (traditions of the Prophet and the Imams) and *tafsīr* (exegesis of the Qurʾān) with his father and his father-in-law, another ʿĀmilī, al-Shaykh ʿAlī b. Hilāl Minshār [d. 984/1576], who was Shaykh al-Islām of Isfahan. He may also have studied jurisprudence and *ḥadīth* in Kāshān with ʿAbd al-ʿĀlī b. ʿAlī al-Karakī [d. 993/1585],[38] and logic and philosophy with Mullā ʿAbd Allāh Yazdī [d. 981/1573] in Mashhad. He later succeeded his father-in-law as Shaykh al-Islām of Isfahan. From

---

[34] Etan Kohlberg, 'Bahāʾ al-Dīn ʿĀmelī', *EIr* III, 429–30; Devin Stewart, 'A biographical note on Bahāʾ al-Dīn al-ʿĀmilī', *JAOS* 101 (1991), 563–71; AA I, 155–60; LB 16–22; *Rawḍāt*, VI, 54–81; RU V, 88–97; *Aʿyān*, IX, 234–49; IBM I, 155–7, II, 967–8; Andrew Newman, 'Towards a reconsideration of the Isfahan school of philosophy', *SIr* 15 (1986), 165–98; Niʿma, *Falāsifat al-Shīʿa*, 398–415; Dalāl ʿAbbās, *Bahāʾ al-Dīn al-ʿĀmilī: adīban, faqīhan wa ʿāliman* (Beirut 1995); Rula Abisaab, *Converting Persia: Religion and Power in the Safavid Empire* (London 2004), 59–70. This last work is a study of the ʿĀmilī circles and their influence to which Shaykh Bahāʾī and Mīr Dāmād were affiliated.

[35] There is an ongoing debate about the nature, extent and significance of this migration. See ʿAlī Murūwa, *al-Tashayyuʿ bayn Jabal ʿĀmil wa Īrān* (London 1987); Jaʿfar al-Muhājir, *al-Hijra al-ʿĀmiliyya ilā Īrān fīʾl-ʿaṣr al-Ṣafawī* (Beirut 1989); Andrew Newman, 'The myth of the clerical migration to Safawid Iran', *Die Welt des Islams* 33 (1993), 66–112; Devin Stewart, 'Notes on the migration of ʿĀmilī scholars to Safavid Iran', *JNES* 55 (1996), 81–103.

[36] On his father, see Devin Stewart, 'The first Shaykh al-Islam of the Safavid Capital Qazvin', *JAOS* 116 (1996), 387–405, 391 on the date of arrival. The date is deduced from a manuscript of his work *Wuṣūl al-akhyār ilā uṣūl al-akhbār* dated Rabīʿ I 960/February 1553 – see M. T. Dānishpazhūh and ʿA. Munzavī, *Fihrist-i nuskha-hā-yi khaṭṭī-yi kitābkhāna-yi markazī-yi Dānishgāh-i Tihrān* (Tehran 1952–79), XV, 4241.

[37] On this powerful jurist known as al-Sayyid al-Ḥusayn *al-mujtahid*, see Abisaab, *Converting Persia*, 45–52.

[38] LB 134–5. Thus he may at this stage also have been a colleague of Mīr Dāmād; cf. AA I, 110.

991/1583 to 993/1585, he travelled as a wandering dervish, passing himself off as a Shāfiʿī jurist when necessary.[39] This experience produced valuable material for his literary anthology *al-Kashkūl*. He returned to Isfahan and then moved to Qazwīn where he succeeded al-Karakī on his death as Shaykh al-Islām of the capital, a post he would also hold in Isfahan when the capital moved in 1006/1597 until his death in 1030/1621. He was buried in the precinct of the shrine of the eighth Twelver Shiʿi Imam ʿAlī al-Riḍā in Mashhad, his first residence in Iran. Along with his friend Mīr Dāmād, he was a confidant and boon companion of Shah ʿAbbās I.

Mullā Ṣadrā studied jurisprudence, *tafsīr* and *ḥadīth* with him, first in Qazwīn and then in Isfahan. The influence on his treatment of *ḥadīth* is clear and it was through Shaykh Bahāʾī that he traced his chain of authority to transmit *ḥadīth*. He referred to his teacher as 'our master upon whom we rely in the traditional scriptural disciplines'.[40] When did he first meet his teacher? It is difficult to determine. We known that Shaykh Bahāʾī visited Shiraz in 998/1588 and they may have met there.[41] But it seems more likely that the pedagogical apprenticeship began in Qazwīn. He may have accompanied his teacher to the shrines of Iraq: an autograph copy of *al-Ḥadīqa al-Hilāliyya* a short commentary on a supplication for welcoming the new crescent of the month of Ramaḍān places Shaykh Bahāʾī in Kāẓimiyya near Baghdad at the beginning of Jumāda I 1003/January 1595. In the margins of the manuscript is a signature of Mullā Ṣadrā dated Dhu'l-Ḥijja 1005/July–August 1593 in Qazwīn.[42] An autograph anthology (the *Jung-i Qazwīn*) that Mullā Ṣadrā penned in Ramaḍān 1004/May 1596 places him in Qazwīn.[43] Thus, we may surmise that the earliest reliable date for his association with Shaykh Bahāʾī is 1003/1595 or 1004/1595. Another manuscript of the text of *al-Ṣirāṭ al-mustaqīm* of Mīr Dāmād in the hand of Mullā Ṣadrā is dated 15 Rabīʿ I 1007/16 October 1598, placing him in their circle. By this time he was with his teachers in the new capital of Isfahan.[44]

---

[39] Devin Stewart, 'Taqiyyah as performance: The travels of Bahāʾ al-Dīn al-ʿĀmilī in the Ottoman Empire', *Princeton Papers in Near East Studies* 4 (1996), 1–70; idem, *Islamic Legal Orthodoxy: Twelver Shiite Responses to the Sunni Legal System* (Salt Lake City, UH 1998), 94–5.

[40] *Sharḥ Uṣūl al-Kāfī*, I, 198.

[41] KH 54.

[42] KH 26.

[43] KH 55 the manuscript is the Kitābkhāna-yi Millī in Tehran.

[44] Stephen Blake has recently argued that the capital was actually moved in 999/1590 when major construction began in the Maydān-i Hārūn Vilāyat. However, this does not strike me as being a particularly convincing case for arguing that from this point Isfahan became the *dār al-salṭanat*. The preparation of a capital is not the same as the actual moving of the state apparatus. See his 'Shah ʿAbbās and the transfer of the Safavid capital from Qazvin to Isfahan', in A. J. Newman (ed.), *Society and Culture in the Early*

His other main teacher, and probably the greater influence on his life, was Mīr Muḥammad Bāqir Astarābādī known as Dāmād (son-in-law in Persian) because his father Mīr Shams al-Dīn Muḥammad was the son-in-law of the powerful *mujtahid* al-Shaykh ʿAlī al-Karakī [d. 940/1534].[45] He was probably born in Astarābād in 969/1561–2 but raised in Mashhad. He studied philosophy in Mashhad with Mīr Fakhr al-Dīn Muḥammad b. Ḥusayn Sammākī Astarābādī. Sammākī had acted as the Shaykh al-Islām of Sabzavār under Shah Ṭahmāsp and had been a student of the philosopher of Shiraz, Mīr Ghiyāth al-Dīn Manṣūr Dashtakī [d. 948/1542].[46] His teachers in jurisprudence and traditions were al-Ḥusayn b. ʿAbd al-Ṣamad al-ʿĀmilī and al-Sayyid al-Ḥusayn al-Karakī in Mashhad and his uncle ʿAbd al-ʿĀlī b. ʿAlī al-Karakī. During the reign of Shah Ṭahmāsp [d. 984/1576] he moved to the capital Qazwīn, and became a close friend of Shaykh Bahāʾī. As a courtier of his successor Shāh ʿAbbās I, he moved to Isfahan in 1006/1597. Later, Mīr Dāmād succeeded Shaykh Bahāʾī as Shaykh al-Islām of Isfahan in 1030/1621, a post he retained until his own death.[47] He conducted the coronation of Shah Ṣafī on 2 Jumāda II 1038/28 January 1629.[48] He died in 1040/1631 on the road from Karbalāʾ to Najaf whilst escorting the Shah to the Shiʿi shrines in Iraq. Mīr Dāmād was buried in the precinct of the shrine of the first Shiʿi Imam ʿAlī b. Abī Ṭālib in Najaf.

With Mīr Dāmād, Mullā Ṣadrā studied philosophy and theology, in particular the Peripatetic works of Avicenna and his student Bahmanyār [d. 458/1066], the pseudo-Aristotelian *Plotiniana Arabica* (in particular the so-called *Theology of Aristotle/Uthūlūjīyā*), the Illuminationist works of Suhrawardī and the commentaries of philosophical theology on *Tajrīd al-iʿtiqād* of Naṣīr al-Dīn al-Ṭūsī [d. 672/1274]. We know that he was associated with him at least from 1004/1595. He was

---

Modern Middles East: Studies on Iran in the Safavid Period (Islamic History and Civilization vol. XLVI, Leiden 2003), 145–64. On the traditional dating of the transfer of the capital, see IBM I, 544.

[45] LB 132–4; AA I, 249–50; *Rawḍāt*, II, 61–7; RU V, 40–4; IBM I, 146–7; Niʿma, *Falāsifat al-Shīʿa*, 394–7; S. Mūsawī Bihbahānī, *Ḥakīm-i Astarābād* 2nd printing (Tehran 1370 Sh/1991); ʿAlī Awjabī, *Bunyān-gudhār-i ḥikmat-i Yamānī* (Tehran 1382 Sh/2003); Andrew Newman, 'Dāmād', *EIr* VI, 623–6; Sajjad Rizvi, 'Mir Dāmād', *EIr* supplement, forthcoming; Abisaab, *Converting Persia*, 71–9.

[46] On Sammākī, see *GAL* S II, 587; C. A. Storey, *Persian Literature: A Bio-bibliographic Survey Vol. I, part I* (London 1970), 17. On Dashtakī, see RU V, 250–2; *Rawḍāt*, IV, 372–3; IBM I, 144–5, 148; Andrew Newman, 'Dashtakī', *EIr* VII, 100–1; Caroline Beeson, 'The Origins of Conflict in the Ṣafawī Religious Institution', unpublished Ph.D. dissertation (Princeton University 1982), Ch. 1; S. A. Arjomand, *The Shadow of God and the Hidden Imam* (Chicago 1984), 134–5, 145.

[47] Muḥammad Maʿṣūm Iṣfahānī, *Khulāṣat al-siyar*, ed. Īraj Afshār (Tehran 1368 Sh/1989), 82, 96, 111–12; cf. Devin Stewart, 'Notes on the migration of ʿĀmilī scholars to Safavid Iran', 85.

[48] IBM II, 632; cf. S. Babaie, K. Babayan, I. Baghdiantz-McCabe and M. Farhad, *Slaves of the Shah: New Elites of Safavid Iran* (London 2004), 47, 163 n.114.

particularly attached to his teacher who may have acted as a spiritual guide and mentor. In a letter dated 1018/1617 that he wrote from Shiraz, he described Mīr Dāmād as

> the apportioner of grace to the hearts of the wise, the eleventh intellect, he who masters both the theory and the practices of the sciences, the *sayyid* and leader, the lord of the philosophers and master of the jurists, teacher of teachers and of scholars, the most noble of scholars and the civiliser of Islamdom.[49]

In this letter, it is clear he has been separated from him for a few years, which is consistent with a speculation that Mullā Ṣadrā completed his studies and left Isfahan in 1010/1600 to return to Shiraz at the death of his father. In this letter he also affirms his association with a luminary scholar of Kāshān (and it is possible he spent some time in the 1010s in that city). This may be a reference to his mystically-inclined father-in-law Mīrzā Żiyā᾿ al-Dīn Muḥammad Rāzī a Sufi known as *Żiyā᾿ al-ʿurafā᾿* who was a native of Kāshān.

In a second letter dated around 1021/1612 possibly from Shiraz, he described his teacher as the sultan of those philosophers who are theosists.[50] The spiritual teachings of Mīr Dāmād are indicated when he is described as

> the gate who opens the spiritual path to God and from whose presence divine grace is acquired; a gate who does not disappoint its seeker and does not betray its confidant ... He knows all that he knows through certain demonstration, and witnessed inner-revelation and ecstatic experience from which the intellect is not severed nor investigation cut off. All this is only through divine grace and lordly inspiration and the guidance of the intellect.[51]

---

[49] Quoted in KH 109.

[50] KH 115.

[51] KH 116–17.

This is very much a description of a 'rationalising mystic'.[52] Later still, in *al-Asfār* he describes him as his spiritual guide (*murshid*) and his teacher, and prays that God preserves his connection with his separated disciple and through his honour and illuminations enlightens the heart of the seeker on the path (i.e. Mullā Ṣadrā).[53] It seems thus that we may speculate that the relationship between Mullā Ṣadrā and Mīr Dāmād was more than that of a teacher of philosophy and his student; it was that of a Sufi master and his disciple. The affection of the teacher for his disciple is further expressed in the fact that Mīr Dāmād named one of his sons Ṣadrā.[54]

We do not have a formal *ijāza* (license to teach and transmit knowledge) from his teachers, that has survived, which can attest to his study with them and to the content of the curriculum; certainly, we know that both Mīr Dāmād and Shaykh Bahā'ī granted a number of these licenses and attestations of study to their students as compiled by Muḥammad Bāqir Majlisī II [d. 1110/1699] in *Biḥār al-anwār*.[55] However, we have one very valuable source that records the intimate relationship of his study and even spiritual discipleship in a literary-poetic collection of the early eleventh/seventeenth century from Qazwīn known as the *Jung-i Qazwīn*. This codex (which is in the National Library in Tehran) includes autograph notes of Mīr Dāmād, Shaykh Bahā'ī and Mullā Ṣadrā. Among these notes are short *ijāza*-like statements. Shaykh Bahā'ī quoted some narrations of the Imams and wrote that he did so at the bequest of his 'illustrious and most excellent, intelligent and witty and pure son (*al-walad al-aʿazz al-afḍal al-dhakī al-zakī al-ṣafī*)'.[56] Similarly, in a note Mīr Dāmād referred to Mullā Ṣadrā as his spiritual son (*walad rūḥānī*).[57] The dual influence of his teachers can be gauged in his early notes (*yāddāsht-hā*) that reveal an interest in Sufism, especially Sufi poetry and the law.[58] These notes were probably written in Shiraz in 1016/1607–8. However, interest in Sufism does not entail affiliation to a Sufi order, which in any case, was highly controversial in this period. Mullā Ṣadrā

---

[52] Philip Merlan coins this term to describe the cognate affiliation of philosophy and mysticism in Late Antiquity – see his *Monopsychism, Mysticism, Metaconsciousness: Problems of the Soul in the Neoaristotelian and Neoplatonic Tradition* (The Hague 1963), 20–1.

[53] *Al-Asfār*, V, 53.

[54] Awjabī, *Bunyān-gudhār-i ḥikmat-i Yamānī*, 37.

[55] *Biḥār*, CVI, 146–59, CVII, 3–5.

[56] KH 59.

[57] KH 56.

[58] Muḥammad Barakat, *Yāddāsht-hā-yi Mullā Ṣadrā* (Qum 1377 Sh/1998), 9, 27–31 (al-Ghazālī), 49–51 (ʿAlā' al-Dawla Simnānī), 58 (Sufi verses).

was not affiliated with any Sufi order; the claim of the Niʿmatallāhī Sufi Maʿṣūm-ʿAlī-Shāh that Mullā Ṣadrā was a Nūrbakhshī Sufi cannot be substantiated.[59]

Contrary to what Corbin and others had claimed,[60] there seems to be no evidence that he studied with another intriguing Astarābādī scholar and associate of Mīr Dāmād, Mīr Abu'l-Qāsim Findiriskī [d. 1050/1640–1].[61] Certainly the story recorded by some of the later biographical dictionaries that claims that Mullā Ṣadrā, on his arrival as a new student in Isfahan, was advised by Findiriskī to study with Mīr Dāmād is apocryphal because we know that he was already associated with his teacher in Qazwīn.[62]

III The Itinerant Philosopher

Completing his training and possibly prompted by the death of his father in 1010/1601–2, he returned to Shiraz to work and teach, but failing to find an adequate patron and facing the opposition and criticism of a city that had forgotten the value of the study of philosophy, he retreated to Kahak, a small village outside the holy city of Qum, to meditate upon his inquiries and initiate the composition of his main works, especially his philosophical and theological summa, *al-Ḥikma al-Mutaʿāliya fī'l-Asfār al-ʿaqliyya al-arbaʿa* (Transcendent Wisdom of the Four Journeys of the Intellect), popularly known as *al-Asfār al-Arbaʿa* (The Four Journeys) which he began in 1015/1606. His retreat (*khalvat*) lasted probably five years in the middle of the 1010s/1600s. He then returned to Shiraz where he is placed by his letters to his teacher, as we have seen, until around 1022/1613. He then began an itinerant life: teaching and writing in Qum, visiting and corresponding with Mīr Dāmād in Isfahan until his death in 1040/1631, and spending time at his family estates in Shiraz. It may have been during this itinerant period that he completed most of his seven pilgrimages to Mecca, which in themselves would suggest interaction with the scholars of that area. Research on his time in Mecca may reveal some information about further influences upon him and his influence on others but we do not have any sources on these travels.

---

[59] Maʿṣūm-ʿAlī-Shāh Shīrāzī, *Ṭarāʾiq al-ḥaqāʾiq*, I, 183.

[60] Corbin, *En Islam Iranien* (Paris 1972), IV, 58; Nasr, *Sadr al-Din Shirazi*, 32.

[61] On him, see RU V, 499–502; IBM I, 145–6; Sajjad Rizvi, 'Mir Fendereski', *EIr* forthcoming [available at http://www.iranica.com].

[62] QU 109.

Manuscript evidence attests to his itinerant life until 1040/1630–1. His commentary on the Throne Verse places him in Qum in 1023/1613. Another letter to Mīr Dāmād was also written from Qum in 1026/1617.[63] A fourth letter dated 1028/1619 places him in Kāshān.[64] Thus the retreat to Kahak ought to be separated from his life as a teacher in Qum (and possibly Kāshān), where he met his student and later son-in-law Muḥsin Fayḍ Kāshānī. It was also in Qum that he had one of his visions which he recounted in his *Risālat al-khulsa.* The episode took place on the last night of Ramaḍān 1028/September 1619 and is preserved by his son Ibrāhīm with his own explanation:[65]

> I had performed some supererogatory prayers without complete attention and then retreated to a high place along the narrow pass between two elongated hills running north to south. I rode some of the time and walked at others, because my steed was weak and at times slow and unable to act otherwise. So I rode at times, and descended at others to relieve its burden until I reached my goal. Suddenly, a handsome man appeared before me and said, "This animal is not made for this". Until then I had failed to notice the force of the burden. It became clear to me that it could not do any more, so I left it and travelled on with complete eagerness and inspired capability.
>
> I suddenly became aware and it struck me that the journey to this high place was a journey to a higher realm of spiritual beings. What journeys is the rational spirit. The narrowness of the path represents the difficulty of the way to the truth. The steed represents the animal soul that is the vehicle of the spirit. As a form, it is an expression for its soundness and its restraint is the command of the Truth on the path of servitude. The path between the two elongated hills is the path between guidance and falling astray and between two sides of opposing things such as health and disease, joy and sorrow, pleasure, love and bliss, and grief, sorrow and despondency, or the opposition between the soul and the body. Justice and equilibrium is the narrow path.

---

[63] KH 135.

[64] KH 141.

[65] *Majmūʿa-yi Rasāʾil,* 265–6.

> Riding part of the way and walking part of it are expressions for the acts of the body approaching God and the acts of the heart that near him through thought and contemplation. That man with the luminous face is the holy spirit that inspires knowledge of realities upon the pure heart by the permission of the Exalted Lord.
>
> The steed that could not bear the burden symbolises the realisation of the heart through inspiration that the paucity of supererogatory acts is due to the weakness of the body and the puissance of certainty and the contamination of the act with doubt and display that damage servitude ...
>
> The discarding of the steed alludes to what my state led me to through the dominance of the wayfaring of the heart and the ascent of the spirit to the realm of spiritual beings without any need of my spirit for a body in the quest for perfection and along the journey to God, the Exalted.

Already at this advanced stage of his life, this episode attests to the strong association of Qum and the contemplative life for Mullā Ṣadrā. It had been a place where he taught but also a retreat from his detractors and a location, particularly the small town of Kahak on the outskirts, for spiritual contemplation and reflection. It was those experiences that he later tried to convert into discursive ideas in his philosophical works. In 1038/1628, he may already have begun to spend more time in his home town although the permanent move did not take place until two years later. This was a transitional period in Safavid history between the reigns of ʿAbbās I and II.

IV Students

He trained a number of significant philosophers in the teaching period in Qum, most important of whom were Muḥsin Fayḍ Kāshānī [d. 1090/1680], and ʿAbd al-Razzāq Fayyāḍ Lāhījī [d. 1072/1661–2] both of whom became his sons-in-law.

Muḥammad b. Murtaḍā known as Muḥsin Fayḍ (his poetic pen-name) Kāshānī was born in 1007/1598.[66] As a young man, he travelled to Isfahan in 1027/1616 where he studied *ḥadīth* and jurisprudence with Shaykh Bahāʾī. Having received a license of transmission, he moved to Shiraz in the next year where he

---

[66] William Chittick, 'Muḥsin Fayḍ-i Kāshānī', *EI²* VII, 475–6; LB 121–31; *Rawḍāt*, VI, 73–97.

obtained a license to transmit *ḥadīth* from al-Sayyid Mājid b. Hāshim al-Ṣādiqī al-Baḥrānī who died later that year in 1028/1619.[67] Making his pilgrimage, he studied *ḥadīth* and jurisprudence in Medina with Muḥammad b. al-Ḥasan al-ʿĀmilī [d. 1030/1621], the grandson of al-Shahīd II. After the death of his teacher, he returned to Iran and met Mullā Ṣadrā in Qum in 1030/1621 and remained his student for the next eight years in Qum and Shiraz until 1038/1628, as attested in Fayḍ's autobiographical treatise *Sharḥ-i Ṣadr.*[68] Later, he spent another two years from 1040/1631 to 1042/1633 with him in Shiraz. A prolific and quite exceptional polymath and specialist in both the scriptural and intellectual disciplines, he was offered the post of Shaykh al-Islām of Isfahan in 1065/1655 during the reign of Shah ʿAbbās II [d. 1077/1666] but he turned it down, concentrating instead on his teaching in Qum where he had a *madrasa* named after him (the famous Madrasa-yi Fayḍiyya).[69] Later in his life he wrote an important epitome of the thought of his teacher entitled *Uṣūl al-Maʿārif.*

ʿAbd al-Razzāq b. ʿAlī Lāhījī, whose pen-name was Fayyāḍ, was a devoted student, although in his mature works, he rejected a number of key doctrines espoused by Mullā Ṣadrā.[70] His *nisba* suggests that he was originally from Lāhījān but nostalgia for the city of Tabriz in his poetry suggests that he may have grown up there.[71] His poetry is in fact a major source for his life with a number of panegyrics that he wrote for his patrons who included the *ṣadr* Mīr Ḥabīb Allāh al-Karakī, the Shahs Ṣafī [d. 1642] and ʿAbbās II [d. 1667], Mīrzā Ṭālib Khān [d. 1044/1634] who was vizier to Shah Ṣafī, and Murtaḍā-qulī Khān who served as the head of the military (*sipahsālār*) under Shah ʿAbbās II. His period of study may have begun in the 1020s/1610s. He had also studied in Isfahan with Mīr Dāmād and was associated with him when he was Shaykh al-Islām of Isfahan.[72] A favourite of Shah ʿAbbās II (for whom he wrote an important manifesto for the Sufi life),[73] he lived the rest of his life in Qum,

---

[67] LB 135; *Biḥār,* CVI, 135; ʿAlī al-Baḥrānī, *Anwār al-badrayn fī tarājim ʿulamāʾ al-Qaṭīf waʾl-Aḥsāʾ waʾl-Baḥrayn,* ed. M. R. Ṭabasī (rpt, Beirut 1994), 78–82.

[68] *Risāla-yi Sharḥ-i Ṣadr* in *Dah Risāla-yi Muḥaqqiq-i buzurg Fayḍ-i Kāshānī,* ed. R. Jaʿfarīyān (Qum 1371 Sh/1992), 33.

[69] Rasūl Jaʿfarīyān, *Dīn va siyāsat dar dawra-yi Ṣafavī* (Qum 1370 Sh/1991), 449–52.

[70] W. Madelung, ''Abd-al-Razzāq Lāhījī', *EIr* I, 154–7; RU III, 114–5; *Rawḍāt,* IV, 192–4; Niʿma, *Falāsifat al-Shīʿa,* 295–6.

[71] Jalīl Misgarnizhād, Introduction to Lāhījī, *Dīwān,* ed. J. Misgarnizhād (Tehran 1373 Sh/1994), 22–3.

[72] *Dīwān-i Fayyāḍ-i Lāhījī,* ed. J. Misgarnizhād, 460–2 (*qaṣīda* 31).

[73] *Gawhar-i murād,* ed. Zayn al-ʿĀbidīn Qurbānī Lāhījī (Tehran 1372 Sh/1993). For studies, see L. Lewisohn, 'Sufism and the school of Isfahan', in L. Lewisohn (ed.), *The Heritage of Sufism Vol. III*

teaching at the Madrasa-yi Maʿṣūma attached to the shrine where he was known as an Avicennian philosopher. Later in life, his major work *Shawāriq al-ilhām fī sharḥ Tajrīd al-kalām*, a valuable and extensive Avicennian commentary on the theological text of al-Ṭūsī, took a number of philosophical positions that were highly critical of the views of his teacher in particular on metaphysics. In his poetry, he celebrated and commemorated his teacher.[74] One *qaṣīda* in particular not only represents his affection for his (recently deceased?) teacher but also sympathy to the philosophical concerns of Mullā Ṣadrā, if not directly espousing his doctrines:

> Each new moon and festival, and hundreds like them, may be blessed in the service of the master,
> The illustrious master, the great Ṣadr, worthy of divinely bestowed mercy,
> River of dignity and mountain of contentment, spring of knowledge, excellence and spiritual direction.
> He has no peer, and in this the heavens are no different from the earth.
> When the edifice of learning has been destroyed,
> Each person comes anew to rebuild it.
> Give thanks that because of his efforts, the house of learning will remain sturdy for eternity.
> There is none like him in the medicine of the soul, nor have I seen one alike who brings ruins to life.
> From the unrivalled warmth of the *Asfār*, the disease of ignorance is cured (*shifā dād*).
> Last night when I was enraptured in thought, my soul sorrowful, my intellect joyful,
> I soared in the Holy Realm (*ʿālam-i quds*) free from the fetters of attachment.
> In the school of the saints where the intellect is master and the soul vizier,
> I contemplated the emanation of the Active Intellect, from which all gain enlightenment,
> And understood that every atom that is a body in this world, along with what engenders it and what it engenders,
> Has in fact a part that is beyond the body, a similitude lacking dimensions.

(Oxford 1999), 63–134; S. Rizvi, 'A Sufi theology fit for a Shiʿi King', in A. Shihadeh (ed.), *Sufism and Theology* (Edinburgh 2007).

[74] *Dīwān-i Fayyāḍ-i Lāhījī*, ed. J. Misgarnizhād, 423–4, 458–60, 462–8 (*qaṣīda* 19, 30, 32, 33).

The master of philosophers (*Ṣadr al-ḥukamā'*) has no equal in time among the offspring of Mother Nature …
People try so hard to find a pearl like you in their hands.
O precious jewel, who makes everything easy,
I wish that I could enumerate your excellence but how can I?
Your thought is the key to many difficulties, each knotted problem, it opens and solves.
Who was Plato and who Aristotle? I just know that I am the disciple and you the master.
We were seated in your service just yesterday, our minds happy and joyful.
But today we hear that that moonface is the master in the school of saints.
I sit in the alleyway, waiting to be released from this school
Until that time that the beloved glances coquettishly at the lover and from him the lover becomes enraptured and aware.
You always did have the qualities of the beloved, joyful, playful and heart-renching.
Those who seek you now share the fate of lovers, and on the face of the earth have little time left.[75]

Other students included the philosophers Ḥusayn Tunikābunī [d. 1105/1693–4],[76] and Muḥammad Riḍā Āqājānī [d. after 1071/1660–1].[77] But we know very little about them: their live are truly just their texts that have survived.[78] Shaykh Ḥusayn b. Ibrāhīm Tunikābunī was a faithful student who wrote a number of treatises on key themes in his teacher's thought, in particular associated with eschatology. He wrote a Sadrian commentary on *Tajrīd al-iʿtiqād* of al-Ṭūsī, perhaps in response to the contrary commentary of Fayyāḍ-i Lāhījī. He shared Mullā Ṣadrā's taste for the

[75] *Dīwān-i Fayyāḍ-i Lāhījī*, ed. J. Misgarnizhād, 458–60 (*qaṣīda* 30).

[76] Corbin and Āshtiyānī (eds), *Anthologie des philosophes iraniens* (Tehran 1974), II, 77–80 (French). It is possible that this date is incorrect. ʿAbd al-Ḥusayn Amīnī, *Shuhadā' al-faḍīla* (Najaf 1936), 208–9 mentions a philosopher called Ḥusayn b. Ibrāhīm Tunikābunī who was attacked by a Sunni mob in 1050/1641 in Mecca and died soon after and was buried in Medina. Cf. Marco Salati, 'Toleration, persecution and local realities: observations on the Shiism in the Holy Places and the Bilād al-Shām', in *La Shīʿa nell'Impero Ottomano* (Rome 1993), 128.

[77] Corbin and Āshtiyānī (eds), *Anthologie des philosophes iraniens*, II, 50–6 (French).

[78] RU III, 114 mentions another student called Muḥammad Yūsuf Alamūtī. I have been unable to trace any mention of him elsewhere.

thought of Ibn ʿArabī [d. 1240] and penned a brief *Risāla fī waḥdat al-wujūd.*[79] Like his teacher, he is also known to have travelled widely to the shrine cities in Iraq and on pilgrimage to Mecca and Medina. Muḥammad-Riḍā b. ʿAlī-Riḍā Āqājānī is an even more elusive character. However, he left behind a massive commentary in 561 large folio pages on *al-Qabasāt* of Mīr Dāmād, which may suggest that he studied with him as well. The only date about his life that we have is taken from this text which is dated 1071/1661 and may have been written in Mashhad.

It is clear that the legacy of Mullā Ṣadrā was rather equivocal. Some of his students faithfully perpetuated his thought, whilst others shared his philosophical tastes but not his particular solutions to problems. Nevertheless from his students one can trace a genealogical line of the 'school of Mullā Ṣadrā' through to the nineteenth century when his works were first championed, taught, copied copiously in manuscript and printed in lithographs. It was the contribution of the thinkers of the Qajar period that established the thought of Mullā Ṣadrā at the heart of the philosophical education of the Shiʿi seminary.

Figure 1. The School of Mullā Ṣadrā

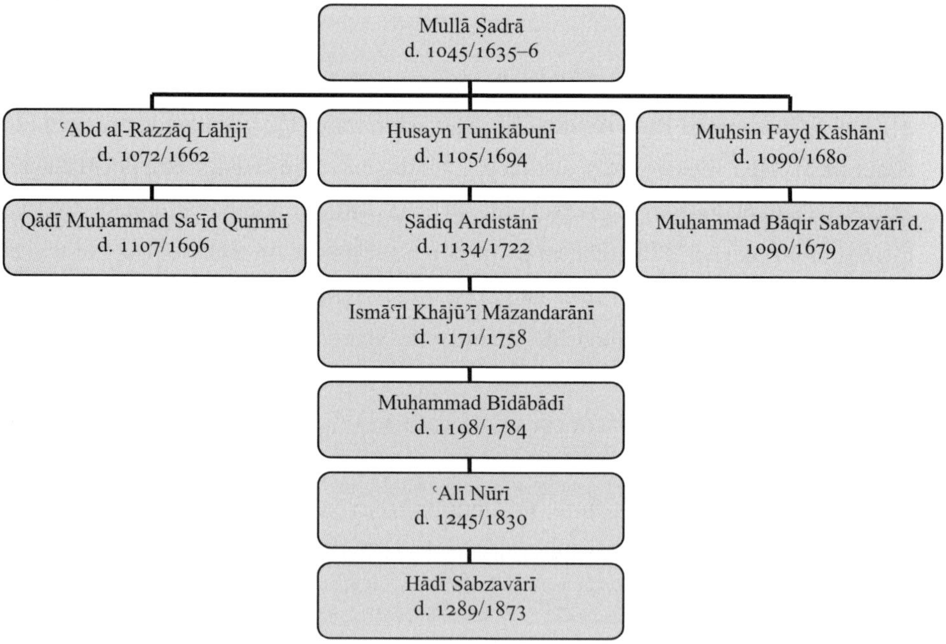

[79] Corbin and Āshtiyānī (eds), *Anthologie des philosophes iraniens*, II, 404–9. There are a number of manuscripts of this work (usually just a few short folios) including MS Raza Library (Rampur) 1027 and 1840.

V Family Life

After returning from Isfahan in around 1010/1601–2, Mullā Ṣadrā probably married in Shiraz or Kāshān in the 1010s/1600s. One modern source suggests that his wife, Maʿṣūma [d. 1061/1651], was the daughter of Mīrzā Żiyāʾ al-Dīn Muḥammad Rāzī a Sufi of Kāshān known as *Żiyāʾ al-ʿurafāʾ*, which would mean that his wife and the mother of Fayḍ were sisters, suggesting a relationship that predates the teacher and student one, and a direct affiliation with Sufis.[80] But Fayḍ never mentioned this relationship, which would raise the question of its reliability. Similarly the claims that Mullā Ṣadrā was directly affiliated to an order are without foundation.

As an affluent man, Mullā Ṣadrā had six children who survived and a large household including retainers and students. He had three daughters.

1) His first-born Umm Kulthūm was born in Shiraz in Ramaḍān 1019/November–December 1610 and later married his student Fayyāḍ-i Lāhījī in Qum.[81] Their first-born Ḥasan [d. 1121/1709], who in turn became a renowned scholar, was born in Qum.
2) Another daughter Zubayda was born in 1024/1615 in Qum, and she later married Fayḍ-i Kāshānī.
3) His third daughter Maʿṣūma was born in Qum in 1033/1623–4 and later married another student, Quṭb al-Dīn Muḥammad Nayrīzī, about whom nothing is recorded.

We do not know anything else about the women of the family. It may be of interest for us to attempt to discern the influence that they may have had (or may have absorbed) upon these illustrious individuals, but pre-modern public sources tend to confine the lives of women to their relationship with their public and more recognisable male relatives.

Mullā Ṣadrā had three sons who became scholars in their own right, having studied with their father:

1) Ibrāhīm who was born in Qum in 1021/1612–3 and died in Isfahan in 1071/1660–1.[82] He is described as a scholar specialising in the law, in *ḥadīth*

[80] Shihāb al-Dīn Marʿashī, Introduction to Muḥammad ʿAlam al-Hudā, *Maʿādin al-ḥikma fī makātib al-aʾimma*, ed. ʿAlī al-Miyānjī (Qum 1407–9/1987–9), 12.

[81] Marʿashī, Introduction to Muḥammad ʿAlam al-Hudā, *Maʿādin al-ḥikma*, 15.

[82] RU I, 26–7; LB 132; ʿAbd al-Nabī Qazwīnī [fl. 1191/1777], *Tatmīm amal al-āmil*, ed. S. A. al-Ḥusaynī (Qum 1987), 51–2.

and *kalām*, and known for forsaking the interests of his father in Sufism and philosophy. The famous Akhbārī tradent Yūsuf al-Baḥrānī [d. 1186/1772] described him as a 'living example of the divine act of bringing forth the living from the dead'! He wrote *marginalia* (*ḥāshiya*) on the compendium of legal precepts *al-Rawḍa al-bahiyya fī sharḥ al-Lumʿa al-Dimashqiyya* of al-Shahīd II, and *marginalia* on the later *Sharḥ al-Tajrīd*, a work that demonstrates that he in fact did continue his father's concerns in philosophy.

2) Niẓām al-Dīn Aḥmad who was born in Kāshān in 1031/1621–2 and died in Shiraz in 1074/1664.[83] No works that are extant are attributed to him.

3) His youngest son Muḥammad Riḍā who was probably born in Qum. Little if anything is recorded about him although it seems that he died in the early twelfth/eighteenth century. ʿAbd al-Nabī Qazwīnī [fl. 1191/1777] mentions him as a recent scholar famed for theology.[84]

Unlike some other famous Safavid scholars (e.g. the Majlisīs), Mullā Ṣadrā did not establish a dynasty of scholars. He did not marry into the major scholarly households of the time and nor did he arrange marriage alliances for his children to build up a network of scholars as his legacy. It seems rather that the intimate circle of his closest students and his family were treated as the same and indeed to an extent were the same group of people. He was a private, contemplative individual; a prominent teacher recognised for his learning but not an individual who used his training and knowledge to gain for himself and his family a status and rank in society and (if one assumes that he was sincere in his writings) nor should one expect him to have done so, considering the many attacks on the world-seeking scholars that he penned. But since patronage was the very sustenance of the time for the scholar, and given his family commitments and his nurturing of his students, he was not averse to seeking out and responding to the assistance and support of the Safavid nobility. In fact, it was precisely this patronage that brought him to settle down finally in Shiraz.

VI Shiraz and the Madrasa-yi Khān in his final years

In 1040/1630–1, he moved permanently to his home town at the bequest of (possibly his former student) Imāmqulī Khān [d. 1042/1633], a notable Georgian *ghulām* who was in charge of the Safavid military administration and the governor of Mullā

---

83 RU I, 27.

84 ʿAbd al-Nabī Qazwīnī, *Tatmīm amal al-āmil*, 153–4.

Ṣadrā's home province of Fārs.[85] He had succeeded his father Allāhvirdī Khān, who had been the governor from 1004/1595–6 until his death in 1022/1613.[86] The Madrasa-yi Khān, founded by Imāmqulī's father just before he died and completed in 1024/1615 had been established with an express purpose of teaching philosophy and science.[87] However, it was only in 1036/1627 that the Madrasa became a *waqf*. The *waqfnāma* is itself an interesting document. It describes Imāmqulī Khān as the patron who harmonised within himself both philosophical wisdom and governance (*jamʿ bayn al-ḥikma waʾl-ḥukūma*), indicating his study of philosophy, perhaps evidence for his association with Mullā Ṣadrā.[88] As a vast and well-endowed complex, the Madrasa was designed to be a place of prayer with a mosque and a minaret and a residential seminary with one large teaching hall above the eivan of the main entrance, four smaller lecture rooms and a hundred bedsits for students.[89] Corbin claimed that Allāhvirdī Khān had originally invited Mullā Ṣadrā to teach in his new Madrasa.[90] But he was in Qum at the time and the governor died before the building was complete. It is thus more likely that the invitation came from his son Imāmqulī, and once the Madrasa was functioning especially as an endowment, our philosopher may have properly begun his association, i.e. in 1036/1627. The *waqf* document insisted that the director of the Madrasa ought to be the person who had mastered the intellectual disciplines and was capable of teaching them.[91] Mullā Ṣadrā was thus a clear choice for the job of the director. He completed his major work the *Four*

---

[85] On Imāmqulī, see R. Savory, 'Emāmqolī Khan', *EIr* VIII, 394; Mihrāz, *Buzurgān-i Shīrāz*, 471–2.

[86] On Allāhvirdī, see Savory, *The History of Shah ʿAbbas*, I, 690, II, 1083–4; idem, 'Allāhverdī Khan', *EIr* I, 891.

[87] KH 253; ʿAlī-Aṣghar Sayfī, 'Madrasa-yi Khān', *Ṣadrā* 11 (1377 Sh/1998), 65–6. On the Madrasa, see Muḥammad Naṣīr Furṣat Shīrāzī, *Āthār-i ʿAjam* (Bombay 1353/1934), 495; B. Karīmī, 'Madrasa-yi Khān', *Īrān-i Imrūz* 3.7–8 (1320 Sh/1941), 31–2; Ḥasan Fasāʾī, *Fārsnāma-yi Nāṣirī*, ed. R. Fasāʾī (Tehran 1367 Sh/1988), II, 1221; H. Khoubnazar and W. Kleiss, 'Die Madrasa-yi Khān', *AMI* 8 (1975), 255–78; R. Hillenbrand, 'Safavid architecture', in P. Jackson and L. Lockhart (eds), *The Cambridge History of Iran Volume 6: Timurid and Safavid Periods* (Cambridge 1986), 795.

[88] KH 254.

[89] The complex was damaged by an earthquake in 1239/1823–4 and by the end of the nineteenth century was no longer functioning as a *madrasa*. The complex is now in ruins although since 1998 SIPRIn has taken on the task of restoration but it is unlikely to return to its former state as a teaching institution.

[90] Corbin, Introduction to *al-Mashāʿir*, 8; S. Babaie et al, *Slaves of the Shah*, 93 repeats this unfounded assertion. The source for the confusion seems to be Iskandar Beg Munshī and Muḥammad Yūsuf, *Dhayl Tārīkh-i ʿĀlam-ārāʾ-yi ʿAbbāsī*, ed. S. Khwānsārī (Tehran 1317 Sh/1938), 299 where it is reported that Mullā Ṣadrā taught at the Madrasa-yi Khān for the last thirty years of his life; cf. Ann Lambton, 'Shīrāz', *EI²* IX, 475. This cannot be the case as the Madrasa was initiated only in 1021/1612 but completed much later.

[91] Zayn al-Dīn Maḥmūd Wāṣifī, *Badāʾiʿ al-waqāʾiʿ*, ed. Alexander Badliev (Tehran 1349 Sh/1970), I, 38–9.

Journeys (al-Asfār al-arbaʿa) in Shiraz in 1038/1628 and in the same year the English traveller Sir Thomas Herbert described the Madrasa: 'and [indeed] Shyraz has a colledge wherein is read Philosophy, Astrology, Physick, Chemistry and the Mathematicks; so as 'tis the more famoused through Persia'.[92]

As we shall see below in Appendix IV, he had works in these subjects in his personal library and it is likely that he taught these texts. From his library and from his own works, one may surmise that the curriculum that he taught included the following sets of works:

1) Philosophical textbooks such as the *Plotiniana Arabica* as well as genuine works of Aristotle (in particular the *Metaphysics*, *Categories*, *Physics* and *De Anima*), *al-Shifāʾ* and *al-Ishārāt* of Avicenna, the works of Suhrawardī, the *Hidāya* of al-Abharī [d. 663/1264], the logical texts *al-Shamsiyya* of Dabīrān Kātibī Qazwīnī [d. 675/1276] and *Tahdhīb al-manṭiq* of al-Taftazānī [d. 792/1389] and their commentaries and glosses, and the commentaries and *marginalia* upon *Tajrīd al-iʿtiqād* of al-Ṭūsī.
2) Scientific works on natural philosophy (Physics) and astronomy, probably the works of al-Ṭūsī and the later tradition.
3) Sufi texts, especially the works of Ibn ʿArabī and his school such as *Fuṣūṣ al-ḥikam* and its commentaries, *al-Futūḥāt al-Makkiyya*, *Sharḥ manāzil al-sāʾirīn*, and works of Sufi etiquette and practical manuals such as *ʿAwārif al-maʿārif*.
4) His own works, attested by the number of manuscripts, including those still in his hometown copied in the hand of his students.
5) Commentary on the Qurʾān and *ḥadīth*, subjects dear to him and popular in Shiraz.

As a prominent student of two major jurists, it is also likely that he acted as a *mujtahid* in his home town and may have taught jurisprudence. Khāminihī mentions a juristic disputation between Mullā Ṣadrā and another student of Shaykh Bahāʾī, Mullā Murād Tafrishī [d. 1051/1641–2] on the problem of whether a small body of water is considered to be pure or impure.[93] The very fact that such a public disputation could occur suggests that Mullā Ṣadrā engaged in *fiqh* publicly. Another testament to the same disputation is his student Fayḍ Kāshānī upheld the position of his teacher on this issue in his *ḥadīth* collection *al-Wāfī*.[94] One should not be surprised that he did act as

---

[92] Thomas Herbert, *Some Years Travel in Divers Parts of Africa and Asia the Great* (London 1677), 129.

[93] Khāminihī, 'Zindagī, shakhṣiyyat va maktab-i Ṣadr al-Mutaʾallihīn', *Ṣadrā* 37 (1383 Sh/2004), 15.

[94] Fayḍ Kāshānī, *al-Wāfī* (Isfahan 1986), juzʾ IV, VI, 15.

a jurist. While he did not leave any works in the discipline, he had been well trained in it. That historiographical school of Safavid studies that insists upon the strict separation between intellectual (and mystical) training and legal training may consider the engagement of Mullā Ṣadrā in the law to be unusual. However, one must remember that the Safavid period was not one in which there was a rupture between intellectual and scriptural disciplines and a number of scholars and teachers were practitioners of both.

This late period of his life was productive and he was much respected as a teacher in his hometown. His instructions to his students to inculcate within themselves the virtues of theosis and the quest for reality and shunning the world and its carnality were unequivocal. In *Sih Aṣl,* he quoted a pseudo-Socratic maxim on the inner states of people, 'The hearts of those plunged in reality are the pulpits of angels and the stomachs of those who take pleasure in carnal desires are the pits of corruptible animals'.[95]

Elsewhere at the conclusion of his *Asrār al-āyāt,* he offered this advice to the student:

> So understand if you can. And if you cannot, avert your gaze from this book, stop studying it and contemplating the complexities of the knowledge of the Qur'ān. [Instead], you must rehearse stories, reports and *ḥadīth,* and the disciplines of biographies and genealogy, and perfect your Arabic and your grammar, and memorise reports without discrimination.[96]

For worthy teachers, he had this warning about unworthy and treacherous students (perhaps reflecting some bitterness of his own early experiences):

> Embrace those who desire it [study] with your company, and leave those who go away in their regret. Teach those whom you can benefit. You will not get wealth from them nor will they achieve a [spiritual] state and beatitude simply through you ...
>
> Know that the brothers who are loud are the enemies of secrets and the friends of the open are the betrayers of the hidden. When they meet you,

[95] *Sih Aṣl,* ed. Khājavī, 21.

[96] *Asrār al-āyāt,* 152.

> they submit to you, but when you are absent from them, they slander you. Whoever from them comes to you, be watchful over him ... these are the people of hypocrisy and treachery. Do not be deluded by their company with you and their show of respect for you. Their goal is not knowledge and a spiritual state but status and wealth. Do not be taken into their circles nor become an ass bearing their weight and burden.[97]

Although he taught openly and expressed himself clearly (unlike his teacher Mīr Dāmād), he was also very protective about his work:

> Take great care with these words ... Do not reduce them to what the deniers and those who think they are philosophers allege ... Protect this treatise and hide it from the eyes of others. You must protect it from fools who are most people nowadays, in fact almost all people except a small band whom only God knows and who he hides under domes of his mercy from the eyes of people.[98]

In his disdain for his contemporaries and his protectiveness, he was no different from his teacher. Mīr Dāmād concluded his introduction to his *al-Ṣirāṭ al-mustaqīm* with this advice to his students (including Mullā Ṣadrā):

> O brothers. I want you to swear an oath and make a covenant with me, and God will be witness over us and he is indeed a sufficient witness, that you will not make licit the study of the issues in this book of mine to the ignorant and those who claim to be philosophers but who cannot be trusted with the purity of a secret, those who do not possess sound taste and superior spiritual energy and upright character. Nor [allow it] to the scum (*li'l-hamaj al-raʿāʿ*) who expend their energies away from the right path of the intellectual way and entry into the spiritual city and circumambulating the Kaʿba of the angels in the uppermost host and seeking the Holy Mosque of perfection which is the greatest orientation ... They seek their carnal desires and acquire wealth and passions and allow their humanity to dominate divinity and allow

---

[97] *Al-Wāridāt al-qalbiyya*, 87.

[98] *Risālat al-ḥashr*, ed. Khājavī, 120.

> their souls to be weighed down by their bodies and make their bodies devourers of their souls.[99]

Such statements, if we are not to dismiss them as tropic arrangements privileging the self over contemporaries, would suggest that he did not seek the position in his home town. While it is likely that he wrote *al-Asfār* as a school text, it does not follow that it was designed to be taught at the Madrasa-yi Khān, not least because he began writing it some time before the Madrasa was even conceived and completed it around the time of his association with it. In this text, he went even further condemning these unworthy from studying his work in language akin to a *fatwā*:

> It is forbidden for most people to undertake to acquire these complex disciplines because those who are worthy of them are a select few and most exceptional. Guidance to them is a grace from God, the Lofty and the Knowing.[100]

True knowledge is thus hierarchically arranged and the rank of a person is dependent upon on their level of knowledge and the gift of divine grace. In a late mystical text *Īqāẓ al-nā'imīn*, he set out his scheme of the hierarchy of humans thus dependent on their level of cognition of the nature of reality in descending order:

> The first level comprises the people of inner-disclosure (*aṣḥāb al-mukāshafa*) who know Reality by forsaking themselves and negating their being ... They continuously contemplate divine signs.
>
> The second includes the excellent philosophers who perceive reality in a purely noetic sense ... Their intellection fashions forms in their imagination appropriate to actual intelligible forms, but they know that those actual forms are far superior to the imaginal forms that they construct in themselves.

[99] Mīr Dāmād, *al-Ṣirāṭ al-mustaqīm*, ed. ʿAlī Awjabī (Tehran 1381 Sh/2002), 12.
[100] *Al-Asfār*, III, 446.

> The third consists of the common folk of faith who are incapable of a higher level and can only manage to construct conjectural forms in their minds ...
>
> The fourth are those who follow authority and submit. They are not even capable of conjecture, let alone imagination. They have a purely material conception of Reality.
>
> The fifth are those who merely rely upon physical manifestations to understand Reality.[101]

The highest level comprises thus those like him and his best students who combine within themselves an excellent training in rational discourse (*al-baḥth*), mystical experience (*al-dhawq*) and inner-disclosure (*al-kashf*) through divine grace.[102] With such unashamedly elitism (and probably arrogance), it is unsurprising that some of his contemporaries were rather critical of him.

VII Death

After an illustrious and prolific career, Mullā Ṣadrā died in Basra on his way to his seventh pilgrimage to Mecca.[103] We know nothing about the events, circumstances and time of his previous pilgrimages and any new evidence on this front would be one way of understanding the influences upon him and his legacy since a pilgrimage was an extended journey passing through numerous stages learning and teaching and conversing with the learned and famous. Did he take the perilous route via Basra (at least from the evidence of his death we can say he did once) or did he ever take the northern route via Syria, perhaps taking in the shrines there and engaging with Sunni and Shiʿi scholars in the Levant as his teacher Shaykh Bahāʾī had done before? It is symptomatic of the paucity of basic life data about him that we cannot say with any certainty (at least we cannot cite an unequivocal reliable first-hand account) when he died. The traditional date given for his death in all the major biographical sources is

[101] *Īqāẓ al-nāʾimīn*, 69.

[102] *Al-Asfār*, IX, 108.

[103] Research into his pilgrimages may yield interesting insights upon his influences and his contacts with the Shiʿi scholarly circles in the Ḥijāz about whom we still know very little. He would normally have taken the pilgrimage route via Basra; on the perils of the route and Shiʿi pilgrims in the period, see S. Faroqhi, *Pilgrims and Sultans: The Hajj under the Ottomans, 1517–1683* (London 1994), 135–9.

1050/1640–1. This account states that he died in Basra and was buried there. It was corroborated by the famous Iranian philosopher-seminarian of the twentieth century al-Sayyid Abu'l-Ḥasan Rafīʿī Qazwīnī [d. 1976] when he reported in 1961:

> About forty years ago, I asked an Arab *sayyid* living in Najaf who used to frequent Basra about the grave of [Mullā Ṣadrā] ... In reply he told me that there was a grave in Basra which was famous as the grave of Mullā Ṣadrā Shīrāzī. However, in more recent times if someone were to go to Basra to verify this, they would find nothing; nor would they find any such known place. It is possible that due to the effect of the changes in the city [through development], the traces of this grave have disappeared. And God the Exalted knows best.[104]

However, there is no clear evidence in support of this date (and also no extant grave). His grandson Muḥammad ʿAlam al-Hudā [d. 1115/1703–4], the son of Fayḍ Kāshānī, reported that his grandfather died in Basra in 1045/1635–6 and was buried in Najaf in the precinct of the shrine of Imam ʿAlī:

> My grandfather the Master of the theosists and hieratics (*Ṣadr al-ʿurafāʾ waʾl-mutaʾallihīn*),[105] the crescent of profound sages, Muḥammad b. Ibrāhīm b. Yaḥyā al-Shīrāzī known as Ṣadr al-Dīn, may God illuminate his proof, died in Basra while intending to make his way to Hajj and the pilgrimage to the Master of the Messengers [in Medina] in the year 1045. His noble body was transferred to Najaf, may God increase its nobility. I have heard from one of my friends – actually it may have been from my father, may God sanctify his spirit[106] – that he is buried in the left side of the illuminated courtyard at the good and noble shrine [of ʿAlī].[107]

He was born according to his own statement in Qum on Thursday 15 Rabīʿ I 1039/1 November 1629 which would mean that he was around six years old when his

---

[104] S. H. Nasr (ed.), *Mulla Sadra Commemoration Volume* (Tehran 1961), 4; cf. KH 413.

[105] Hieratic as a translation for *ʿārif* is derived from the late antique usage for the function of a holy man who is also a mystic and a thinker. See Damascius, *The Philosophical History*, ed./tr. P. Athanassiadi (Athens 1999).

[106] This indicates that it was written after the death of his father, i.e. after 1090/1681. It thus still presents the possibility that his memory was mistaken.

[107] Muḥammad ʿAlam al-Hudā, *Maʿādin al-ḥikma fī makātib al-aʾimma*, I, 9; KH 414.

grandfather died.[108] It seems that his evidence is probably based on what his father told him later.

This seems to be corroborated by the fact that the date of completion for his last works, including those left incomplete, is 1044/1635–6. One piece of evidence that seems to question this is the suggestion of the editor that there is a manuscript of *al-Masāʾil al-qudsiyya* dated 1049/1639–40.[109] However, this manuscript is not an autograph and may have been copied after his death. In fact the internal evidence suggests a complete date of what is extant as 1034/1624. Although one cannot be unequivocal in stating with certainty and given closure to his life, the most probable date of his death is exactly the one mentioned by his grandson, namely 1045/1635–6. But it remains the case that no grave of his is known to the people of Najaf.

---

108 Muḥammad ʿAlam al-Hudā, *Maʿādin al-ḥikma*, I, 9.

109 *Al-Masāʾil al-Qudsiyya* in *Rasāʾil*, ed. Āshtiyānī, 3.

Appendix I
The Harassment of Mullā Ṣadrā

It has been alleged that Mullā Ṣadrā was accused of heresy and driven out of Isfahan whence he fled to Kahak.[110] It should be clear from the preceding account that I suggest he left Isfahan when he wanted and moved back to his hometown of Shiraz; it was only later that he retreated to Kahak for a more complex set of reasons. Nevertheless, there is a historiographical approach to the Safavid period that insists upon two doctrinal positions: first, there was a paradigm shift of power from the Shah as a charismatic *pīr* of a Sufi *ṭarīqat* to a royal figure who ruled a state legitimated by the *sharīʿa*; second, the Safavid period, in which legitimacy was contested and Twelver Shiʿism imposed, witnessed a perennial conflict between *eros* and *nomos*, between Sufis and philosopher-mystics advocating an eclectic approach to God and hard-nosed jurists hostile to Sufism and popular religion. It is thus natural that someone like Mullā Ṣadrā would be attacked in particular for his condemnation of *taqlīd* and juristic authority.[111] The nomocentric jurists (the shariʿa-minded in Hodgson-speak)[112] began with attacks on popular religion and the *Abū-Muslim-nāma* and then wrote attacks on Sufism and philosophy such as *Ḥadīqat al-Shīʿa*, written around 1055/1645 and falsely ascribed to the ascetic and philosophically-minded jurist Aḥmad al-Ardabīlī [d. 1585] and *Tuḥfat al-akhyār* written by Muḥammad Ṭāhir Qummī [d. 1098/1686] the Shaykh al-Islām of Qum in 1075/1664–5.[113] By the end of the seventeenth century, the victory of the jurists was complete.

---

[110] Corbin, Introduction to *al-Mashāʿir*, 3; James Morris, Introduction to *al-Ḥikma al-ʿArshiyya*, 16; M. Mūsawī, *al-Jadīd fī falsafat Ṣadr al-Dīn al-Shīrāzī* (Baghdad 1978), 9.

[111] Khājawī, *Lawāmiʿ al-ʿārifīn*, 34–40; S. Amir Arjomand, *The Shadow of God and the Hidden Imam* (Chicago 1984); Kathryn Babayan, 'Sufis, dervishes and Mullas', in C. Melville (ed.), *Safavid Persia* (Pembroke Papers 2, London 1996), 125–31; L. Lewisohn, 'Sufism and the school of Isfahan', 95–8.

[112] Marshall Hodgson, *The Venture of Islam* (Chicago 1974), I, 238–9.

[113] [Ps-Ardabīlī] *Ḥadīqat al-Shīʿa*, ed. S. Ḥasanzāda (2 vols, Qum 1377 Sh/1998); Qummī, *Tuḥfat al-akhyār* (Qum 1973). On these anti-Sufi texts and trends, see Andrew Newman, 'Sufism and anti-Sufism in Safavid Iran', *Iran* 37 (1999), 95–108; Jaʿfarīyān, *Dīn va siyāsat dar dawra-yi Ṣafavī*, 220–98; Kathryn Babayan,

What can we make of this? First, there is no evidence that Mullā Ṣadrā opposed the juristic theory that divided believers into jurists and followers, i.e. *taqlīd*. Wherever he condemned *taqlīd*, he was referring to the blind imitation and rehearsal of rational arguments without understanding; the context makes it clear that he was not discussing juristic theory.[114] In *al-Shawāhid al-rubūbiyya*, he placed the *mujtahids* at a rank just below the Imams as their representatives:

> He [The Prophet] said: "There is no prophet after me". But he preserved the authority (*al-ḥukm*) of the revelations (*al-mubashshirāt*) and the authority of the Imams who are preserved from error, and the authority of the *mujtahids*. Even if their name does not survive, their authority does. He ordered those without knowledge to consult them following the divine order to "ask those who know if you do not know" [Qurʾān 16:45]. They [the *mujtahids*] give *fatwas* on the basis of their *ijtihād* and they differ just as previous dispensations of religious law have differed. He [God] said: "For everyone we have created a path" [Qurʾān 5:52]. Similarly for every *mujtahid*, he has created for a juristic path from his proof and a method, and has determined his proof ton establish his authority and forbidden him to diverge from it so that he may pronounce on the divine law.[115]

This is clearly not a statement rejecting juristic authority. Second, the 'eclectic-minded' wrote works condemning deviant Sufis and worldly jurists themselves: Mullā Ṣadrā himself wrote *Kasr aṣnām al-jāhiliyya* and *Sih Aṣl*, Sayyid Aḥmad ʿAlawī [d. 1054/1644], the son-in-law of Mīr Dāmād wrote *Iẓhār al-ḥaqq* in 1043/1633–4, and Fayḍ Kāshānī wrote a *Muḥākama* in 1072/1662–3 adjudicating between false and true Sufis.[116] Such works were not merely going against the grain but serious attempts at articulating the way in which they saw reality and its pursuit and understanding. Third, the reconciliation between the jurist and the philosopher occasioned in the person of Mīr Dāmād, for example, did not die out. Even later in the century, when nomocentrism is seen to have triumphed, prominent philosopher-jurists

---

Mystics, Monarchs and Messiahs: Cultural Landscapes of Early Modern Iran (Cambridge, MA 2002), 121–60, 398–428.

[114] E.g. *Iksīr al-ʿārifīn* in *Rasāʾil*, 138; *Sih Aṣl*, ed. Khājavī, 27, 79, 83, 107; *Sharḥ al-hidāya*, 3.

[115] *Al-Shawāhid al-rubūbiyya*, Mashhad edn, 377.

[116] This last text was published in *Nashriyya-yi Dānishkada-yi Adabiyyāt-i Tabrīz* 2 (1336 Sh/1957).

such as Muḥammad Bāqir b. Muḥammad Mu'min Sabzavārī [d. 1090/1679],[117] and Jamāl al-Dīn Muḥammad b. Ḥusayn Khwānsārī [d. 1125/1713] flourished.[118]

What about actual critiques and condemnations of our philosopher? Based on two hostile nineteenth century accounts, the first the unreliable *Qiṣaṣ al-ʿulamā'* of Muḥammad Tunikābunī and the second the more reliable but exoteric *Mustadrak al-wasā'il* of Mīrzā Ḥusayn Nūrī, a contemporary historian ʿAbd al-Rafīʿ Ḥaqīqat has devised the following charge sheet explaining the flight from Isfahan, a result of his excommunication (*takfīr*) as Arjomand fancifully puts it.[119] First, he was accused of Sunni sympathies advocating the beliefs of the Sunni Sufi Ibn ʿArabī [d. 1240] including the infamous doctrine of Pharaoh and his death as a believer. The eighteenth century *muḥaddith* and *akhbārī* Yūsuf al-Baḥrānī in particular attacked his belief in the unity of being and his espousal of the views of that 'heretic' Ibn ʿArabī.[120] The late Safavid theologian Muḥammad Bāqir Majlisī [d. 1110/1699] condemned the belief in the unity of being as a most serious heresy and clear disbelief.[121] Second, he was accused of denying the (allegedly) Qur'ānic doctrine of eternal punishment in hellfire for the unbelievers. Third, he allegedly asserted that divine and profane love were identical. Fourth, he denied the resurrection of the physical body of this earth. Fifth, he articulated a hierarchical heaven in which rank was determined by knowledge and action in this world.

These accusations are problematic. First, he is accused of having held these doctrines in Isfahan and expressed them in his commentaries on the Qur'ān and *Uṣūl al-Kāfī* and his treatise *Ṭarḥ al-kawnayn.* Since the first two works are late compositions from his time in Qum and Shiraz, it is unlikely that as a young man he would have been hounded out of Isfahan for works he had yet to write! The third text is more slippery since there is little agreement on which text this is. If it is the *Sarayān*

[117] See RU V, 44–5; AA II, 250: he wrote a number of works in jurisprudence and commentaries on *al-Ishārāt* and on the metaphysics of *al-Shifā'* of Avicenna. Cf. Norman Calder, 'Legitimacy and accommodation in Safavid Iran: the juristic theory of Muḥammad Bāqir al-Sabzavārī (d. 1090/1679)', *Iran* 25 (1987), 91–105.

[118] On this Avicennian philosopher, see *Rawḍāt*, II, 350; RU I, 114; *Tadhkirat al-mulūk: A Manual of Safavid Administration*, tr. V. Minorsky (E. J. W. Gibb Memorial Series XVI, London 1943), 41, 110cf. Corbin, *Histoire de la philosophie islamique* (Paris 1986), 467. His commentary on the legal text *al-Rawḍa al-bahiyya* was lithographed in the nineteenth century (Tehran 1856), and his *scholia* on the metaphysics of *al-Shifā'* of Avicenna was published recently (Qum 1998).

[119] QU 109; Nūrī, *Mustadrak al-wasā'il* (Qum n.d.), IV, 422–3; Ḥaqīqat, *Tārīkh-i ʿulūm va falsafa-yi Īrān* (Tehran 1372 Sh/1993), 767–9; cf. Arjomand, *The Shadow of God*, 149.

[120] LB 131–2.

[121] Majlisī, *ʿAqā'id al-Islām* (Beirut 1993), 48.

wujūd al-Ḥaqq written in the first years after he moved to Isfahan and probably before 1008/1600, then it is not mentioned in early accusations. Besides, if it were such a poisonous work, how did he manage to survive another seven years or so in Isfahan?

Second, Isfahan at the time of Shah ʿAbbās I was not hostile to Sufi metaphysics. Philosophically and mystically-minded jurists were much in vogue, ultimately represented by the like of Mīr Dāmād who had been Shaykh al-Islām of Isfahan in the later years of Shah ʿAbbās (he succeeded his friend Shaykh Bahāʾī), had conducted the coronation ceremony of Shah Ṣafī in 1629, and later died in Najaf in 1040/1631 whilst escorting the Shah to the Shiʿi shrines in Iraq. Another good example was the prominent courtier Sayyid Ḥusayn b. Rafīʿ al-Dīn Marʿashī known as Sulṭān al-ʿulamāʾ [d. 1064/1654] who served as the grand vizier at roughly the same period from 1034/1624–1042/1632.

Third, an accusation of Sufism might be seen as compromising the faith of a Shiʿi, and this remains the case, as Cooper says of the contemporary period, '[Sufism] was, and indeed still is, seen by some Persian ʿulema to dilute a person's Shiism and draw him towards Sunni sympathies and the label Sufi is sometimes used pejoratively in this sense'.[122]

However, the accusation made by Arjomand that a number of the thinkers of the school of Isfahan constructed a philosophy and mysticism that seemed to bypass Shiʿi dogma does not hold up to scrutiny.[123] It is not true to say that Qāḍī Saʿīd Qummī [d. 1107/1696] wrote his early *Kalīd-i Bihisht* without recourse to central Shiʿi concepts such as the authority and power of the Imams and devotion to them encapsulated in that key notion of *walāya*.[124] Nor is it correct to say that Lāhījī wrote *Gawhar-i murād* for Shah ʿAbbās II by concealing his true philosophical intent within a Shiʿi framework.[125] In fact, the success of this Persian work was to demonstrate that a more profound understanding of faith entailed recognising that Shiʿi theology, Sufi metaphysics and Avicennian philosophy were reconciled at a higher transcendent level.[126] Similarly, it cannot be said that Mullā Ṣadrā became oblivious of either the nomological aspect of Shiʿism or its theology. The theme of *walāya* remains central to his thinking. It mediates between the origins and the return of creation (*al-mabdaʾ*

---

[122] John Cooper, 'Rūmī and ḥikmat', in L. Lewisohn (ed.), *The Heritage of Persian Sufism I* (rpt, Oxford 1999), 432.

[123] Arjomand, *The Shadow of God*, 150.

[124] Ed. Sayyid Muḥammad Mishkāt (Tehran 1936).

[125] Ed. Zayn al-ʿĀbidīn Qurbānī Lāhījī (Tehran 1372 Sh/1993).

[126] On the Sufi aspects of the text, see Lewisohn, 'Sufism and the school of Isfahan', 101–12.

wa'l-ma'ād) and is the sole access to true knowledge of God. In *al-Ḥikma al-'Arshiyya* that was probably written in the last years of his life after 1040/1631, he wrote:

> In order actually to attain and comprehend divine insights and inner truths, it is necessary to acquire lights from the lamp-niche of the Seal of prophecy (*mishkāt khātam al-nubūwa*) through the intermediary of the first of his successors [i.e. 'Alī], the most excellent of his friends and the most noble gate to the city of his knowledge. For it is only through the seeds of Sainthood (*al-walāya*) and the tree of guidance (*al-hidāya*) that divine knowledge and spiritual insights can be disseminated and expanded in the hearts of those prepared and capable of receiving their guidance.[127]

This is a good instance of an explicit connection between prophetic and Imamic teaching and the pursuit of philosophy which Corbin famously dubbed 'philosophie prophétique'.[128]

Thus the evidence for Mullā Ṣadrā being driven out of Isfahan is meagre. However, this does not mean that he was not harassed and criticised. I would argue that the real opposition that he faced came from his home town. After leaving Isfahan, he returned to Shiraz but facing the opposition of teachers of *ḥadīth* who now dominated the city, he retired to Kahak near Qum. It was these people that he criticised in *al-Asfār* and in *Sih Aṣl.*[129] There is one contemporary source that appears to be critical of Mullā Ṣadrā and his approach to religion. It seems that sometime in the early 1040s/1630s Shah Ṣafī commissioned Mullā Ṣadrā to produce a Persian translation of *Iḥyā' 'ulūm al-Dīn*, the *magnum opus* of the Sunni Sufi al-Ghazālī [d. 505/1111].[130] At such a later stage in his career, it is unlikely that he seriously considered fulfilling the commission; besides, his own interest and his prolific composition lay elsewhere in this period, in particular with his later works of philosophical theology and his great commentary on *Uṣūl al-Kāfī*. In 1044/1634–5, his fellow townsman a prominent judge called Sayyid 'Alī-Naqī Kamarihī [d.

[127] *'Arshiyya*, 63; cf. Morris, *The Wisdom of the Throne* (Princeton, NJ 1981), 231–2.

[128] Corbin, 'De la philosophie prophétique en Islam Shī'ite', *Eranos Jahrbuch* XXXI (1962), 49–116.

[129] *Al-Asfār*, I, 4–5; *Sih Aṣl*, ed. Nasr, 5–7.

[130] It was his student Fayḍ Kāshānī who eventually undertook the commission and produced a Persian Shi'i version entitled *al-Maḥajja al-Bayḍā fī tahdhīb al-Iḥyā'*. 'Alī-Akbar Ghaffārī produced the standard edition which was published in the 1980s by the seminary in Qum.

1060/1650] wrote a work entitled *Humam al-Thawāqib* for the Shah in which he criticised the commission of a Sufi work such as the *Iḥyā'* but it did not include a critique of Mullā Ṣadrā himself.[131] In fact, he reported that it was Mullā Ṣadrā himself (*mawlānā al-fāḍil al-ʿAllāma al-fahhāma Ṣadrā Muḥammad Shīrāzī*) who informed him of the commission and his reluctance to deliver it.[132]

Ultimately, the question of the harassment of philosophers and mystics in the Safavid period is caught up in the polemics and ideology of those who study religious history. In particular, one is faced with two extremes. The idyllic golden age theorists argue that the flowering of Safavid culture was due to a large extent to the patronage of major figures, who combined expertise in the arts, a profound mystical insight and intuition, a training in law and theology and accomplished philosophical acumen. On the other side, there are those who insist on the primordial conflict between *eros* and *nomos* and see in the conflicts between some jurists and some Sufis and the state apparatus the seeds of a divergence on legitimate authority that since the 1970s in Twelver Shiʿism is known as the debate about *wilāyat al-faqīh.*[133] One suspects that the truth, if that indeed is the correct term to use here, lies somewhere in between.

[131] On him, see AA II, 207; RU IV, 271–2; Fasā'ī, *Fārsnāma-yi Nāṣirī*, II, 1147. Rasūl Jaʿfarīyān, 'Guzārish-i andīsha-yi siyāsī-yi yik ʿālim-i Shīʿī', in *Maqālāt-i Tārīkhī IV* (Qum 1379 Sh/2000), 13–41, who bases his study on MS Madrasa-yi Sipahsālār (Muṭahharī in Tehran) 161, especially fol. 24–40. Another manuscript is indicated in Aḥmad Munzavī, *Fihrist-i nuskha-hā-yi khaṭṭī-yi Fārsī* (Tehran 1969), II, 1716; cf. Babayan, *Mystics, Monarchs and Messiahs*, 416; *al-Dharīʿa* XXV:145. Of course, his criticism of a Sufi text does not mean that he was an Akhbārī; we know that he wrote a strong defence of the method of *ijtihād* in *Risāla dar ithbāt-i luzūm-i wujūd-i mujtahid dar ʿaṣr-i ghaybat*, ed. Abu'l-Ḥasan Muṭṭalibī in *Mīrāth-i Islāmī-yi Īrān VI*, ed. R. Jaʿfarīyān (Qum 1376 Sh/1997), 399–430.

[132] MS Madrasa-yi Sipahsālār 161, fol. 36 cited in Jaʿfarīyān, 'Guzārish-i andīsha-yi siyāsī-yi yik ʿālim-i Shīʿī', 39.

[133] There is an almost insurmountable literature on this topic. But a good introduction to the historical background to the issue within Shiʿi jurisprudence is Ahmad Kazemi Moussavi, *Religious Authority in Shīʿite Islam: from the Office of Muftī to the Institution of the Marjaʿ* (Kuala Lumpur 1996).

Appendix II
Mullā Ṣadrā and the Akhbāriyya: some notes

The early seventeenth century witnessed the formulation of an important (new?) school within Twelver Shiʿism known as the Akhbāriyya.[134] The latter part of the century and much of the eighteenth century was a title of conflict between this school with a particular emphasis on the *ḥadīth* and a thorough dislike for the use of reasoning in pursuit of discovering the law and making sense of theology, and the rationalist *mujtahids* who as a body were called the Uṣūliyya. The Akhbāriyya insisted that religious knowledge had to be founded upon sound principles in the *ḥadīth* and categorically rejected the rational and critical classification of the texts propounded by the Uṣūliyya.[135] The manifesto of the school was *al-Fawāʾid al-Madaniyya* written by the *muḥaddith* Mullā Muḥammad Amīn b. Muḥammad Sharīf Astarābādī [d. 1033/1623–4 or 1036/1626–7] and completed in Mecca in Rabīʿ I 1031/January–February 1622.[136] The response to his polemic came in the form of two major refutations: *al-Shawāhid al-Makkiyya* by Nūr al-Dīn ʿAlī al-ʿĀmilī [d.

[134] For a useful introduction, see E. Kohlberg, 'Akbārīya', *EIr* I, 716–8. For a study of the Safavid period focusing on one late Safavid text *Munyat al-mumārisīn* of ʿAbd Allāh al-Samāhījī [d. 1135/1722], see Andrew Newman, 'The nature of the Akhbārī-Uṣūlī dispute in late Ṣafawid Iran', *BSOAS* 55 (1992), 22–51, 250–61.

[135] We still lack a good, historically grounded study of the development of *ḥadīth* criticism in Twelver Shiʿism. It is often assumed that the process began late with works in the sixteenth century such as *Dirāya fī ʿilm muṣṭalaḥ al-ḥadīth* (Najaf 1960; tr. N Virjee, London 2002) of al-Shahīd II. Asma Afsaruddin has argued that the process of critically evaluating these texts on a rational basis began much earlier in Ḥilla and singles out the role of Jamāl al-Dīn Aḥmad b. Mūsā Ibn Ṭāwūs [d. 1274] and his *Bināʾ al-maqāla al-Fāṭimiyya* (ed. ʿAlī al-ʿAdnānī al-Ghurayfī, Qum 1411/1990) – see her 'An insight into the *Ḥadīth* methodology of Jamāl al-Dīn Aḥmad b. Ṭāwūs', *Der Islam* 72 (1995), 25–46. It was Ibn Ṭāwūs who established the four-fold division of *ḥadīth* into *ṣaḥīḥ* (sound, reliable), *ḥasan* (good, acceptable), *muwaththaq* (trustworthy) and *ḍaʿīf* (weak, unreliable).

[136] Astarābādī, *al-Fawāʾid al-Madaniyya*, ed. Raḥmat Allāh Raḥmatī al-Arākī (Qum 1424/2003), 544. On Astarābādī, see E. Kohlberg, 'Astarābādī', *EIr* II, 845–6.

1086/1657–8],[137] and *al-Sihām al-māriqa min aghrāḍ al-zanādiqa* by al-Shaykh ʿAlī b. Muḥammad b. al-Ḥasan b. Zayn al-Dīn al-ʿĀmilī [d. 1103/1691–2], a virulent attack based on his personal experience of Astarābādī who had been a colleague of his father.

Scholarly debates on the conflict usually take one of two positions. First, the Akhbārī-Uṣūlī conflict is seen as a long-running struggle between traditionalism and rationalism, between the scholars who specialised in the traditions (*akhbār*) of the Imams as the basis of religious knowledge and those who insisted that rational principles could be utilised to make sense of the revealed sources for law and theology.[138] With the increasingly Muʿtazilī tendencies of the Shiʿi theologians of Baghdad from the time of al-Shaykh al-Mufīd [d. 413/1022], traditionalists were condemned as crude literalists (*ḥashwiyya*) and attacked for their neglect of reason.[139] ʿAbd al-Jalīl al-Qazwīnī, a late twelfth century source from Rayy, in his *Kitāb al-naqḍ* distinguished between his own position as a rationalist (*uṣūlī*) and the position of the Akhbārīs whom he called the *ḥashwiyya*.[140] A few years later, the pivotal jurist al-ʿAllāma Ibn al-Muṭahhar al-Ḥillī [d. 726/1325] in his *Nihāyat al-wuṣūl ilā ʿilm al-uṣūl*, completed in 704/1305, labelled the two positions as Uṣūlī and Akhbārī.[141] Astarābādī insisted on calling the ancient traditionalists Akhbārī and argued that well before the time of al-ʿAllāma al-Ḥillī the terms Uṣūlī and Akhbārī were established in usage.[142] Modarressi argues that the successful school of al-ʿAllāma al-Ḥillī [d. 725/1325] had led to the victory of the Uṣūliyya and it was only with the composition

[137] Despite the fact that Akhbārīs have not been a significant factor in Shiʿi thought since the mid-nineteenth century, it is revealing that *al-Fawāʾid* was originally published alongside this refutation in the lithograph of 1312/1894–5, and again most recently in 2003 it was edited by Raḥmat Allāh Raḥmatī al-Arākī (probably just a new typesetting of the lithograph with readings from one manuscript) and published by the seminary. The only edition of the text that has been produced by modern descendents of the Akhbārīs was published in Qum by al-Shaykh Abū Aḥmad Āl ʿUṣfūr in 1981.

[138] Hossein Modarressi, 'Rationalism and traditionalism in Shīʿī jurisprudence: A preliminary survey', *SI* 59 (1984), 141–58; W. Madelung, 'Imāmism and muʿtazilite theology', in T. Fahd (ed.), *Le Shīʿisme imāmite* (Paris 1970), 13–28; Devin Stewart, *Islamic Legal Orthodoxy*, 175–208 with the modified approach that the Akhbāriyya were an anti-*madhhab* movement.

[139] Al-Shaykh al-Mufīd, *Awāʾil al-maqālāt*, ed. ʿAbbās-Qulī Chandarābī and Abū ʿAbd Allāh Zanjānī (Tehran 1364/1945), 81, 82, 86. On the semantic range of *ḥashwiyya* and discussions in classical Islamic law and theology, see A. Halkin, 'The Ḥashwīya', *JAOS* 54 (1934), 1–28.

[140] Al-Qazwīnī, *Kitāb al-naqḍ*, ed. Jalāl al-Dīn Urmawī (Tehran 1954), I, 2–3, 17, 236, 272, 282, 285 *inter alia*.

[141] Al-Ḥillī, *Nihāyat al-wuṣūl ilā ʿilm al-uṣūl*, MS Princeton Arabic New Series 376, fol. 201r, cited in Stewart, *Islamic Legal Orthodoxy*, 182.

[142] Astarābādī, *al-Fawāʾid al-Madaniyya*, 91, 97.

of *al-Fawā'id* that the Akhbāriyya came back into the reckoning.[143] However, he does note that the school of al-Shahīd II [d. 965/1558] prepared the way through their turn to traditions and their criticism of previous independently rational legal positions.[144]

Devin Stewart has recently questioned this and instead suggested that Astarābādī was directly reacting to the rationalism of this school.[145] This seems to be confirmed by studying *al-Fawā'id*. Astarābādī himself stated that his teacher Mīrzā Muḥammad Astarābādī [d. 1028/1619] urged him to revive the way of the Akhbārīs,[146] and to carry forward the project by composing an attack on rationalism within the school of al-Ḥillī with its insistence upon the use of Aristotelian logic and legal reasoning (*ijtihād*) as its first target, and the school of al-Shahīd II as the more immediate and timely opponent.[147] In another text, *Dānishnāma-yi Shāhī* written probably just after *al-Fawā'id* for Muḥammad Quṭb-Shāh [d. 1035/1626] the Shiᶜi ruler of Golconda in India, he made the claim about reviving the way of the Akhbāriyya; indeed that is the theme of the text.[148]

The opposing view considers the Akhbārī movement to be at its origins a seventeenth century phenomenon and is dismissive of the invented genealogy that Astarābādī claims.[149] The traditional biographical sources concur by condemning him for creating a school of slander against the *mujtahids*.[150] These sources do not mention that his teacher was an Akhbārī; he is merely described as a pious scholar and an expert in the study of the narrators of traditions.[151] The Uṣūlī ᶜAlī al-ᶜĀmilī in

---

[143] MT 40–56.

[144] MT 52–3.

[145] Stewart, 'The genesis of the Akhbārī revival', in M. Mazzaoui (ed.), *Safavid Iran and Her Neighbours* (Salt Lake City, UH 2003), 169–93.

[146] Introduction to Astarābādī, *al-Fawā'id al-Madaniyya*, 14.

[147] Astarābādī, *al-Fawā'id al-Madaniyya*, 30; Shaykh Bahā'ī and his work *Mashriq al-Shamsayn* (now ed. M. Rajā'ī, Mashhad 1414/1994) is a particular target – see *al-Fawā'id al-Madaniyya*, 120, 147–60, 478, 486–95. Newman, 'The nature of the Akhbārī-Uṣūlī dispute', 260–1 suggests that the fact that al-Samāhījī does not mention Astarābādī as the founder of the school or even an important member corroborates the position of a long history. However, there may be other reasons for his omission and al-Samāhījī himself could be seen as indulging in a similar invented tradition of his school.

[148] Astarābādī, *Dānishnāma-yi Shāhī*, MS Majlis-i Shūrā 3071, fol. 1r–1v; I am grateful to Dr Robert Gleave for providing me with a copy of this manuscript. Cf. *Rawḍāt*, I, 129–30; MT 52.

[149] Norman Calder, 'The structure of authority in Imāmī Shīᶜī jurisprudence', unpublished Ph.D. dissertation (School of Oriental and African Studies, University of London 1980), 231; Robert Gleave, *Inevitable Doubt: Two Theories of Shīᶜī Jurisprudence* (Studies in Islamic Law and Society vol. 12, Leiden 2000), 7–10; A. Hairi, *Shiᶜism and Constitutionalism in Iran* (Leiden 1977), 66–7.

[150] *Rawḍāt*, I, 120; even the Akhbārī Yūsuf al-Baḥrānī, *Lu'lu'at al-baḥrayn*, 117 says that he was the first to attack the *mujtahids* and divide the community into the Akhbārīs and followers of *mujtahids*.

[151] AA II, 281; RU V, 116; LB 119–20; *Rawḍāt*, VII, 38.

his valuable source *al-Durr al-manthūr min al-maʾthūr wa-ghayr al-maʾthūr* is very complimentary about the elder Astarābādī, which given his virulent *ad hominem* attack on the younger Astarābādī and his dislike of Akhbārīs, would be unlikely if he had considered him to be a member of a group that he detested.[152]

Whichever particular interpretation one prefers, the real issue came down to the use of reason as an independent means for discerning religious knowledge and more broadly the practice of legal reasoning (*ijtihād*). Returning to Mullā Ṣadrā, is there any evidence for any contact between him and this line of argument, in particular with Astarābādī himself? My inquiry is prompted by an abstract proposed by Devin Stewart that suggests that Mullā Ṣadrā wrote *Sharḥ Uṣūl al-Kāfī* as an attack on the Akhbāriyya.[153] The biographical sources do not mention any encounter between them. But circumstantial evidence suggests that a meeting was not inconceivable. Astarābādī spent the first few years of his education in Shiraz where he studied *kalām, uṣūl al-fiqh* (in particular he mentions *Sharḥ al-mukhtaṣar* of al-Ījī) and philosophy with Muḥammad Shāh Taqī al-Dīn Nassāba [d. 1019/1610], a student of Shāh Fatḥ Allāh Shīrāzī [d. 997/1589].[154] He then studied jurisprudence in Iraq and received an *ijāza* in Najaf (*al-mashhad al-muqaddas al-Gharawī*) in 1007/1598 from al-Sayyid Muḥammad b. ʿAlī al-ʿĀmilī [d. 1009/1600], the author of the text in *furūʿ al-fiqh* entitled *Madārik al-aḥkām fī sharḥ Sharāʾiʿ al-Islām.*[155] This confirms that he originally trained as an Uṣūlī. This teacher was a particular influence as he was known to be a *mujtahid* who disliked issuing precepts solely on the basis of legal reasoning and preferred to base his opinions on *ḥadīth.*[156] He continued his travels, returning to Shiraz and may have visited India, which would explain the dedication of *Dānishnāma-yi Shāhī* to an Indian ruler. In *al-Fawāʾid* he tells us that he studied with

---

[152] Al-ʿĀmilī, *al-Durr al-manthūr min al-maʾthūr wa-ghayr al-maʾthūr*, ed. S. A. al-Ḥusaynī (Qum 1978), II, 209–10.

[153] The paper was supposed to be delivered at the World Congress on Mullā Ṣadrā in Tehran in 1999 but never was. In fact, I have been informed by e-mail correspondence with him (26 January 2005) that he never wrote it but that he suspected it to be correct.

[154] Astarābādī, *al-Fawāʾid al-Madaniyya*, 265; RU V, 194; SA 498. I am grateful to Dr Robert Gleave for sharing with me some of his research on the life of Astarābādī which he has prepared for a forthcoming book on the Akhbāriyya provisionally titled *Islamic Literalism: The History and Doctrines of the Akhbārī School of Imāmī Shīʿism.*

[155] Astarābādī, *al-Fawāʾid al-Madaniyya*, 59; RU V, 35–6; *Rawḍāt*, I, 147 who says that the place of the issuance of the license was Mashhad. I am not sure how Devin Stewart arrives at the conclusion that the license was issued in Karbalāʾ – see Stewart, 'The genesis of the Akhbārī revival', 170–1.

[156] MT 53 gives evidence for him and other *mujtahids* who insisted on discerned a *ḥadīth*-based legal system.

the elder Astarābādī in Mecca for ten years beginning in 1015/1606.[157] He probably remained in the Ḥijāz until his death in 1036/1626–7. We have already seen that Mullā Ṣadrā probably visited Iraq with Shaykh Bahāʾī sometime in the middle of the last decade of the sixteenth century. He may also have been in Shiraz at least briefly at the beginning of the seventeenth century, and given that he went on seven pilgrimages to Mecca, an encounter with a fellow Iranian there would not have been out of the question.[158] His student Fayḍ Kāshānī did meet Astarābādī in Mecca and was appreciative of his views on *ḥadīth.*[159] First, in *Kitāb al-Uṣūl al-aṣīla*, written probably between 1041/1631 and 1044/1634–5, he criticised recent scholars for failing to understand the correct procedures in evaluating *ḥadīth*, and upheld one scholar who had actually explained the problem correctly, by whom he meant Astarābādī (*baʿḍ al-fuḍalāʾ, al-fāḍil*).[160] Second, in a later work *al-Ḥaqq al-mubīn fī kayfiyyat al-tafaqquh fīʾl-dīn* which was composed in 1068/1658, he mentioned meeting a scholar of Astarābād in Mecca who was a pioneer in the way of the *ḥadīth.*[161]

Did Mullā Ṣadrā take a position on Astarābādī?[162] Was his commentary on *Uṣūl al-Kāfī* written in the early 1040s/1630s a critique of Astarābādī and his commentary on the same *ḥadīth* collection?[163] Astarābādī was highly critical of philosophy and philosophical theology. The last two chapters on his *al-Fawāʾid* are a systematic attack upon the mistakes of philosophers and theology, in which he focuses his attack on the *Tajrīd* cycle of texts, in particular the *marginalia* of Jalāl al-Dīn Davānī and Ṣadr al-Dīn Dashtakī on the later commentary (*sharḥ jadīd*).[164]

---

[157] Astarābādī, *al-Fawāʾid al-Madaniyya*, 59.

[158] Shiʿi scholarship and presence in the Holy Cities remains largely *terra incognita.* But see Marco Salati, 'Toleration, persecution and local realities: observations on the Shiism in the Holy Places and the Bilād al-Shām', in *La Shīʿa nell'Impero Ottomano* (Rome 1993), 121–48 [see the addenda and corrections provided by Rasūl Jaʿfariyān, 'Tārīkh-i tashayyuʿ dar Makka', in *Maqālāt-i Tārīkhī IV* (Qum 1379 Sh/2000), 43–64]; idem, 'A Shiite in Mecca: The strange case of the Mecca-born Syrian and Persian Sayyid Muḥammad Ḥaydar', in R. Brunner and W. Ende (eds), *The Twelver Shia in Modern Times* (Social, Economic and Political Studies of the Middle East and Asia vol. 72, Leiden 2001), 3–24, especially 4–5 sources.

[159] I am relying upon the excellent study of Etan Kohlberg, 'Aspects of Akhbārī thought', in N. Levetzion and J. Voll (eds), *Eighteenth Century Renewal and Reform* (Syracuse, NY 1987), 133–6, especially 136–8.

[160] Fayḍ Kāshānī, *Kitāb al-uṣūl al-aṣīla*, ed. Jalāl al-Dīn Urmawī (Tehran 1970), 1, 34, 49, 58 *inter alia.*

[161] Fayḍ Kāshānī, *al-Ḥaqq al-mubīn*, ed. Jalāl al-Dīn Urmawī (Tehran 1970), 12.

[162] Kohlberg, 'Aspects of Akhbārī thought', 145 says that Mullā Ṣadrā remained aloof from the Akhbārī-Uṣūlī debate unlike his student.

[163] Astarābādī, *al-Fawāʾid al-Madaniyya*, 35 tells us that he wrote such a work, corroborated by the biographical sources. See Appendix III below for details.

[164] Astarābādī, *al-Fawāʾid al-Madaniyya*, 405–515, especially 500ff.

Defending a traditionalist position, he further strengthened his claim in his conclusion where he implied that his interpretation was directly sanctioned by the Imams themselves who appeared to him in dreams and visions urging him to write the work, and appeared to others as well urging them to travel to Medina to urge him to write the work.[165] Thus any refutation of his position would need to deal with both the traditionalism of the text and the foundational claim of being supported in his endeavours by the Imams.

Mullā Ṣadrā focused on traditionalism. He was sympathetic to visionary experiences of the Imams and would not have criticised such a claim out of hand.[166] In a number of works Mullā Ṣadrā criticised the exoteric scholars of *ḥadīth*, whom he dismissed as *ḥashwiyya*. Muḥammad Khāminihī, the best modern biographer, suggests that these are attacks on Astarābādī.[167] However, the evidence that he presents is insufficient and nowhere in his works does Mullā Ṣadrā ever mention Astarābādī by name. But consider these attacks on the *ḥadīth* folk.

In the famous introduction to *al-Asfār*, he complained:

> I saw that the custom of our time was to inculcate ignorance and disseminate misguidance and stupidity. We became afflicted by a group who attacked understanding, whose eyes could not bear the lights of wisdom and its secrets, whose sight had become consumed like the sights of bats barred from the illumination of knowledge and its effects. They consider a profound meditation and reflection upon divine matters in the divine verses to be a heresy, they consider attempts to convert the masses from being scum as misguidance and a betrayal, as if they are Ḥanābila whose literalist books of *ḥadīth* assimilate the Necessary and the contingent, the Eternal and the incipient. Their gaze does not go beyond the material ... Ignorance has become the most facetious of banners. They have extinguished knowledge and its excellence and harassed spiritual knowledge and its upholders ...
>
> Everyone who is plunged in the sea of ignorance and stupidity and who orbits around the intellectual and the transmitted disciplines, and emerges to

[165] Astarābādī, *al-Fawā'id al-Madaniyya*, 536.

[166] His detractor ʿAlī al-ʿĀmilī in his refutation *al-Shawāhid al-Makkiyya* does not hold back and condemns him for his hallucinations and his arrogance for considering himself so superior to others – see Astarābādī, *al-Fawā'id al-Madaniyya*, 536 at the bottom of the page.

[167] KH 161, 278.

> the height of acceptance and submission, is seen as having arrived and among the people of our time is considered to be the most knowledgeable and the most excellent.[168]

In this passage, he attacked the literalism and anthropomorphism of the Shiʿi *ḥadīth* folk and associated them with the classical example of the *ḥashwiyya* among theologians, the Ḥanbalīs.[169]

Elsewhere, in *Sih Aṣl*, he attacked the view that only *ḥadīth* is knowledge, a position associated with the Akhbāriyya and, again in the same text, he attacked *ḥadīth* folk who seek favour and patronage and are enamoured of worldly status.[170] These citations are not conclusive; for those who would like to rally Mullā Ṣadrā to the Uṣūlī cause, the lack of any explicit engagement is frustrating.

Can the commentary on *Uṣūl al-Kāfī* resolve the impasse? The first place to look is the introduction:

> Know, O my believing brothers and righteous companions – may God guide you to the path of certainty and the way of the pious – that sometimes it is thought that felicity results from sensory pleasures and achieving the highest carnality. But it is clear to one who has investigated matters and tasted the drink of knowledge and experienced light and been conditioned to be safe from evil and purified from this arrogant world, which is but a place for graves, that none of these sensory pleasures are real. They are merely tenebrous veils and changes of bodies and imaginary dreams, reflections in fantastic mirrors like mirages ...[171]

It thus becomes clear at the outset that his commentary will stress the spiritual and affirm knowledge that is beyond the material. True felicity for him lies in an understanding of metaphysical reality and in this he sees a reconciliation and corroboration in the complementary teachings of the sound intellect and the sayings of the Imams:

---

[168] *Al-Asfār*, I, 6.

[169] KH 278 thinks that reference to the Ḥanābila confirms his suspicion that Astarābādī is the intended target; however, this is based on the assumption that the Ḥijāz in this period was dominated by them and that is certainly quite anachronistic.

[170] *Sih Aṣl*, ed. Nasr, 87, 118.

[171] *Sharḥ Uṣūl al-Kāfī*, I, 164.

> It is known axiomatically by those whose correct intellect is guided by explicit tradition that everyone created by God in a correct and sound creation ... must perceive the truth of faith and know and understand through them both the first truth, the angels, the prophets, the scriptures ... They must not stop striving nor be exempt by laziness to acquire knowledge and enlightenment, and purify themselves from the evil of their souls by studying the revealed verses of God and the inspirations of the Prophet and his family.[172]

As we have seen before, true knowledge is Prophetic knowledge and involves meditating upon the Qur'ān and the *ḥadīth* of the Imams. But it is easy to claim to understand these sources through superficial study:

> We have seen that many of those who possess knowledge and understanding and who study the Qur'ān and the *ḥadīth* assiduously are quickly satisfied by the discipline ... due to the lack of their experience of their reality, hastened as they are by corrupt goals and invalid motivations. Thus the wretched among them through their study fail to become felicitous.[173]

He claimed that his own method of deep study that incorporated an understanding of the text and openness to the realities that it may yield is to be preferred:

> I have selected from these *ḥadīth* pearls of knowledge from the sea of wisdom and understanding, conveyed by jewels of the essence of the verities of faith, in which are hidden pure pearls of the meaning of the Qur'ān supported by the rules of demonstration and I have for some time devoted myself to contemplating the secrets of their meaning, delving deeply into the sea of their foundations, maintaining by the power of thought and demonstration the purity of their pearls ...

---

[172] *Sharḥ Uṣūl al-Kāfī*, I, 166.

[173] *Sharḥ Uṣūl al-Kāfī*, I, 167.

> I have glossed them to ease their difficulty and to separate the kernel from the husk and explain the jewels of meaning and the realities of their supports so that this is a book that comprehends the variety of the principles of the faith, disclosed from the minute difficulties of the secrets of certainty. You will find in it a summary of the sayings of the scholars rooted in knowledge and the purity of the experiences of philosophers and theosists. In it are the symbols of Qur'ānic verses and treasures of its lights and the interpretation of the sayings of the Prophet and the secrets of the words transmitted from the people of the house of prophecy and sainthood.[174]

On the face of this, the general trend seems to be at odds with an Akhbārī tendency to limit religious knowledge to explicit sayings, in the absence of which meaning cannot be disclosed and positions not ascertained. For Mullā Ṣadrā, there is never closure in the meaning of truth and revelation, no limit beyond which there is not truth and interpretation available to those willing to receive it. The main point that Astarābādī was making was that, at least since al-Ḥillī, Shiʿi jurists had undergone a Sunni turn and had adopted three illegitimate methods: Sunni method in discerning the law, the use of Aristotelian logic and reasoning, and forsaking the *ḥadīth.* As a result they had illegitimately confined the options for believer to two: either an Uṣūlī *mujtahid* or a follower (*muqallid*). Mullā Ṣadrā does not directly addresses any of these points; nor does he provide a defence for al-Ḥillī or discuss the question of *ijtihād.*[175]

So at this stage, the position of Mullā Ṣadrā with respect to the Akhbāriyya remains elusive, although one is tempted to say that he was critical of anti-rationalism and literalist traditionalism but not the Akhbāriyya in particular.[176] Perhaps once a

---

[174] *Sharḥ Uṣūl al-Kāfī*, I, 168.

[175] One jurist-philosopher and contemporary of Mullā Ṣadrā who did criticise Astarābādī was Sayyid Aḥmad ʿAlawī, the son-in-law of Mīr Dāmād. In 1034/1625, he wrote a brief treatise criticising a work on the impurity of intoxicants (*fī najāsat al-khamr*) – see MS Tehran University Central Library 3749 (fol. 56–8, *nastaʿlīq*, in an Indian *majmūʿa* compiled in Agra and Lahore between 1038/1628–9 and 1080/1669–70).

[176] It is interesting to note that the modern Akhbārī editor of *al-Fawāʾid* (14) mentions in the introduction that Astarābādī wrote a treatise attacking the author of *al-Asfār.* This point is also made by Manṣūr Ṣifatgul, *Sākhtār-i nihād va andīsha-yi dīnī dar Īrān-i ʿaṣr-i Ṣafavī* (Tehran 1381 Sh/2002), 524. They have both been misled by homonymy: when Astarābādī criticised Ṣadr al-Dīn Shīrāzī, he meant Dashtakī [d. 1497] – see *al-Fawāʾid al-Madaniyya*, 500 where he refers to his work refuting the positions of al-Sayyid al-Shīrāzī [Dashtakī] and Dawānī on *Sharḥ al-Tajrīd.* The context is clear elsewhere too: Ṣifatgul quotes *Dānishnāma-yi Shāhī* in which the criticism comes alongside a dismissal of the views of Dawānī – see MS Majlis-i Shūrā 3071, fol. 6v where he mentioned their views in their *marginalia* on the later *Sharḥ al-Tajrīd*,

thorough examination of this text is undertaken alongside the works of Astarābādī, we may be in a position to provide a more definitive answer.

a work which Mullā Ṣadrā never wrote and again he mentioned al-Sayyid al-Shīrāzī (and Mullā Ṣadrā was not a *sayyid*). See the Appendix to Chapter 2 on these two figures and these works. The biographical dictionaries note that he wrote a critique of these two *marginalia* and correctly identify the authors – RU V, 36–7; *Rawḍāt*, I, 147; LB 118.

Appendix III
Commentaries on *al-Kāfī* of al-Kulaynī in the Safavid Period

The establishment of Shiʿism as the official confession of the Safavid dynasty entailed a commitment to propagate and disseminate what had been until then a minority school within Iran. At the forefront of attempts to introduce Shiʿi doctrines and piety to the people was the presentation of the direct sayings of the Imams and their traditions. The classical four books of Shiʿi *ḥadīth* were copied and disseminated and a systematic attempt made to make them accessible through commentaries and translations. This almost pioneering state-led effort was such that some major commentaries in Arabic and Persian were produced in the Safavid period.

The oldest of the four books, a work that encapsulated the totality of the theology and law of Twelver Shiʿism was *al-Kāfī fī ʿilm al-Dīn* compiled by the tradent Abū Jaʿfar Muḥammad b. Yaʿqūb al-Kulaynī [d. 329/941].[177] The text is divided into three sections: *uṣūl*, an exposition of doctrines of the faith beginning with the significant section on the intellect and its excellences; *furūʿ*, on ritual practices and legal prescriptions and prohibitions; and *rawḍa*, a miscellany of texts. Given the central significance of the text for law and theology, it is perhaps surprising that no commentary was written on it before the Safavid period. As commentaries are often a vehicle for expressing theological assumptions and positions, one can discern within them the rival Uṣūlī, philosophical and Akhbārī tendencies. The following is the list

[177] For studies of the text, see Andrew Newman, *The Formative Period of Twelver Shiʿism* (Richmond 2000); ʿAbd al-Rasūl Ghaffār, *al-Kulaynī waʾl-Kāfī* (Qum 1416/1996); I. K. A. Howard, 'Shīʿī theological literature', in M. J. L. Young, J. D. Latham and R. B. Serjeant (eds), *Religion, Learning and Science in the ʿAbbasid Period* (Cambridge 1990), 24–7; idem, 'al-Kāfī by al-Kulaynī', *Al-Serat* 2 (1976), 1–10; M. I. Marcinkowski, 'A glance at the first of the four canonical *ḥadīth* collections of the Twelver-Shīʿites: *al-Kāfī* of al-Kulaynī', *Hamdard Islamicus* 24 (2001), 13–30; Saiyad Nizamuddin Ahmad, 'Twelver Šīʿī ḥadīth', *Oriente Moderno* 82 (2002), 125–45.

of the most important extended commentaries and *marginalia* in chronological order.[178]

1) *Sharḥ* of Muḥammad ʿAlī b. Muḥammad al-Balāghī al-Najafī [d. 1000/1591], which does not seem to be extant. This seems to have been the first commentary ever written.
2) *Al-Rawāshiḥ al-samāwiyya* of Mīr Dāmād [d. 1040/1631] is often described as a *Sharḥ*, but it is really an independent treatise on *ḥadīth* that includes a commentary on the *khuṭba* of *al-Kāfī.*[179] He did write an incomplete philosophical-theological *Ḥāshiya* on the *uṣūl* up to a section of *kitāb al-Ḥujja.* This may be the beginning of the rational approach to the traditions in the commentaries. See *al-Dharīʿa* XI:257. There are a number of manuscripts of this work, e.g. MS Marʿashī (Qum) 4263 (3v–115v, *naskhī,* ownership seal of Muḥammad Ashraf b. Muḥammad ʿAbd al-Ḥasīb Ḥusaynī, his great-grandson, dated 1096/1685); MS Marʿashī 6339 (5v–127r, *nastaʿlīq,* 12th century H); MS Marʿashī 6461 (3v–56v, *naskhī,* 12th century H).
3) *Sharḥ* of Muḥammad Amīn Astarābādī attempts to demonstrate Akhbārī methodology with respect to traditions. The text is rather short and focuses on a section of the *uṣūl.* Manuscript copies include: MS Marʿashī 4594 (1v–44r, *naskhī* dated Ṣafar 1063/January 1653 copied from autograph); MS Marʿashī 6665 (75v–108v, *nastaʿlīq* of Mīr Ḥusayn b. Sayyid Amīr Māzandarānī, Mecca 1072 H).
4) *Sharḥ Uṣūl al-Kāfī* of Mullā Ṣadrā will be discussed in more detail below in Chapter Two. Suffice it to mention here that it is a detailed philosophical and mystical commentary that includes discussions of hermeneutic issues that arise in *uṣūl al-fiqh.*
5) *Ḥāshiya* on the *uṣūl* was written by Sayyid Niẓām al-Dīn Aḥmad ʿAlawī, student and son-in-law of Mīr Dāmād and continues the rationalist project on the text. I have come across one manuscript: MS Marʿashī 2849 (141v–370r, *naskhī,* Muḥarram 1070/September–October 1659). The codex also contains

[178] ʿAbd al-Rasūl Ghaffār, *al-Kulaynī wa'l-Kāfī,* 443–52. For a study of the genre focusing upon the work of Mullā Ṣadrā, see ʿAlī ʿĀbidī Shāhrūdī, *Sharḥ Uṣūl al-Kāfī,* I, 19–161. For a complete listing, see *al-Dharīʿa* VI: 180–84, XIII: 95–100, XIV: 26–28; Fuat Sezgin, *Geschichte des arabischen Schrifttums* (Leiden, 1967), I, 541–42.

[179] There is no critical edition of this text despite the numerous manuscript exemplars. The lithograph is consistently reprinted in offset, especially in Qum.

a *marginalia* by his son Badr al-Dīn Ḥusayn (fol. 1v–136v, *nastaʿlīq*, 1094/1683).

6) *Sharḥ* composed by the Avicennian philosopher and jurist Sayyid Muḥammad Rafīʿ al-Dīn b. Ḥaydar al-Ṭabāṭabāʾī known as Mullā Rafīʿā Nāʾinī [d. 1083/1672–3] on the *uṣūl.*[180] See *al-Dharīʿa* VI:184, XIV:27. There are a number of manuscripts of this commentary that again focuses on doctrinal issues, e.g. MS Marʿashī 3748 (174ff, *nastaʿlīq* of Mīr Maʿṣūm Hiravī before 1091/1680]; MS Marʿashī 6342 (250ff, *nastaʿlīq* of Mullā Khalīl Qazwīnī before 1089/1678); MS Marʿashī 7121 (106v–322v, *nastaʿlīq*, ownership stamp dated Ṣafar 1163/January–February 1750); MS Āstān-i Quds-i Raḍawī (Mashhad) 7582 (*shikaste*, 12th century H); MS Āstān-i Quds-i Raḍawī 10099 (*naskhī*, 12th century H); MS Princeton Arabic New Series (157ff, *nastaʿlīq*, Shaʿbān 1110 H).

7) Mullā Khalīl b. Ghāzī Qazwīnī [d. 1089/1678], a student of Fayḍ Kāshānī, wrote two traditionalist commentaries: *al-Shāfī fī sharḥ al-Kāfī* in Arabic, and *al-Ṣāfī fī sharḥ al-Kāfī* in Persian.[181] See *al-Dharīʿa* XIV:27. An extensive commentary focusing on the traditions relating to ritual prescriptions, there are a number of extant manuscripts, e.g. MS Marʿashī 2334 (183ff, *naskhī* of Muḥammad Qāsim Ḥusaynī Ṭāliqānī, 8 Ṣafar 1112 H).

8) Muḥammad Ṣāliḥ b. Aḥmad Māzandarānī [d. 1081/1670], son-in-law of Majlisī I, wrote a monumental commentary in Arabic on the *Uṣūl*, the *rawḍa* and sections of *furūʿ*, and is probably the most commonly found commentary in manuscript collections.[182] There is even a modern edition.[183] He also commented on other *ḥadīth* collections and works of *fiqh*. See *al-Dharīʿa* XIV:27. This is a thoughtful theological commentary that often appeals to philosophical argument in its discussion, and even approves of Sufi

---

[180] On this important thinker of the reigns of Shah Ṣafī and ʿAbbās II, see Ghulām-Riḍā Zavāra, 'Muʿarrifī-yi āthār-i kalāmī az ʿaṣr-i Ṣafavī', *Kitāb-i Māh: Dīn* 4.11–2 (1380 Sh/2001), 32–9; Corbin, *Histoire de la philosophie islamique*, 467. He wrote a short theological text for the Shah Ṣafī entitled *Shajara-yi Ilāhiyya* dated Rabīʿ II 1047/August-September 1637. Two early manuscripts are: MS British Museum Or. Add. 7612 (fol. 1–42, *nastaʿlīq* dated Shawwāl 1056/November–December 1646), and MS Marʿashī 8252 (*nastaʿlīq* of Muṣṭafā b. Muḥammad Ḥusaynī Najafī dated 29 Jumāda I 1078/16 November 1667).

[181] There is an old Lucknow lithograph from 1831 of the Persian commentary. On him, see *Rawḍāt*, III, 257–62; AA II, 112; Ardabīlī, *Jāmiʿ al-ruwāt*, I, 297; SA 491.

[182] On him, see RU V, 110; *Rawḍāt*, VI, 87.

[183] Edited by al-Sayyid ʿAlī ʿĀshūr (12 vols, Beirut 2000).

approaches. However, it is systematically critical of the approach of Mullā Ṣadrā.

9) Perhaps the best known and most comprehensive commentary is *Mirʾāt al-ʿuqūl* of Majlisī II [d. 1110/1699], the best example of a traditionalist approach.[184] See *al-Dharīʿa* XI:279–80.

What is clear is that despite the focus on Akhbārī thought in the seventeenth century and their use of commentaries on *ḥadīth* to propagate their views on the foundations of religious knowledge, most major commentaries in the period were not of that tendency but were rather open to philosophical, rational and even mystical approaches to the traditions.[185]

[184] Majlisī, *Mirʾāt al-ʿuqūl fī sharḥ akhbār Āl al-Rasūl*, ed. Sayyid Ḥ. Rasūlī Maḥallātī (25 vols, Tehran 1984–90).
[185] E.g. Māzandarānī, *Sharḥ Uṣūl al-Kāfī*, I, 12–18.

Chapter 2
An Annotated Bibliography of Mullā Ṣadrā Shīrāzī[186]

A major polymath of the Safavid period and arguably the greatest philosopher in Islam after Avicenna, Mullā Ṣadrā has suffered from presumptuous interpretation and neglect partly due to the lack of availability of reliable editions and translations of his work. In order for those interested in Islamic thought to be able to engage seriously with his work, a first-order requirement is access to a reliable bibliography of his works and tools for research that will point the investigator in a useful direction.

My hope is to provide such a tool in this chapter. I have set out to cover three areas: a full bibliography of his works, explanatory comments on the nature of his

---

[186] Previous bibliographies include:

Sayyid Jalāl al-Dīn Āshtiyānī, *Sharḥ-i ḥāl va ārā'-yi falsafī-yi Mullā Ṣadrā* (Mashhad 1350 Sh/1971), 251–67. Henceforth Āsh.

Muḥsin Bīdārfar, Introduction to Mullā Ṣadrā, *Tafsīr al-Qur'ān al-Karīm*, ed. M. Khājavī (Qum 1987), I, 90–111. Henceforth Bīd.

Cécile Bonmariage, 'Le réel et les réalités: La structure de la réalité de l'être chez Mullā Ṣadrā Shīrāzī', unpublished Ph.D. dissertation (Université Catholique de Louvain 1998), II, 2–24. Henceforth Bonmariage.

Corbin, Introduction to Mullā Ṣadrā, *Kitāb al-mashā'ir*, ed. H. Corbin (Tehran 1964), 27–41. Henceforth Corbin.

Dānishpazhūh, 'Fihrist', in Nasr (ed.), *Sadra Commemoration Volume* (Tehran 1961), 107–20. Henceforth *SCV*.

Trad Hamade, 'Dieu, le monde et l'âme chez Molla Sadra al-Shirazi', unpublished Ph.D. dissertation (Université de Paris I-Panthéon-Sorbonne 1992), 181–215.

Ibrahim Kalin, 'An annotated bibliography of the works of Mullā Ṣadrā with a brief account of his life', *Islamic Studies* 42 (2003), 21–62.

S. Rajaie Khorassani, 'Mulla Sadra's Philosophy and its Epistemological Implications', Unpublished Ph.D. dissertation (Durham University 1976), 19–33.

Muḥammad Riḍā al-Muẓaffar, Introduction to *al-Asfār*, I, ʿayn–tā.

Seyyed Hossein Nasr, *Sadr al-Din al-Shirazi and his Transcendent Theosophy* (Tehran 1977), 30–53.

A recent work claims to be an exhaustive bibliography including manuscript information but is not. See Nāhīd Bāqirī Khurramdashtī with the assistance of Fāṭima Aṣgharī, *Kitābshināsī-yi jāmiʿ-yi Mullā Ṣadrā* (Tehran 1378 Sh/1999).

works and their content, and some key references to manuscripts of his work (of particular relevance given the paucity of critical editions of his work and their relative value). Significant manuscript copies (including autographs) are given in bold. However, the situation is changing through the efforts of the Sadra Islamic Philosophy Research Institute based on Tehran that has convened conferences on his work and is systematically publishing critical editions, studies and translations of his works.

I Major metaphysical works

1) *Asfār.*
al-Ḥikma al-mutaʿāliya fī'l-asfār al-ʿaqliyya al-arbaʿa.
The Transcendent Philosophy of the Four Journeys of the Intellect.
See *GAL* S II: 588, *al-Dharīʿa* VI:9–20.
The standard edition is edited by Riḍā Luṭfī, Ibrāhīm Amīnī, and Fatḥallāh Ummīd, 3rd printing (Beirut 1981). It is not clear (at least we are not told) which manuscripts were the basis of the edition. This 1981 edition, though not a critical one, contains the marginalia of ʿAlī Nūrī [d. 1831], Hādī Sabzavārī [d. 1873], ʿAlī Zunūzī [d. 1891], Ākhūnd-i Hīdajī [d. 1930], and ʿAllāma-yi Ṭabāṭabāʾī [d. 1981].
A new critical edition with the marginalia of Hādī Sabzavārī under supervision of Sayyid Muḥammad Khāminihī, the president of SIPRIn (Tehran 1380–83 Sh/2001–5). This edition is more user-friendly with paragraphing, notes and identification of key sources. But unlike the earlier edition, it only includes the marginalia of Sabzavārī which are gathered at the end of the volume and not given at the foot of the page.
Vol. I, ed. Ghulām-Riḍā Aʿvānī ((Tehran 1383 Sh/2005). This volume covers marḥala I–IV of the 1st safar. Although the introduction does not detail the manuscripts used, a comparison of the critical apparatus with other volumes shows that it is based on the following: Majlis-i Shūrā 1707 and 1708, Sipahsālār 1403 and 1430, Āstān-i Quds-i Raḍavī 317, Kitābkhāna-yi Gulpāyigānī 21/3, and an extremely important codex from the private Kitābkhāna-yi Tuysirkānī (372ff, based on an autograph dated Jumāda I 1051).
Vol. II, ed. Maqṣūd Muḥammadī (Tehran 1380 Sh/2001). This volume covers marḥala IV–VI of the 1st safar and has a brief introduction prefaced. The edition is

based on the following MSS: Majlis-i Shūrā 1707 and 1708, Sipahsālār 1403 and 1430, Āstān-i Quds-i Raḍavī 317, and Kitābkhāna-yi Gulpāyigānī 21/3.
Vol. III, ed. Maqṣūd Muḥammadī (Tehran 1381 Sh/2002). The edition is based on MSS Majlis-i Shūrā 1707 and 1708, Sipahsālār 1403, Āstān-i Quds-i Raḍavī 317, and Kitābkhāna-yi Gulpāyigānī 21/3 and the codex from the private Kitābkhāna-yi Tuysirkānī.
Vol. IV, ed. Maqṣūd Muḥammadī (Tehran 1380 Sh/2001). This volume from the 2nd safar is based on MSS Majlis-i Shūrā 1707, Sipahsālār 1403, Āstān-i Quds-i Raḍavī 317, Tehran University Central Library 2279 and the codex from the private Kitābkhāna-yi Tuysirkānī.
Vol. V, ed. Riḍā Muḥammadzāda (Tehran 1381 Sh/2002). This volume covers the discussion of substantiality (*jawhariyya*) in the 2nd safar, fann IV. This critical edition is based on the following MSS: Sipahsālār 1403, Āstān-i Quds-i Raḍavī 317, Majlis-i Shūrā 1707, the nineteenth century lithograph, Tehran University Central Library 2279, and the codex from the private Kitābkhāna-yi Tuysirkānī.
Vol. VI, ed. Aḥmad Aḥmadī (Tehran 1381 Sh/2002). This volume deals with aspects of theology from the 3rd safar. It is based on the following MSS: Sipahsālār 1404, Majlis-i Shūrā 1706 and 1707 and 1708, Tehran University Central Library 9989, Āstān-i Quds-i Raḍavī 317, and the private Kitābkhāna-yi Tuysirkānī codex, as well as the lithograph.
Vol. VII, ed. Maqṣūd Muḥammadī (Tehran 1380 Sh/2001). This volume covers the beginning of the 3rd safar. It is based on the following MSS: Majlis-i Shūrā 1706 and 1707 and 1708, Tehran University Central Library 9989, Āstān-i Quds-i Raḍavī 317, Sipahsālār 1404, and the private Kitābkhāna-yi Tuysirkānī codex.
Vol. VIII, ed. ʿAlī-Akbar Rashād (Tehran 1382 Sh/2003). This volume from the 4th safar on the nature of the soul is based on MSS Majlis-i Shūrā 1706 and 1707, Sipahsālār 1404, Āstān-i Quds-i Raḍavī 317, and the codex from the private Kitābkhāna-yi Tuysirkānī.
Vol. IX, ed. Riḍā Akbarīyān (Tehran 1381 Sh/2002). This volume deals with the culmination of the 4th safar and the discussion of the resurrection. It is based on these MSS: Majlis-i Shūrā 1706 and 1707, Sipahsālār 1404, Āstān-i Quds-i Raḍavī 317, Tehran University Central Library 385, and the lithograph.
There is another edition with scholia by the seminarian and philosopher Ḥasanzāda Āmulī (3 vols so far, Tehran 1415/1995–). As yet incomplete, this is another non-critical edition. The editor has provided extensive scholia in the footnotes and references to relevant works and citations.

The *Asfār* was lithographed in four volumes in Tehran in 1282/1865 with the marginalia of Hādī Sabzavārī [d. 1873], Āqā Muḥammad Bīdābādī [d. 1783], ʿAlī Nūrī [d. 1831], Ismāʿīl Iṣfahānī [d. 1861], Āqā Muḥammad Riḍā Qumshihī [d. 1888–9], ʿAlī Zunūzī [d. 1891], and Mīrzā Hāshim Rashtī Ashkivarī [d. 1914]. The copyist was Muḥammad Ṣādiq Gulpāyigānī and the editor was ʿAlī Dāmghānī.

There are two good Persian translations of the text: one incomplete effort is by a philosophy professor at Tehran University Javād Muṣliḥ translated as *Falsafa-yi ʿālī*, (3 vols, Tehran 1337 Sh–/1958–); the second one is more satisfactory and complete, translated by the well-known editor Muḥammad Khājavī (Tehran 1378–82 Sh/1999–2003), dividing each volume of the Arabic into three in Persian. The main drawback of this large undertaking is that the translator has chosen not to translate key terminology from the Arabic which may make it inaccessible for some Persian readers.

Signalling its importance in India, there is an Urdu translation of the first safar completed by a group working under Sayyid Manāẓir Aḥsan Gīlānī at Osmania University (Hyderabad 1947). A fairly poor effort, there are claims that the famous Islamist Abu'l-Aʿlā Mawdūdī was involved in the project.

Thus far, there is no translation of the text in a European language except for a partial German translation that can be found in Max Horten, *Die Gottesbeweise bei Schirazi* (Strassburg 1912).

This is his *magnum opus*. It was commenced in Kahak in 1015/1606 and completed in Shiraz on Friday 7 Jumāda I 1037/14 January 1628. We know his birth year because he mentions that at the time he was fifty-eight years old.

The work is divided into four parts or journeys: 'I have arranged my book to correspond to their movement through lights and signs in four journeys and I have named it the transcendent philosophy of the journeys of the intellect' (*Asfār* I: 13). The first journey from creation to God (*min al-khalq ilā'l-ḥaqq*) encompasses Sadrian ontology and metaphysics and comprises volumes I to III. It is divided into ten stages (*marḥala*). It deals with the logic of being and non-being, the basic divisions of being and its senses, and problems of essence, universals and definition, as well as causation. The first journey sets out the ontological foundations of his approach to philosophy. The main thrust of the argument is to demonstrate that being has primary sense and reference (*aṣālat al-wujūd*), that there is a critical distinction between the notion and reality of being, and its referents are modulations within a singular reality (*tashkīk al-wujūd*). Being is shown to possess modes, concrete, propositional and mental (*al-wujūd al-dhihnī*). Causation within the hierarchy of being is explained in terms of degrees of intensity, illuminative relations and the doctrine of 'noble future contingency' (*al-imkān al-ashraf*). The dynamics of the system are also discussed: time and substantial motion (*al-ḥaraka al-jawhariyya*). At the culmination of this stage, the philosopher-wayfarer acquires a mastery over preliminaries into divinalia.

The second journey in God with God (*biʾl-ḥaqq fīʾl-ḥaqq*) is somewhat strangely the framework for his study of physics, of substance, accidents, hylomorphism and categories and corresponds to volumes IV to V. It is divided into sciences (*funūn*) following the Avicennan term for a section on natural philosophy. It includes his proof for Platonic forms, his critique of Aristotelian categories and the ontological realm of the 'Imaginal' (*ʿālam al-mithāl*).

The third journey from God to creation (*min al-ḥaqq ilāʾl-khalq*) deals with the descent from the divine realm into the realm of *intelligibilia*, and comprises volumes VI to VII of the edition. It is divided into stations (*mawāqif*). This stage includes an inquiry into the nature of the divine essence, attributes and acts. This journey focuses upon the theological core of the work. It includes the famous proof for the existence of God known as '*burhān al-ṣiddīqīn*' that proceeds through a pure analysis of being. It explains the God-world relationship and posits the doctrine of the simple whole (*basīṭ al-ḥaqīqa kull al-ashyāʾ*) that draws upon the description of the pure Intellect in the Theologia Aristoteles. He also discusses the nature of revelation and prophecy, divine providence and theodicy.

The final journey in creation with God (*fīʾl-khalq biʾl-ḥaqq*) is a discussion of psychology, soteriology and eschatology and makes up the final two volumes. It includes an initiation into the pyschology of the soul, and is an illustration of the maxim that 'he who knows his self, knows his Lord' (*man ʿarafa nafsahu fa-ʿarafa rabbah*). What is significant about the culmination of his thought is the shift from Avicennan psychology to a mystical account of the soul and its afterlife based upon the Sufi metaphysics of Ibn ʿArabī.

There is an excellent research aid for this text: M. J. ʿIlmī and S. M. Mīrī, *Fihrist-i mawḍūʿī-yi Kitāb al-Ḥikma al-mutaʿāliya fīʾl-asfār al-arbaʿa al-ʿaqliyya* (Tehran 1374 Sh/1995).

Another contemporary work that is an extensive and useful commentary in Persian (which incorporates large sections of the text in Persian translation) is Āyat Allāh ʿAbd Allāh Jawādī Āmulī, *Raḥīq-i makhtūm: Sharḥ-i Ḥikmat-i mutaʿāliya* (10 vols, Qum 1376–80 Sh/1997–2001). This is an excellent guide to the sources, influences and intellectual history of the ideas and arguments in the work.

Manuscripts:[187]

Cambridge University Library Or. 734 (1st safar, 229ff, naskhī, 1273 H), 735 (2nd safar, 194ff, naskhī, 1230 H), 736 (3rd safar, 209ff, naskhī, 1272 H), 737 (4th safar, 220ff, naskhī, 1273 H).

British Museum Or. 6420 (3rd safar, 76v–117r, nastaʿlīq, 19th century), 6423 (4th safar, 199ff, naskhī, 1245/1829), 6320 (4th safar, 174ff, nastaʿlīq, Shaʿbān 1250 H).

Institute of Ismaili Studies (London) 609 (1st safar, 447ff, shikaste, 19th century H).

Imām Jumʿa-yi Kirmān Collection (Tehran University) 157 (nastaʿlīq, 13th century H), 479 (naskhī, 1259 H).

Tehran University Central Library 257 (1st safar, 232ff, taʿlīq, 1245 H), 258 (2nd safar, 152ff, taʿlīq, 1244 H), 259 (3rd safar, 153ff, taʿlīq, 1244 H), 260 (4th safar, 124ff, taʿlīq, 1239 H), **385 (4th safar, 288ff, naskhī, 1087 H autograph of Muḥammad ʿAlam al-Hudā b. Fayḍ Kāshānī)**, 386 (1st safar, 243ff, shikaste of Muḥammad Riḍā Tabrīzī, 29 Ṣafar 1232 H Isfahan), 1506 (1st safar, 151ff, naskhī, 1201 H), 1170 (164ff, naskhī, 1276 H), 2270 (1st safar, 355ff, naskhī, 1277 H), **2279 (1st safar, 263ff, naskhī of Ismāʿīl b. Hādī Qā'inī Bīrjandī, Ṣafar 1203 H date of marginalia of ʿAlī Nūrī)**, 2298 (2nd safar, 198ff, nastaʿlīq, 12th or 13th century H), 2370 (1st safar, 224ff, naskhī, 1264 H), 6580 (306ff, naskhī, 1204 H), 6608 (1st safar, 306ff, naskhī of Muḥammad Gūyā, 12 Rajab 1204 H), 6621 (2nd and 3rd safar, 269ff, nastaʿlīq, 13th century H), 7237 (1st safar, 146ff, nastaʿlīq, 1249 H), 7327 (3rd safar, 160ff, nastaʿlīq, 13th century H), 7279 (89ff, nastaʿlīq, 13th century H), 8322 (1st safar, 155ff, naskhī, 13th century H), 9987 (3rd safar, 104ff, naskhī, 12th century H), 9988 (221ff, naskhī, 11th century H), **9989 (1st safar, 262ff, naskhī of Mīrzā Ismāʿīl b. Hādī Qā'inī, Jumāda I 1051 H)**, 10001 (3rd safar, 159ff, 1274 H).

Tehran University Law Faculty 6 (3rd safar, 221ff, naskhī, late 12th century H), 87 (1v–229r, naskhī, 1222 H), **113 (1st safar, 307ff, nastaʿlīq, 11th century H)**.

Millī-yi Īrān (National Library, Tehran) 1228 (1st safar, 283ff, nastaʿlīq, 1236 H), 1401 (2nd safar, 149ff, nastaʿlīq, 1241 H), 2527 (1st safar on substance and accident, 162ff, shikaste, 1206 H).

Madrasa-yi Marvī (Tehran) 292 (1st safar, naskhī of Ismāʿīl, 1240 H), 683 (4th safar, late 12th century H), 709 (3rd safar, naskhī, late 12th century H).

---

[187] I have provided details of as many manuscripts as I have been able to locate and in parentheses, I have stated the number of folios, the type of script, and the date of the copy if available. Of course, the list is neither complete nor exhaustive in details; I have relied upon the information available in the catalogues, which in many cases is far from satisfactory. One major lacuna is the absence of references from Turkish libraries.

Sipahsālār (Tehran) 1403 (nastaʿlīq of Muḥammad Muqīm b. ʿAbd al-Nabī, 559ff, 1076–7 H), **1404 (3rd and 4th safar, naskhī/nastaʿlīq, 11th century H)**, 1425 (2nd safar, naskhī of Muḥammad Jaʿfar Iṣfahānī, Rabīʿ I 1251 H), 1426/1 (3rd safar, 412ff, naskhī, 12th century H), 1428 (4th safar, naskhī of Ismāʿīl b. Karbalāʾī Ḥasan, 19 Ṣafar 1251 H), 1429 (3rd safar, 235ff, naskhī of Muḥammad b. ʿAlī Ṭabāṭabāʾī Quhpāʾī, 1248 H), **1430 (1st safar up to causation, 134ff, nastaʿlīq, 11th century H)**, 6315 (3rd safar, 253ff, nastaʿlīq, Rabīʿ II 1238 H), 6317 (1st safar, 73ff, naskhī of Muḥammad ʿAbd al-Karīm, Tuesday 29 Rajab 1212 H Isfahan), 6319/1 (1st safar, 30v–302v, naskhī, 12th century H), 8199 (185ff, nastaʿlīq of ʿAlī b. Muḥammad Ḥusayn Ḥusaynī Tunikābunī, Dhuʾl-Ḥijja 1246 H).

Majlis-i Shūrā-yi Millī (Tehran) 78 (1st safar, 322ff, shikaste, 1270 H with *marginalia* of Jilva), 97 (1st safar, 267ff, nastaʿlīq, 1266 H), 169 (205ff, naskhī, 1160 H), 199 (3rd safar, 328ff, naskhī, 19th century), **1706 (2nd and 3rd safar, 705ff, nastaʿlīq/naskhī of Muḥammad Qawām al-Dīn Tūnī/Rāzī?, 1051 H)**, 1707 (4th safar, 914ff, nastaʿlīq of ʿAbd Allāh and ʿAlī Zunūzī, 1222 H), **1708 (1st and 2nd safar, 914ff, naskhī, n.d but based on autograph)**, 1989 (1st safar, 624ff, naskhī, 1257 H), 1990 (2nd safar, 382ff, naskhī, 1274 H), 1991 (3rd safar, 363ff, naskhī, 1261 H), 1992 (4th safar, 407ff, naskhī, 1262 H), 1993 (1st safar, 366ff, naskhī, 1267 H), 1994 (1st safar, 566ff, nastaʿlīq, 12th century H), 2942 (4th safar, 344ff, naskhī, 1254 H), 3762 (1st safar, 28ff, naskhī, 13th century H), 4189 (4th safar, 310ff, nastaʿlīq of Muḥammad Khurāsānī, 1101 H), **4797 (3rd safar, 373ff, shikaste of Muḥammad Hādī Ghiyāth al-Dīn Manṣūr, 11th century H)**, 4979 (3rd safar, 1–289ff, nastaʿlīq, 12th century H).

Majlis-i Sīnā (Tehran) 280 (portions of 3rd safar and other sections, shikaste, 1191 H).

Kitābkhāna-yi Chihil Sutūn Masjid Jāmiʿ-yi Tehrān 49 (3rd and 4th safar, nastaʿlīq, 1274 H with marginalia of ʿAlī Zunūzī and Muḥammad Riḍā Qumshihī).

Mashhad University Faculty of Theology 22 (1st safar, 144ff, naskhī, 1237 H), 1339 (346ff, nastaʿlīq, 1240 H), 1608 (81ff, shikaste, 13th century H), 1903 (399ff, naskhī, 11th century H).

Āstān-i Quds-i Raḍavī (Mashhad) 26 (342ff, naskhī, 1262 H), 317 (504ff, nastaʿlīq of ʿAlī-panāh Ḥusayn Zunūzī Tabrīzī, 1206 H), 318 (1st safar, 313ff, nastaʿlīq, 1264 H, 319 (216ff, nastaʿlīq of Faḍl Allāh Ḥusaynī, 1237 H), 320 (208ff, naskhī of Ḥasan Khwānsārī, Rabīʿ I 1224 H), 321 (2nd safar, 119ff, nastaʿlīq, 19th century), 322 (nastaʿlīq of Ḥasan ʿAlī, 1257 H), 6968 (naskhī, 1237 H), 6991 (nastaʿlīq, 1235 H), 7433 (naskhī, 1271 H), 9933 (incomplete), 11221 (1st safar, 359ff, nastaʿlīq of Muḥammad b. ʿAbd al-Karīm, Shawwāl 1219 H), 12181 (naskhī), 14298 (shikaste, 1222 H).

Jāmiʿ-yi Gawharshād (Mashhad) 102 (207ff, naskhī, 1262 H), 103 (146ff, naskhī, 1265 H), 332 (155f, nastaʿlīq shikaste, 19 Jumāda I 1223 H), 478 (204ff, nastaʿlīq, 13th century H), 514 (3rd safar, 81ff, nastaʿlīq of Muḥammad Taqī, 25 Ramaḍān 1215 H Isfahan).

Malik (Āstān-i Quds-i Raḍavī, Mashhad) 473 (2nd and 3rd safar, 335ff, shikaste, 1237 H), 1237 (1st and 2nd safar, 171ff, shikaste, n.d.), 1398 (3rd safar, 200ff, naskhī, 13th century H), 2184 (1st safar, 140ff, naskhī, 12th century H), 2218 (1st safar, 232ff, shikaste, 13th century H), 2417 (1st safar, 225ff, naskhī, 1285 H), 2900 (1st safar, 343ff, nastaʿlīq, 1235 H), 2952 (1st safar, 399ff, naskhī, 1222 H).

Āstāna-yi Shāh-i Chirāgh (Shiraz) 285 (43ff, naskhī, n.d.).

Kitābkhāna-yi ʿUmūmī-yi Āyat Allāh Marʿashī (Qum) 5648 (2nd safar, 203ff, nastaʿlīq of Aḥmad b. Muḥammad Ḥusaynī, 12 Ramaḍān 1238 H), 6136 (incomplete 1st safar, 348ff, nastaʿlīq, 13th century H in hand of ʿAlī Nūrī)), 7078 (lithograph), 12148 (only 2nd safar, 254ff, nastaʿlīq, 1321 H).

Kitābkhāna-yi Gulpāyigānī (Qum) majmūʿa 21/3 (naskhī, Shaʿbān 1051 H)

Kitābkhāna-yi Vazīrī (Yazd) 1515 (1st safar, 221ff, naskhī of Muḥammad Mahdawī Raḍawī, Muḥarram 1094 H).

Kitābkhāna-yi Namāzī (Khūʾī) 156 (3rd and 4th safar, naskhī of Muḥammad al-Ḥusaynī, Dhuʾl-Qaʿda 1096 H).

Maktabat Amīr al-Muʾminīn al-ʿāmma (Najaf) 1091 (1st safar, 302ff, naskhī of his son Qawām al-Dīn, Isfahan 1072 H), 1090 (1st safar, 380ff, naskhī, 12th century H).

Sālār Jung (Hyderabad) 3 (1st safar only, 176ff, naskhī, dated 1843), 4 (3rd and 4th safar, 343ff, Shafīʿa, dated 1072/1661), **24 (3rd and 4th safar, 343ff, naskhī of Shafīʿ Shujāʿ al-Dīn Maḥmūd Raḍawī in Isfahan 1072 H)**.

Asiatic Society of Bengal (Calcutta) 852 (shikaste, 1190 H), 52 (3rd safar, shikaste, 1813 CE).

Būhār Library (Calcutta) 331 (3rd safar, 204ff, naskhī, 1289 H).

Raza Library (Rampur) 3648 (nastaʿlīq, 1st safar, 423ff, 19th century), 3649 (nastaʿlīq, 2nd safar, 146ff, 1222/1808), 3650 (nastaʿlīq, 1st and 3rd safar, 97ff, 19th century), 3468 (naskhī, 117v–124r, 18th century).

Āṣafiyya (Ḥyderābād) 207.

Dār al-Kutub (Cairo) 2345 (171ff, mixed script, 12th century H), 2346 (2nd safar, 170ff, mixed script, 1184 H).

Bibliothèque Nationale (Paris) 6994.

Princeton (Arabic New Series) 680 (1st safar, 215ff, naskhī, 1222 H), 891 (4th safar, 110ff, naskhī, 18th century), 1301 (3rd safar, 1261 H), 1873 (3rd safar, 1230 H).

2) *Shawāhid.*

Al-Shawāhid al-rubūbiyya fī'l-manāhij al-sulūkiyya.

Witnessing the Divine along the Path of the Wayfarers.

Ed. S. J. Āshtiyānī with *marginalia* of Sabzavārī (Mashhad 1967). An uncritical edition, the editor notes that he based his edition mainly on the lithograph supplemented by MS Tehran University Library 4549, a manuscript from Āstān-i Quds-i Raḍavī (no details given), a manuscript from the Malik Library dated 1102 H (not clear which one this is) and a manuscript in the private collection of Mullā Ismāʿīl Iṣfahānī Darbkūshkī. The edition is prefaced with a large (158 page) introduction by Āshtiyānī on the contents of the text and the history of the school of Mullā Ṣadrā into the 20th century.

Pirate reprint of the edition (Beirut 2000).

A new critical edition by Sayyid Muṣṭafā Muḥaqqiq Dāmād (Tehran 1382 Sh/2003). This is an excellent edition based on nine manuscripts, the 19th century lithograph and the Āshtiyānī edition. The *aṣl* is MS Tehran University Central Library 406. The others used as MSS Tehran University Central Library 4549, 1541, 274; MS Malik 2403; MS Madrasa-yi Fayḍiyya 1748; MS Majlis-i Shūrā 1917; MS Marʿashī 9066; and a private MS of Muḥammad Bāqir Iṣfahānī copied 29 Shawwāl 1312/25 April 1895.

A new Persian translation and commentary undertaken by Jawād Muṣliḥ (Tehran 1383 Sh/2004).

It was lithographed in 1286/1870 with the *marginalia* of Sabzavārī and copied by Muḥammad ʿAlī Iṣfahānī, a student of ʿAlī Zunūzī.

See *GAL* S II: 589, and *al-Dharīʿa* XIII:339, XIV:243.

It was completed in the 1030s H, or at least before 1041/1631 since Mīr Dāmād ('our noble teacher and master of the great scholars') is mentioned as alive ('may his shadow prevail over us', 74). Well-known *scholia* were composed on the text by ʿAlī Nūrī and Muḥammad Riḍā Qumshihī. A rather substantial work of philosophical theology, it reveals a mystical taste not always evident in the *Asfār*. It contains a considerable number of quotations from the *Theologia Aristotelis* (the epitome of Plotinus' *Enneads* IV–VI) and other sources from the *Plotiniana Arabica.*

A truly hefty tome, the text is divided into five 'loci of witnessing' (*mashāhid*), which are each divided into 'witnesses' (*shawāhid*) and further subdivided into 'illuminations' (*ishrāqāt*). The first concerns preliminary and foundational issues in metaphysics and is divided into five 'witnesses' (*shawāhid*) and discusses the properties of existence, the nature of knowledge and the problem of 'mental existence' (*wujūd dhihnī*), the nature of divine Being and its attributes in particular divine unity, aspects of the Aristotelian categories, and the properties of essence and other *universalia*. The second, examining philosophical theology, is divided into two witnesses on the supra-sensible realm, the nature of divine being, creation and God's agency, and Imaginal and Platonic forms. The third *mashhad*, on the psychology of the reversion to the One, comprises three witnesses on cosmogony, the nature of the soul and 'philosophical anthropology', and on the return to the One by progressing through the stages of the intellect. The fourth encompasses three discussions on bodily resurrection, eschatology and the afterlife, and the three Neoplatonic realms of being. The final *mashhad* discusses the nature of prophecy and sainthood (*al-walāya*).

MSS:

King's Pote (Cambridge) 255 (naskhī, 1109/1707).

British Library Or. 6420 (2r–62r, shikaste, 19th century), **Delhi Arabic 1630 (38ff, damaged but excellent shikaste, late 17th century)**, Delhi Arabic 1667 (fol. 116–50, incomplete, shikaste, 18th century).

Tehran University Central Library 274 (264ff, 1284 H lithograph from autograph), **406 (280ff, nastaʿlīq, 1039 H)**, 1290 (122ff, naskhī with *marginalia* of Sabzavārī, 1229 H), **1541 (92ff, nastaʿlīq of Muḥammad Qummī, 26 Rabīʿ II 1093 H)**, 2202 (158ff, nastaʿlīq, 11th century H), **4549 (153ff, nastaʿlīq of Abu'l-Ḥasan Shīrāzī, 1039-40 H)**, 6474 (nastaʿlīq of Fatḥ Allāh Ṭabīb, 1268 H Shiraz), 7275 (incomplete at beginning and end, naskhī, 11th century H), **8818 (219ff, naskhī of Muḥammad Bāqir b. Malik Ḥājjī Murtaḍā, 11th century H)**.

Tehran University Faculty of Theology dāl 519 (274ff, nastaʿlīq, 1078 H), dāl 658 (110ff, nastaʿlīq, 15 Ṣafar 1137 H).

Millī 155/1 (122ff, nastaʿlīq of Muḥammad Riḍā b. Mullā Ṣafī-qulī 1085–6 H), 1452 (94ff, naskhī, 12th century H), 1881 (12–41ff, nastaʿlīq of Muḥammad Zanjānī, 1276 H), 2871 (188ff, shikaste, 1275 H).

Majlis-i Shūrā 169 (205ff, naskhī, 1160 H), 1913 (309ff, nastaʿlīq of Hidāyat Allāh Kurdistānī replete with errors, 1261 H), 1914 (naskhī, 1236 H), 1915 (244–362ff, mixed script, 13th century H), 1916 (17–242ff, nastaʿlīq, 19th century), **1917 (1–109ff, shikaste of Shāh-qulī b. Imām-qulī, Ṣafar 1078 H)**.

Kitābkhāna-yi Chihil Sutūn Masjid Jāmiʿ-yi Tehrān 129 (naskhī of Ḥusayn b. Qāsim Rawḍa-khwān, 1213 H).

Mashhad University Faculty of Theology 373 (192ff, shikaste, 11th century H), 374 (139ff, naskhī, 1204 H), 375 (148ff, nastaʿlīq, 13th century H), 1727 (115ff, nastaʿlīq, 11th century H).

Āstān-i Quds-i Raḍavī 174 (139ff, nastaʿlīq, waqf 1166 H), 778 (175ff, naskhī), 779 (142ff, naskhī, 1250 H), 780, 781 (111ff, naskhi, 1227 H), 783 (197ff, shikaste of Muḥammad Jaʿfar, 1255 H), 15131 (naskhī of ʿAbd al-Karīm), 15055.

Jāmiʿ-yi Gawharshād 649 (182ff, naskhī with *marginalia* of Nūrī, 1220 H), 1965 (lacuna at beginning, naskhī of ʿAbd al-Ḥayy, Shaʿbān 1256 H).

Malik 1445 (193ff, nastaʿlīq, 13th century H), **2403 (150ff, naskhī of Ibn Muḥammad Sharīf Kāshānī based on autograph, 1068 H).**

Āstāna-yi Shāh-i Chirāgh 324 (75ff, naskhī, 18th century?).

Marʿashī 1948/2 (7r–57r, naskhī, 13th century H), 6652 (128ff, naskhī, 14 Muḥarram 1210 H), **9066 (124ff, nastaʿlīq, 1087 H)**, 9310 (137ff, naskhī, 1125 H), 9557 (86ff, nastaʿlīq, 13th century H), 11027 (fol. 68–135, incomplete, nastaʿlīq, 24 Dhuʾl-Qaʿda 1242 H), 12737 (nastaʿlīq, 113ff, 1269 H).

Madrasa-yi Fayḍiyya (Qum) 1748 (226ff, naskhī of Muʿīn al-Dīn b. Naʿīm al-Dīn, 1075 H).

Kitābkhāna-yi Vazīrī (Yazd) 963 (111ff, naskhī, Ṣafar 1075 H).

Kitābkhāna-yi Namāzī (Khūʾī) 624 (thuluth of Ibn Sayyid Muḥammad, 15 Muḥarram 1141).

Sālār Jung 295 [Ilāhīyāt 109] (108ff, nastaʿlīq of Aḥmad Munajjim-i Shīrāzī, 1272/1855), 1273 (108ff, nastaʿlīq, 1856).

Raza Library (Rampur) 1925 (nastaʿlīq of ʿAlī-naqī Gīlānī, fol. 2v–65v, 1081/1670), 1926 (nastaʿlīq of Mullā Niẓām al-Dīn Sihālvī, 92ff, 18th century), 1927 (nastaʿlīq, 157ff, 19th century).

Bankipore/Khudā Bakhsh 629 (170ff, nastaʿlīq, 1122 H).

Princeton (Arabic New Series) 873 (130ff, 13th century H).

ʿAllāma Ṭabāṭabāʾī (private in Qum, copied by Sayyid Jalāl al-Dīn Āshtiyānī, 1389 H)

3) *ʿArshiyya*

al-Ḥikma al-ʿArshiyya.

The Wisdom of the Throne.

Ed./tr. into Persian by G. Āhānī (Isfahan 1340 Sh/1961). The edition, which has some semblance of a critical apparatus, is based on the lithograph of the commentary by Aḥsāʾī and two manuscripts, both rather late: one from the Mahdavī collection dated

1235 H and another belonging to the editor dated 1315 H which includes the commentary by Iṣfahānī. This edition was reprinted in Tehran in 1361 Sh/1982.
Tr. by J. W. Morris as *The Wisdom of the Throne* (Princeton 1981). An excellent introduction and annotation to a workable translation, it will be reprinted in the near future by White Cloud Press in Ashland, Oregon.
Persian translation by Aḥmad Ḥusaynī Ardakānī (Tehran 1363 Sh/1984).
A new Arabic uncritical edition by Muḥammad Khalīl al-Labūn and Fuʾād Dakār (Beirut 2000).
See *al-Dharīʿa* VI:149, and *GAL* S II: 588.
It was lithographed in 1315/1898 with *al-Mashāʿir*. The text was completed between 1041 and 1044/1631–4. There is a famous and hostile commentary by Shaykh Aḥmad al-Aḥsāʾī for Mullā Mashhad Shabistarī in 27 Rabīʿ I 1236/1821 [see MS Āstāna-yi Haḍrat-i Maʿṣūma in Qum 6009, naskhī of Mahdī b. ʿAbd al-Raḥīm, Jumāda I 1236 H, for part I; and MS Majlis-i Shūrā 1857, naskhī of Aḥmad b. Muḥammad Rashtī, 1237, for part II both based on the autograph] and was lithographed in *octavo* with 447 pages in 1278/1861 (Corbin, 29). It was also printed in Kirman in 1979, and again in Kuwait/Damascus by Muʾassasat al-Fikr al-Awḥad, a Shaykhī research body founded by Mīrzā ʿAbd al-Rasūl Iḥqāqī the present head of the Tabrīz/Karbalāʾ branch of the movement. Another commentary by the philosopher Ismāʿīl Iṣfahānī, defending Mullā Ṣadrā against the critique of al-Aḥsāʾī, was lithographed in Tehran in 1315 H. The commentary by his contemporary Mullā ʿAlī Nūrī [d. 1831] is in manuscript.
Being a late work, he mentions many others such as *Asfār* (237–48), *Risālat al-ḥudūth* (262*), al-Shawāhid al-rubūbiyya* (245), and *scholia* on *Sharḥ Ḥikmat al-ishrāq* (237–9). The text, which is a later theological epitome, is divided into two loci of illumination. It draws upon the metaphysics of the Peripatetic school to articulate metaphysical bases for the eschatology of Shiʿi theology. The first discusses the ontological foundations of theology and the nature of God. The second concerns the return to the One and is sub-divided into three 'illuminations': the first deals with psychology and the nature of the human soul and its faculties, the second with the nature of Resurrection providing a defence of the theological doctrine of bodily resurrection, and the third with the states of the afterlife. The final two sections contain extensive illustrations from *ḥadīth* literature and, unlike *Asfār* IX, are not based upon the speculations of Ibn ʿArabī [d. 1240]. The eschatological passages should be read alongside the relevant passages at the end of *Asfār* IX. The

Neoplatonic tendency of the work is evident in the numerous citations of the *Plotiniana Arabica* corpus.

MSS:

Tehran University Central Library 897 (89–97ff, naskhī, 1096–7 H), 2273 (89v–117r, naskhī, 1279 H), **3638 (296–375ff, nastaʿlīq, 12th century H).**

Tehran University Law Faculty 30 (94v–144v, nastaʿlīq, 1294 H).

Millī 1539 (179–267ff, naskhī, 13th century H), 1639 (83–162ff, naskhī, 1250 H).

Majlis-i Shūrā 1412 (240ff, naskhī, 1306 H), 1802 (4–50ff, naskhī, 1244 H), **1806/3 (181–261ff, shikaste, 11th century H)**, 1813 (87–127ff, shikaste of ʿAlī b. Rajab-ʿAlī, 1275 H), 1814 (130ff, nastaʿlīq, 1237 H), 1815 (1–85ff, naskhī, 1236 H), 1816 (1–119ff, nastaʿlīq, 19th century H), 3106 (160ff, nastaʿlīq, 1263 H), **4942 (63v–82r, shikaste, 11th century H)**, 5438 (1v–38r, naskhī, 1238 H).

Majlis-i Sīnā (Tehran) 97 (39–55ff, nastaʿlīq, 13th century H).

Āstān-i Quds-i Raḍavī 508 (35ff, shikaste of ʿAlī Akbar b. Muḥammad Karīm Sāliyānī, Dhuʾl-Ḥijja 1263 H), 509 (39ff, shikaste, 1241 H), 8213 (30ff, naskhī, 19th century), 11735 (40ff, shikaste, 19th century), 11892 (naskhī, early 12th century H).

Madrasa-yi Fayḍīya (Qum) 1143/4 (32ff, naskhī of Ṣādiq Mūsawī Māzandarānī, 1124 H Isfahan).

Marʿashī 6717/2 (8v–38r, nastaʿlīq, 28 Ramaḍān 1280 H), 7577 (124r–155v, nastaʿlīq of ʿAbd al-Malik Bawānātī, 1128 H), 9717 (2v–78v, naskhī, 1260 H), 11992/1 (shikaste, fol. 1–48, 1259 H).

Princeton (Arabic New Series) 80 (2v–78v, naskhī, 13th century H).

4) *Mabdaʾ.*

al- Mabdaʾ waʾl-maʿād.

The Alpha and the Omega.

Ed. S. J. Āshtiyānī with *marginalia* of Sabzavārī (Tehran 1976). This is not a critical edition and there is little indication of its basis. It does have an introduction on the text in Persian and another short one in English by S. H. Nasr. It was reprinted without the introductions in Beirut in 2000; the *marginalia* of Sabzavārī were printed in a separate volume.

A new critical edition by M. Dhabīḥī and J. Shāhnaẓarī (2 vols, Tehran 1381–2 Sh/2002–3). The apparatus is based on MSS Āstān-i Quds-i Raḍavī 255, 868, Majlis-i Shūrā 1952, 1953, 1959, Tehran University Central Library 421, 2302, 2698, Mahdavī 712, and the Shiraz autograph.

There is a Persian translation by Aḥmad Ḥusaynī Ardakānī, edited by ʿAbdullāh Nūrānī, (Tehran 1983), but this is another uncritical edition albeit with some useful comments in the preface.

See *GAL* S II: 589, and *al-Dharīʿa* XIX:52, XX:107.

It was lithographed with the *scholia* of Sabzavārī (Tehran 1314/1897). The calligraphy was by ʿAbd al-Karīm Shīrāzī and corrected by Sayyid Ibrāhīm Ṭabāṭabāʾī.

It was completed in 1015/1606 according to MS Tehran University Central Library 421. It closely follows the Avicennan text of the same name. The first section (*al-fann al-awwal*) deals with the One, His attributes and actions and the procession of being from it. It is divided into two chapters (*maqālāt*), the first of which discusses the nature of the pure One as principle, unity and necessity and in it, he examines some of Suhrawardī's arguments about the Light of Lights. The second chapter deals with the One as determined being through His attributes and the procession of existents from the One in the chain of being. This chapter is the core of the philosophical theology of the work. The second section (*al-fann al-thānī*) discusses the return to the One, corporeal resurrection and the spiritual path. It is divided into three chapters. The first chapter deals with hierarchy in the cosmos and the panpsychist doctrine that all that exists is conscious and seeks to return to its principle. It discusses in detail human psychological states and ethics in the face of divine grace. It is in this chapter that one encounters his political philosophy. The second chapter is a critical evaluation of proofs for corporeal resurrection after death. The final chapter on resurrection 'according to the doctrine of the gnostics' is an extensive literary exposition of the thought of Ibn ʿArabī on the soul's journey to the One and contains within it many Qurʾānic citations as corroborating texts and illustrates the Sadrian hermeneutic of scripture to explain his philosophical method. The fourth chapter deals with the nature of prophecy and its attributes of miracle working, legislation and interpretation of dreams. It proffers a theory that links the imaginative and rational faculties with the functions of prophecy.

MSS:

Tehran University Central Library 421 (275ff, naskhī, possibly in hand of author dated 1015 H or closely copied, purchase date of 1194 H), 1506 (161ff, naskhī of Muḥammad Bāqir b. Aḥmad, 14 Jumāda I 1201 H), 2146 (262ff, nastaʿlīq, 11th century H), 2276 (216ff, naskhī, 1236 H), 2283 (237ff, naskhī, 1276 H), 2302 (270ff, naskhī of Sharaf b. Muḥammad, 18 Rabīʿ 1095 H), 2698 (175ff, naskhī of

Muḥammad Amīn b. ʿAbd al-Wahhāb, 12 Muḥarram 1103 H), 5400 (nastaʿlīq, 11th century H).

Millī 1448 (215ff, nastaʿlīq, 1194 H), 1639 (239–403ff, naskhī, 1250 H).

Majlis-i Shūrā 1952 (38ff, naskhī of Muḥammad Amīn b. ʿAbd al-Wahhāb, 14 Dhu'l-Ḥijja 1113 H), 1953 (1–388ff, nastaʿlīq, 1110 H), 1954 (311ff, shikaste, 1212 H), 1955 (332ff, shikaste of ʿAbdallāh Zunūzī, 1228 H), 1956 (100ff, shikaste, 1249 H), 1957 (89ff, shikaste, 13th century H), 1958 (1–327ff, naskhī, 1108 H), 1959 (42–200ff, naskhī, 12th century H), 5003/3 (29–226ff, nastaʿlīq of Sayyid Muḥammad Ḥusaynī, Shaʿbān 1097 H).

Kitākhāna-yi Mahdavī 712 (206ff, naskhī, 4 Shaʿbān 1086 H).

Āstān-i Quds-i Raḍavī 255 (154ff, nastaʿlīq, 1065 H in Qazwin from autograph), 866 (222ff, naskhī, 1254 H), 867 (200ff, shikaste of Muḥammad ʿAlī Daylamī, Isfahan 1227 H), 868 (266ff, nastaʿlīq, 1237 H), 869 (228ff, naskhī, damaged, n.d.), 6959 (224ff, nastaʿlīq, n.d.), 7894 (173ff, naskhī, 1243 H), 13110 (naskhī, n.d.), 11343 (141ff, nastaʿlīq, 1241 H), 11434 (nastaʿlīq).

Jāmiʿ-yi Gawharshād 1575 (nastaʿlīq, 1267 H).

Malik 929 (250ff, naskhī, 11th century H), 954 (190ff, shikaste, n.d.).

Marʿashī (Qum) 8306 (191ff, nastaʿlīq of Muḥammad Gīlānī, 28 Shaʿbān 1193 H), 9373 (1314 H lithograph).

Kitābkhāna-yi Namāzī (Khū'ī) 606/1 (thuluth of Ḥasan b. Muḥammad Ṣādiq Qummī, Ṣafar 1094 H).

Maktabat al-awqāf al-ʿāmma (Baghdad) 3239 (248ff, naskhī, 1201 H), 3240 (24ff, naskhī, 1181 H).

Sālār Jung 88 (188ff, nastaʿlīq, 1122/1710).

Raza Library (Rampur) 3651 (nastaʿlīq, 133ff, 18th century).

Bankipore (Khudā Bakhā, Patna) 2391 (190ff, naskhī, 1102 H), 2392 (267ff, nastaʿlīq, 13th century H).

Princeton (Arabic New Series) 33 (2v–144v, 1277 H), 369 (241ff, 1238 H).

Maktabat al-Fayḍ al-Mahdawī (Kirmānshāh) (nastaʿlīq in hand of Ghulām ʿAlī b. Muḥammad Ṣāliḥ Māzandarānī, 1222 H).

ʿAllāma Ṭabāṭabā'ī (private in Qum in hand of ʿAbd al-Razzāq Lāhījī in lifetime of author).

Madrasa-yi ʿĀliyya-yi Imām-i ʿAṣr (Shiraz) (autograph, nastaʿlīq, 281ff, n.d.).

5) *Mashāʿir.*
Kitāb al-Mashāʿir.
The Book of Ontological Inspirations.
Persian translation by G. Āhānī (Isfahan 1961); reprinted in 1361 Sh/1982 in Tehran.
Ed. S. J. Āshtiyānī with (mediocre) commentary of Jaʿfar Langarūdī (Lāhījānī) (Mashhad 1963). The editor provides extensive footnotes in Persian, but again an uncritical edition. It was reprinted in Tehran in 1376 Sh/1997.
Ed. H. Corbin with his French translation as *Le Livre des Pénétrations Métaphysiques*, and the Persian translation of Mīrzā ʿImād al-Dawla (Tehran 1964). The most reliable edition of the text, it is based on the lithograph of the original and of the commentary of al-Aḥsāʾī and MS Majlis-i Shūrā 100 which includes the Persian translation/commentary. The edition is appended with a magisterial study of the ontology of the text in French and appended with a fully annotated French translation, drawing heavily on the commentary of al-Aḥsāʾī. It was reprinted in 1363 Sh/1984 in Tehran and on numerous occasions since the late 1990s.
Pirated re-issue of the Corbin edition without his introduction and notes in a 'new' edition by Muḥammad Khalīl al-Labūn (Beirut 2000).
Another re-issue of the Corbin edition by Khālid Tirāzī (Beirut 2002).
Translated into English by P. Morewedge as *The Metaphysics of Mullā Ṣadrā* (New York 1992). A reprinting of the Corbin edition with a few corrections for Qurʾānic citations, it is a clumsy and jargon-ridden attempt that is rather difficult to read and replete with typographical and transliteration errors.
Translated into Japanese by T. Izutsu as *Sonzai ninshiki no michi: sonzai to honshitsu ni tsuite* (Tokyo 1993).
It was lithographed in Tehran by Aḥmad Shīrāzī in 1315/1898 with the commentaries of Sabzavārī, Nūrī, Iṣfahānī, and Mīrzā Aḥmad Ardakānī Shīrāzī, edited by Muḥammad Bāqir Kāshānī.
It was completed on 7 Jumāda I 1037/14 January 1628, which is the date of MS Tehran University Central Library 7698.
See *GAL* S II: 589, and *al-Dharīʿa* XIV:65, XXI:37. There is also a hostile commentary by Shaykh Aḥmad al-Aḥsāʾī dated 27 Ṣafar 1234 H for Mullā Mashhad Shabistarī. It was printed in Kirman in 1979, and again in Kuwait/Damascus by Muʾassasat al-Fikr al-Awḥad, a Shaykhī research body founded by Mīrzā ʿAbd al-Rasūl Iḥqāqī the present head of the Tabrīz/Karbalāʾ branch of the movement.
This work focuses upon the Sadrian doctrine of being. It comprises eight *mashāʿir* on ontology that follows closely the order and argument (and even the wording at times)

of the first *manhaj* of the *Asfār* (it may well be an epitome of it), and three *manāhij* on the theological issues of the nature of God, His attributes and His creation. It is a dense and excellent summation of Mullā Ṣadrā's doctrine of singular yet modulated being and provides a key description of his logic of being.

The first *mash'ar* is on the *a priori* intuition of existence: *wujūd* requires no proof. The second discusses the scope of existence and its application to entities. The third introduces his critical notion of mental existence, providing eight arguments for its validity. The fourth defends the proposition that the term existence has reference (*'ayniyya*), responding to seven objections from the Ishrāqī tradition beginning with Suhrawardī. The fifth deals with the existential predication of quiddity. The sixth examines the individuation of entities that exist, drawing heavily upon Avicenna. The seventh defends the proposition that existence is what emanates from the One and is created by it and not quiddity, refuting eight arguments from the Ishrāqī tradition to the contrary. The final *mash'ar* is on the nature of the One and his attributes as relations with everything.

The second path is divided into four *mashā'ir* on theological aspects of the divine attributes. The final path is divided into three *mashā'ir* and discusses the divine act of creation and origination and concludes with a significant summary of his defence of the doctrine of *creation ex nihilo* supported by his own doctrine of substantial motion and process. He ends the treatise with an epilogue urging the mystical path and summarising the decent of being from the One in its hierarchy.

MSS:

Browne Collection (Cambridge) N.5 (112ff, naskhī, n.d. probably 13th century H).

Kirmān Collection 124/2, 328/5, 335.

Tehran University Central Library 148/3 (114–151ff, naskhī of Mūsā b. Riḍā Mashhadī, 1104 H), 1422 (105–30ff, naskhī, 1256 H, introduction and two chapters), 2289 (53ff, nastaʿlīq, 13th century H), 2680 (61ff, shikaste, 1274 H), 3362 (109v–144v, nastaʿlīq, 1244 H), 3419 (8v–82v, nastaʿlīq, 13th century H), 4517 (1–52ff, naskhī, 1308 H), 6275 (124–70ff, naskhī, 13th century H of translator ʿImād al-Dawla Badīʿ al-Mulk Mīrzā), 6474 (nastaʿlīq, 1268 H), 6519 (incomplete, nastaʿlīq, 13th century H), 7318 (incomplete, nastaʿlīq, 13th century H), **7698/5 (40–60ff, nastaʿlīq probably of author when he was 58 years old, 7 Jumāda I 1037 H)**, 7746 (nastaʿlīq , 1233 H), 8290 (complete, nastaʿlīq, 1220 H), 9112 (1r–43v, incomplete, nastaʿlīq, 1256 H).

Tehran University Faculty of Theology 135 jīm (122r–206r, nastaʿlīq with *marginalia* of Nūrī and Mullā Ismāʿīl, 1231 H), 111 dāl (47v–65v, naskhī, 1235 H), 123 dāl (111v–136v, nastaʿlīq, 1233 H), 146 dāl (171v–229v, naskhī, 1201 H), 467 dāl (1v–22v, naskhī with *marginalia* of Nūrī, 1244 H), 482 dāl (36r–57r, nastaʿlīq, 1209 H), 790 dāl (75v–111v, mixed script, 1215 H), 802 dāl (53v–67r, naskhī, 12th century H).

Tehran University Law Faculty 30 (58v–94v, nastaʿlīq, 1294 H).

Millī 1264 (45ff, nastaʿlīq, 1262 H), 1607 (1–68ff, naskhī, 1195 H), 1614 (57ff, naskhī, 12th century H), 1639 (179–238ff, naskhī, 1250 H), 1681 (37–122ff, nastaʿlīq, 1199 H), 1769 (99ff, naskhī, 1267 H).

Majlis-i Shūrā 83 (39ff, shikaste, 1252 H), **1721 (naskhī of Muḥammad Bāqir b. Ismāʿīl, 1087–91 H)**, 1970 (68ff, nastaʿlīq, 13th century H), 1971 (1–109ff, nastaʿlīq, 1302 H), 1972 (1–42ff, naskhī, 13th century H), 1973 (190–238ff, nastaʿlīq, incomplete 19th century), 1974 (93ff, naskhī, 1295 H), 4779 (53ff, naskhī, 1209 H), **5003 (1r–20r, nastaʿlīq of Sayyid Muḥammad Ḥusaynī, Ramaḍān 1092 H)**, **5279 (158v–176r, nastaʿlīq, 11th century H)**, **6339/4 (48–105ff, shikaste of Mullā ʿAlī Gīlānī, 1125 H)**, 6340 (48–105ff, shikaste, 1228 H).

Majlis-i Sīnā (Tehran) 280 (portions, shikaste, 1280 H).

Mashhad University Faculty of Theology 655 (nastaʿlīq, 1269 H), 1342, 1658 (nastaʿlīq, 1246 H), 1342 (nastaʿlīq of Muḥammad Ḥasan Ṭabasī, 1204 H).

Āstān-i Quds-i Raḍavī 665 (23ff, nastaʿlīq, 1297 H), 892 (35ff, shikaste, 1235 H), 893 (29ff, shikaste, 1254 H), 894 (shikaste of Faḍl Allāh, 1287 H), 930 (40ff, nastaʿlīq, 1247 H), 5665 (nastaʿlīq, 1297 H), 11892 (naskhī, early 12th century H), 13256 (shikaste), 14864 (nastaʿlīq, 1310 H), 15328.

Jāmiʿ-yi Gawharshād 649/2 (182ff, naskhī, 1220 H), 877 (118ff, nastaʿlīq, 12th century H), 1010 (108ff, naskhī, 1265 H), 1067 (227ff, naskhī, 1249 H).

Malik 1636 (31ff, shikaste, 1238 H), 1867 (49ff, shikaste, 1207 H).

Āstāna-yi Shāh-i Chirāgh 318 (79ff, naskhī and nastaʿlīq, 1292 H), 319.

Marʿashī 38/2 (15v–64v, nastaʿlīq, 1232 H), 674 (13v–39r, nastaʿlīq), 6717 (41v–62v, nastaʿlīq, 1279 H), 7102 (1–41v, naskhī, 13th century H), 9917 (5v–38v, nastaʿlīq, 1264 H), 10353/1 (1v–25v, nastaʿlīq of Muʿīn b. Ḥusayn Gīlānī, 1183 H), 11798/1 (fol. 1–45, naskhī, 13th century H), 11020/1 (fol. 1–28, naskhī, Rajab 1211 H).

Maktabat al-Imām al-Ḥakīm (Rashtī collection, Najaf) 62 (1–22ff, naskhī, 1233 H).

Sālār Jung 96 (49ff, Shafīʿa, 1218/1803).

Princeton (Arabic New Series) 10 (36ff, 1231 H), 40 (1v–23r, 13th century H), 699 (1v–30r, 1223 H).

II Commentaries

1) *Taqdīs.*
Ḥāshiya ʿala ʿArsh al-taqdīs of Mīr Dāmād [d. 1040/1631]. (See *Dībāja* below).
Marginalia on the Throne of Sanctification.

2) *Rawāshiḥ.*
Ḥāshiya ʿalaʾl-Rawāshiḥ al-samāwiyya fī sharḥ uṣūl al-Kāfī of Mīr Dāmād.
Marginalia upon the Heavenly Percolations commenting upon the Sufficient Principles.
Dānishpazhūh (*SCV*, 120) says that it is suspect, although Muẓaffar (*Asfār* I: āīn) and Corbin (29) find no reason to dispite its authenticity. On the margins of the lithograph of *al-Rawāshiḥ* dated 1311/1894 are notes signed with a *ṣād*, and there is a manuscript of the text in his hand with *marginalia*, which would confirm the authorship. The *marginalia* are brief and far from complete upon a text that is an introduction to a commentary, laying down some hermeneutic principles for reading *ḥadīth*. Since we know that Mullā Ṣadrā copied a number of works of his master, it is possible that he penned a few marginal notes on those manuscripts as well.

3) *Taqwīm.*
Ḥāshiya ʿala Taqwīm al-īmān of Mīr Dāmād.
Marginalia on the Establishment of the Faith.
The text, a work of philosophical theology from the Illuminationist school, has been published with the *marginalia* of another student of Dāmād, his son-in-law Sayyid Aḥmad ʿAlawī, *Taqwīm al-īmān*, ed. ʿAlī Awjabī (Tehran 1377 Sh/1998).
I have been to trace only one manuscript, which I have not been able to consult – Āstān-i Quds-i Raḍavī 110 (150ff, nastaʿlīq, waqf 1166 H).

4) *Hidāya.*
Sharḥ al-hidāya of Athīr al-Dīn Mufaḍḍal b. ʿUmar al-Abharī [d. 663/1264].
Commentary on the Guidance in Philosophy.
Ed. ʿAbd al-Karīm Shīrāzī (Tehran lithograph 1313, facsimile rpt, Qum 1998); re-typesetting of Tehran lithograph (Beirut 2003).
Previous (lithograph) printings include:
With the *marginalia* of ʿAbd al-ʿAlī Baḥr al-ʿUlūm [d. 1810] (Lucknow 1262/1846).

With *marginalia* of Saʿd Allāh Rāmpūrī (Madras 1270/1854).
With *marginalia* of Maulvī Abuʾl-Ḥasan Lakhnavī, Ḥāfiẓ Muḥammad ʿAbd al-Ḥayy, Irtiḍā ʿAlī Khān, and Muḥammad Saʿd Allāh (Hyderabad 1291/1875).
With *marginalia* of ʿAbd al-Ḥayy Lakhnavī (Lucknow 1291/1875).
(Delhi 1916).
(Lucknow 1921).
The Persian translation of Aḥmad Ḥusaynī Ardakānī as *Mirʾāt al-akwān*, ed. ʿAbd Allāh Nūrānī (Tehran 1375 Sh/1996). This uncritical edition is based on MS Majlis-i Shūrā 1967 and MS Kitābkhāna-yi Millī 2223 and is prefaced with a useful discussion of the issues raised in the text.
See *GAL* I: 608 and S II: 589, and *al-Dharīʿa* XIV:243.
This is an important commentary of a Peripatetic work from his youth, probably completed around 1015 H and then re-worked and completed 29 Ramaḍān 1029/August 1620. He mentions the *Asfār* (213, 223) in it and the introductory chapter on the definition of philosophy closely overlaps with the first chapter of the *Asfār*. Other important commentaries on the *Hidāya* include those of the Timurid philosophers and courtiers from Central Asia Mīrak Muḥammad b. Mubārakshāh Bukhārī [d. ca. 880/1440] and Mīr Ḥusayn Maybudī [d. 910/1504]. The commentary of Mullā Ṣadrā eclipsed theirs and became the dominant school text in India.
The introduction discusses the division of the sciences and the relationship between metaphysics and physics. The text is divided into three parts (*aqsām*) on physics, theology and psychology and metaphysics. The first section (*fann*) is on physics and deals with issues of space-time, atomism, form and matter, and motion. The second section discusses astronomy, the cosmology of the sub-lunary and supra-lunary worlds. The second part deals with theology and divine action and impetus in the sub-lunar world and is divided into three sections. The third part discusses metaphysics and theology and is divided into three sections on substance and accident, modalities and the Necessary Being, and the emanative cosmogony. These are then followed by a conclusion (*khātima*) concerning the nature of the return to the One and eschatology, and a concluding guidance (*hidāya*) on the nature of the soul. It was very popular in Indian *madrasa*-s, where it was simply known as 'Ṣadrā' and was (indeed still is) an integral part of the *Dars-i Niẓāmī* curriculum. The section manily studied was the physics. This popularity accounts for the numerous extant copies of

manuscripts from the subcontinent and the many *marginalia* that were composed upon it that are found in Indian libraries.[188]

MSS:

British Library Or. 5759 (410ff, naskhī, 18th century), India Office Islamic British Library 1357 (224ff, nastaʿlīq, 18th century copied in Hyderabad in India from autograph), Delhi Arabic 1645 (232ff, rough naskhī, 19th century).

Tehran University Central Library 254[4574] (292ff, shikaste of ʿAbd al-Razzāq b. Muḥammad Yūsuf Raḍawī for author, 1046 H), 295 (262ff, taʿlīq, 1046 H), 1422 (1v–103r, nastaʿlīq, 1260 H, until end of the physics), 1502 (283ff, naskhī, 17 Dhuʾl-Qaʿda 1144 H), 6275 (368–77ff, naskhī, 13th century H).

Millī 1012 (201ff, naskhī, 12th century H), 1023 (184ff, nastaʿlīq, 11th century H), **1298 (254ff, nastaʿlīq of Muḥammad Muʾmin Jarbādqānī, 1071 H)**, 1541 (190ff, naskhī and nastaʿlīq, 1281 H).

Madrasa-yi Marvī 561 (1201 H), 645 (13th century H), 674 (1267 H).

Majlis-i Shūrā 82 (157ff, nastaʿlīq, 19th century), 127 (317ff, naskhī, 1244 H), 1813 (1–87ff, shikaste, 1275 H), 1877 (282ff, shikaste of ʿAbdallāh Zunūzī, 1201 H), 1878 (1–320ff, nastaʿlīq, 1281 H), 1879 (2nd *fann* of metaphysics, 87ff, naskhī, 13th century H).

Mashhad University Faculty of Theology 366 (115ff, shikaste, n.d.), 908 (99ff, shikaste, n.d.), 1370 (naskhī, 1303 H), 1651 (135ff, nastaʿlīq, 12th century H), 1678 (111ff, naskhī, 1225 H).

Āstān-i Quds-i Raḍavī 173 (243ff, nastaʿlīq of Hādī b. ʿAbd al-Wāḥid Shāh Maḥmūd Fīrūzābādī, Ramaḍān 1071 H), 175 (196ff, nastaʿlīq shikaste, 1211 H), 757 (shikaste, 1234 H), 9717 (177ff, nastaʿlīq of Muḥammad Riḍā Tabrīzī, Jumāda I 1256 H), 13221 (nastaʿlīq, 1218 H), 14682 (naskhī, 19th century).

Jāmiʿ-yi Gawharshād 1012 (naskhī of ʿAlī-qulī b. Ismāʿīl-Bīk, 16 Shaʿbān 1124 H Isfahan), 1363 (236ff, nastaʿlīq, 12th century H).

Malik 1340 (243ff, naskhī, 1269 H), 1659 (207ff, nastaʿlīq, 12th century H), 1909 (285ff, nastaʿlīq, 12th century H), **2124 (185ff, nastaʿlīq of ʿAbd al-Rashīd Shūstarī, 23 Jumāda I 1051 H)**, 2422 (398ff, naskhī, 11th century H).

Marʿashī 1153 (physics and metaphysics, 232ff, naskhī), 8569 (physics 202ff, naskhī), 9994 (254ff, naskhī, 1206 H), **11778 (240ff, incomplete at beginning, nastaʿlīq, 11th century H).**

---

[188] See Akbar Thubūt, *Faylasūf-i Shīrāz dar Hind* (Tehran 1380 Sh/2001).

Madrasa-yi Raḍaviyya (Qum) 72 (1v–256v, nastaʿlīq, 1291 H).

Madrasa-yi Imām-i ʿAṣr (Shīrāz) 15 (165ff, ʿAlī b. ʿAbd al-Ghālib, 1059 H).

Kitābkhāna-yi Namāzī (Khūʾī) 151 (nastaʿlīq of Muḥammad Ibrāhīm Riḍwānī, autograph *marginalia* of Mullā Naʿīmā Ṭāliqānī, Shaʿbān 1077 H), 476 (shikaste of Ṣadr al-Dīn Ḥusaynī, Ṣafar 1078 H).

Maktabat al-Imām al-Ḥakīm (Rashtī collection) 88 (291ff, nastaʿlīq, 1276 H).

Dār al-Kutub 2789 (319ff, naskhī, 1259 H).

Sālār Jung 66 (236ff, nastaʿlīq 1072/1661), 67 (303ff, naskhī, 11th century, maybe 1072 H), 68 (399ff, naskhī, 1124/1712), 69 (162ff, nastaʿlīq, n.d.), 70 (483ff, Shafīʿa, 13th century H), 107/2 (77-118ff, nastaʿlīq, 1202/1787), 1833 (335ff, nastaʿlīq, 1141/1729).

Asiatic Society of Bengal 416 (shikaste, 1164 H), 919 (shikaste, 1164 H), 958 (shikaste, 1164 H).

Būhār Library (Calcutta) 324 (130ff, shikaste, 1174 H), 334 (169ff, nastaʿlīq, 18th century), 335 (33ff, nastaʿlīq, 19th century).

Āṣafiyya 377.

Government Oriental Library (Madras) 153 (716ff, nastaʿlīq, 17th century), 225 (100ff, nastaʿlīq, 1228 H).

Raza Library (Rampur) 3555 (nastaʿlīq, 478ff, 1127/1715, notes of Mullā ʿAbd ʿAlī Baḥr al-ʿUlūm in margins), 3556 (nastaʿlīq, 211ff, 1212/1798), 3557 (nastaʿlīq, *de cælo* only, 80ff, 19th century), 3558 (nastaʿlīq, 56ff, 19th century), 3559 (naskhī, 211ff, 19th century), 5356 (nastaʿlīq, incomplete, 17ff, 19th century).

Bankipore (Khudā Bakhsh) 2368 (351ff, naskhī, 12th century H), 2369 (239ff, nastaʿlīq, 12th century H), 2370 (nastaʿlīq, 13th century H).

34 Muṣṭafā Āshir Efendi (Istanbul) 419/4 (taʿlīq, 16v–233r).

Princeton (Arabic New Series) 1146 (13th century H), 1816 (13th century H), 1845 (13th century H, incomplete).

Chester Beatty (Dublin) 4721 (231ff, nastaʿlīq, 11th century H).

5) *Kāfī.*

Sharḥ Uṣūl al-Kāfī.

Commentary on the Sufficient Principles.

Ed. M. J. Khājavī with the *marginalia* of ʿAlī Nūrī (3 vols, Tehran 1367 Sh/1988). Although lacking critical apparatus, this is a good edition based on the lithograph and 5 manuscripts: MS Marʿashī 4322 (the holograph), MS Majlis-i Shūrā 89, 32 (dated 1233 H for the *marginalia* of ʿAlī Nūrī), 4806 and MS Tehran University Faculty of

Arts 6630 (dated 1105 H). The edition includes a long introduction by ʿAlī ʿĀbidī Shāhrūdī.
It was lithographed in 1282/1865.
See *GAL* S I: 320 and S II: 589, *GAS* I: 541, and *al-Dharīʿa* XIII:96, 99.
The completion date often provided is 1044/1634, but it was incomplete at his death. It mentions many of his Quranic works as well as the *Asfār*. A major work commenting upon the classical Shiʿi collection of *ḥadīth* compiled by al-Kulaynī [d. 329 /941], it ends in the midst of his commentary upon *Kitāb al-ḥujja* ḥadīth number 153 in the chapter on 'The Imams are entrusted with the affair of God and are treasure stores of His knowledge'. The commentary on the twelfth tradition (the numerical value is not insignificant) is extensive and divided into a number of 'loci of witnessing' (*mashāhid*). The tradition concerns the true nature of the intellect (*al-ʿaql*). The first *mashhad* describes the people of intellect and the stages of their intellectual development. The second analyses God's facilitation and grace that provides for the spiritual and intellectual development of humans. A long third section, divided into 'chapters' (*fuṣūl*) discusses the nature of God, his attributes, his agency and the critical God-world relationship. Further sections deals with ethics and *moralia*. *Mashhad* seven returns to the nature of the intellect. The discussion continues for another eighteen sections on the nature of the people of intellect and their moral virtues and the vices of the ignorant. The nature of this long commentary is primarily a philosophical digression that corroborates what he argues in his other works on the nature of the intellect and the soul and the progression of the human soul to reversion to the One. The commentary on the fourteenth tradition on the creation of the intellect is similarly lengthy but stylistically it represents a more indicative blend of scriptural reasoning and philosophical argumentation.
An analysis of this text is critical to demonstrating the importance of Shiʿism in his philosophical method.

MSS:
Browne Collection (Cambridge) C.19 (210ff, naskh, 1841 CE).
Institute of Ismaili Studies 618 (*kitāb al-tawḥīd*, 452ff, naskhī, 17th century).
Kirmān Collection 8 (naskhī, 11th century H), 9, 179, 386 (nastaʿlīq, 13th century H), 429 (naskhī, 1235 H).
Tehran University Central Library 1630, 5902 (Ch. 25 of *kitāb al-tawḥīd*, nastaʿlīq, 13th century H), 6630 (298ff, naskhī of Muḥammad Ashraf b. Muḥammad Hādī, 7

Jumāda I 1105 H), 8506 (up to *ḥadīth* 212, 586ff, naskhī of Muḥammad Qāsim Shīrāzī, Rabīʿ I 1063 H).

Tehran University Faculty of Theology 36 (273ff, naskhī of ʿAbd al-Bāqī Gīlānī, 18 Ṣafar 1077 H), 50 (200ff, naskhī, 11th century H).

Tehran University Faculty of Arts 8 jīm (up to *ḥadīth* 210, 315ff, naskhī of ʿAlī b. ʿAbd al-Ghālib Fīrūzābādī for author, Ramaḍān 1061 H), 9 jīm (*ḥadīth* 211–513, 311ff, nastaʿlīq of Ṣāliḥ b. Sharīf, 8 Jumāda 1074 H).

Millī 1459 (*kitāb al-ʿaql waʾl-ʿilm*, 130ff, nastaʿlīq shikaste, 1212 H)

Majlis-i Shūrā [31]89 (417ff, nastaʿlīq, 1194 H), 123 (245ff, lacuna at beginning, nastaʿlīq, 1084 H), 124 (first 23 chapters with lacuna at beginning, 417ff, nastaʿlīq, 1194 H), 133 (*kitāb al-ḥujja*, 195ff, naskhī, 1232 H), 164 (*kitāb al-ʿaql waʾl-ʿilm*, 245ff, shikaste of ʿAlī b. ʿAbd al-Ghālib Fīrūzābādī, 1084 H), 1264 (*kitāb al-tawḥīd*, 220ff, naskhī, 1209 H), 1265 (*kitāb al-tawḥīd*, 540ff, naskhī, 1209 H), 4806 (445ff, nastaʿlīq, 1320 H), 5772 (658ff, naskhī of ʿAbd Allāh b. Salām Allāh Junaydī Shīrāzī, 1054 H).

Madrasa-yi Marvī 707 (*kitāb al-ʿaql*, naskhī of ʿAbd al-Ṣamad, 1202 H).

Sipahsālār 234 (327ff, 1199 H), 235 (84ff, 1269 H).

Kitābkhāna-yi Mahdavī (Tehran) 764 (nastaʿlīq of Niʿmat Allāh Shūlistānī, 1052 H).

Mashhad University Faculty of Theology 571 (naskhī, 1241 H).

Āstān-i Quds-i Raḍavī 1705 (naskhī of Zayn al-ʿĀbidīn, 1232 H), 6817 (517ff *kitāb al-ʿaql*, naskhī, 10 Rabīʿ II 1198 H, incomplete), 7139, 9610 (naskhī of Muḥammad Ḥusayn Lāhījī, 1095 H), 9879 (naskhī, 1206 H), 11369 (nastaʿlīq, n.d.).

Jāmiʿ-yi Gawharshād 1355 (nastaʿlīq, 12th century H).

Malik 891 (260ff, naskhī, 12th century H), 1878 (199ff, naskhī, 1335 H), 2743 (334ff, naskhī, 1277 H).

Millī (Tabriz) 3096 (100ff only *kitāb al-ʿaql*, nastaʿlīq of author, 1044 H).

Marʿashī 4322 (255ff, naskhī, holograph), 7747 (195ff, naskhī, close to his time and marginal corrections from autograph dated 1083 H with an ownership seal of 1076 H), 8831 (407ff, nastaʿlīq, Dhuʾl-Qaʿda 1214 H), 11200 (259ff, naskhī of Muḥammad Riḍā Dashtakī, Rabīʿ II 1219 H), 12189 (naskhī, 264ff, 12th century H).

Madrasa-yi Fayḍiyya (Qum) 134 (34ff, naskhī, 1325 H), 135 (490ff, naskhī, 1367 H seal of Burūjirdī), 136 (naskhī, 1323 H), 137 (naskhī, 1377 H), 138 (308ff, naskhī, waqf 1370 H), 139, 140, 141, 142, 143.

Madrasa-yi Gulpāyigānī (Qum) 2/25 (autograph 1044 H).

Kitābkhāna-yi Vazīrī (Yazd) 3534 (462ff, naskhī of Muḥammad Riḍā b. ʿAlī-qulī, 1072 H).

Sālār Jung 928 (165ff, naskhī, 11th century H).

Raza Library (Rampur) 1146 (267ff, nastaʿlīq, 19th century, *Kitāb al-ʿaql*).

Princeton (Arabic New Series) 713 (265ff, nastaʿlīq, 13th century H); **Princeton (Yahuda) 2660 (119ff *kitāb al-ʿaql*, naskhī, 1080/1669).**

Wadham College Oxford 70 (naskhī, 1098 H Kirman).

6) *Shifāʾ.*

Taʿlīqa ʿalāʾl-ilāhiyyāt min kitāb al-Shifāʾ of Avicenna [d. 428/1037].

Scholia upon the metaphysics section of the Cure.

Ed. Najafqulī Ḥabībī, 2 vols. (Tehran 1382 Sh/2003). This is a new critical edition based on the following MSS: Tehran University Central Library 327, Majlis-i Shūrā 1777, Sipahsālār 1444, Marʿashī 914, and the lithograph.

On margins of the lithograph of Avicenna's text (Tehran Dār al-Funūn lithograph 1303/1885–6). There is an offset printing of this (Qum 1991).

See *al-Dharīʿa* XVIII:436, and Sayyid Iʿjāz Ḥusayn Kintūrī, *Kashf al-ḥujub waʾl-astār ʿan asmāʾ al-kutub waʾl-asfār* (Calcutta 1330/1912), 182.

It was completed between 1041–4/1631–4.

In it, he mentions the *Asfār* and *al-Shawāhid al-rubūbiyya* repeatedly. It was lithographed on the margins of the *Shifāʾ* in two volumes, calligraphed by ʿAbd al-Karīm Shīrāzī. It is incomplete and does not cover the whole of Avicenna's text. Some manuscripts also include sections on the natural philosophy and the logic. As a gloss, this work is a useful aid to understanding the Avicennan text and demonstrates how Mullā Ṣadrā reads Avicennan metaphysics in his own terms.

MSS:

Tehran University Central Library 327 (226ff, taʿlīq of ʿAbd al-Rashīd Shūstarī, 1053 H from holograph in Madrasa-yi Āṣafīya in Shīrāz), 2255, 2295 (295ff, nastaʿlīq, late 11th century H with *marginalia* of ʿAlī Nūrī and Ḥusayn Khwānsārī), 3348 (289ff, nastaʿlīq, 1113 H), 5093 (213ff, naskhī of Muḥammad Ḥusayn Gulpāyigānī, late 11th century H), 6684 (259ff, nastaʿlīq, 11th century H).

Tehran University Faculty of Theology 238 (244ff, naskhī, 1075 H, includes commentary on *Posterior Analytics/al-burhān* of logic), 236 (182ff, naskhī, on margins of the text)

Nūrbakhsh (Tehran) 525 (490ff, naskhī of Muḥammad Riḍā Tabrīzī, 23 Ṣafar 1077 H).

Millī 1477 (178ff, naskhī, 12th century H).

Sipahsālār 1441 (220ff, nastaʿlīq of ʿAbd Allāh Qāʾinī, 1105 H), **1442 (434ff, naskhī of 'Gadā-yi ʿAlī', 26 Shaʿbān 1068 H)**, 1444 (nastaʿlīq, 11th century H), 6480 (400ff, nastaʿlīq, 11th century H).

Majlis-i Shūrā 1777 (624ff, naskhī of ʿAbd Allāh Shūstarī, 1056 H), 1778 (543ff, naskhī, n.d.), 1779 (144ff, naskhī, 12th century with *ʿArshiyya* of ʿAlī Zunūzī), 1780 (shikaste, 13 Rabīʿ I 1205 H, Isfahan), 1911 (257ff, shikaste, 1135 H), **4778 (156ff, nastaʿlīq of ʿAbd Allāh Qurra-Bīk, 5 Jumāda II 1070 H)**.

Āstān-i Quds-i Raḍavī 5662 (naskhī, 1082 H).

Marʿashī 914 (284ff 1st 6 maqālāt, naskhī of Ṭāhmasp-qulī Farāhānī, 1074 H Qum), 7667 (2v–25v, nastaʿlīq, 11th century H), **13260 (nastaʿlīq, autograph incomplete, 96ff)**.

Asiatic Society of Bengal 956 (naskhī).

Āṣafiyya 236.

Bankipore/Khudā Bakhsh 2227 (146ff, nastaʿlīq, 12th century H), 2228 (274ff, naskhī, 12th century).

Raza Library (Rampur) 3489, 3490.

7) *Ishrāq.*

Taʿlīqa ʿalā Sharḥ Ḥikmat al-Ishrāq of Quṭb al-Dīn al-Shīrāzī [d. 1311], itself the commentary on the work of Shihāb al-Dīn Suhrawardī [d. 1191].

Scholia upon the commentary on the Wisdom of Illumination.

Copied by Muḥammad b. Mīrzā ʿAbd al-ʿAlī Darjazīnī, ed. Asad Allāh Hirātī under the direction of Sayyid Ibrāhīm Ṭabāṭabāʾī (Tehran lithograph 1313 H).

Partial translation by H. Corbin in *Le Livre de la Sagesse Orientale*, ed. C. Jambet (Paris 1986), 439–666.

There is a forthcoming edition by Hossein Ziai (Tehran 1384 Sh/2006).

See *GAL* I: 565; *al-Dharīʿa* VI:121, and Kintūrī (Calcutta 1330 H), 179.

In it, he mentions his teacher, Mīr Dāmād (238 and 318; page 580 of the translation), so it must predate 1041/1631. He also mentions many other works of his own such as *Tafsīr Fātiḥat al-kitāb* (379), *Risāla fīʾl-ḥudūth* (392, 449, 513), *al-Mabdaʾ waʾl-maʿād* (452, 485, 513), and *al-Shawāhid al-rubūbiyya* (373, 429, 535). Though incomplete, it reveals the importance of the *Ishrāqī* tradition upon his thought and his attempt at adjudicating between Peripatetic and Illuminationist arguments in light of his own ideas. The main text is divided into two sections (inspired by Stoic curricular teaching?) on logic and metaphysics and physics (On divine Lights). The *scholia* are extensive.

<u>MSS:</u>

Cambridge Or. 495 (240ff, naskhī, 1260/1844).
Tehran University Central Library 281 (97ff, taʿlīq of ʿAlī Nūrī, 1264 H).
Majlis-i Shūrā 1768 (454ff, naskhī, 1260 H in hand of ʿAlī Zunūzī).
Āstān-i Quds-i Raḍavī 13955 (nastaʿlīq).
Marʿashī 13207 (shikaste, 241ff, 11th century H in life of author).
Madrasa-yi Navvāb (Mashhad) 3 ḥikmat (137ff, nastaʿlīq, n.d.).
Malik (Mashhad) 2156 (370ff, naskhī, 1111 H Shiraz).
Bankipore/Khudā Bakhsh 2351 (304ff, nastaʿlīq, 12th century H).
Manikji (Bombay) 36 (429ff, draft of Muḥammad Ḥusayn Māzandarānī Mashhadī, Ramaḍān 1066 H).
Princeton (Arabic New Series) 34 (95v–356v, 14th century H).

III Qur'ānic works

1) *Asrār.*
Asrār al-āyāt wa-anwār al-bayyināt.
Secrets of the verses/signs and their manifest lights.
Ed. M. Khājavī with *marginalia* of Nūrī (Tehran 1363 Sh/1984). A good but uncritical edition. He also published a translation in the same year.
Reprint of Persian translation (Tehran 1380 Sh/2001).
It was lithographed by Aḥmad Shīrāzī in Tehran in 1319/1902 with the *marginalia* of ʿAlī Nūrī.
See *GAL* S II: 589 and *al-Dharīʿa* II:39.
It was completed between 1041–4/1631–4.
The text begins with an introduction on the philosophical and hermeneutical method of mystics and those rooted in knowledge (*al-rāsikhūn fī'l-ʿilm*), in which the nature of scripture is discussed alongside a definition of philosophy. The main body of the text is divided into three aspects (*ṭaraf*). The first is divided into three loci of witnessing (*mashhad*-s) on theology and focuses upon the proof for the existence of God, the nature of His oneness and monorealism (*waḥdat al-wujūd*) and the reality of attributes. The second is divided into four witnesses on the creation of the universe, the Muhammadan reality, the emanation of the many from the One, and the divine law and prophecy. This section deals with the God-world relationship. The third witness discusses the resurrection and the return to the One and is divided

significantly into twelve witnesses ranging from the states in the grave to degrees within heaven and hell.

MSS:

Kirmān Collection 315 (nastaʿlīq, 11th century H).

Tehran University Central Library 417 (218ff, naskhī, 1262 H), 2273 (1v–89r, naskhī, 1279 H), 3092 (1–200ff, naskhī of Muḥammad Hādī Qazwīnī, 1233 H), **3638 (1–247ff, nastaʿlīq, 12th century H)**, 3699 (83ff, nastaʿlīq, 1267 H), 7679 (naskhī, 13th century H), 7746 (nastaʿlīq of Muḥammad Mahdī Astarābādī, 1233 H).

Tehran University Faculty of Arts 189/1 (naskhī of ʿAbd al-Wāḥid Shīrāzī, 1095 H).

Tehran University Faculty of Theology 147 (89ff, nastaʿlīq, 1234 H), 212 (231ff, naskhī, 1244 H).

Millī 1539 (339–536ff, naskhī, 13th century H).

Majlis-i Shūrā 1206 (200ff, naskhī of Muḥammad Abu'l-Ḥasan, 1240 H), 1719 (127–57ff, naskhī, 13th century H), 2715 (1–189ff, naskhī, n.d.).

Āstān-i Quds-i Raḍavī 5672, 6144 (nastaʿlīq, 1216 H), 6953 (shikaste), 13619 (naskhī).

Malik (Mashhad) 2472 (72ff, naskhī, 12th century H).

Marʿashī 7577/1 (1v–103v, nastaʿlīq of ʿAbd al-Malik Bawānatī, 1128 H), 11027/1 (shikaste of Ḥusayn ʿAlī Nihāvandī in Isfahan, Shaʿbān 1244 H).

Bibliothèque Nationale (Paris) 1366 (158ff, nastaʿlīq, 18th century).

Princeton (Arabic New Series) 489 (91ff, naskhī, 13th century H, *marginalia* of Sabzavārī).

2) *Mafātīḥ.*

Mafātīḥ al-ghayb.

Keys to the unseen.

A Persian translation by the courtier Ḥusām al-Dīn Shīrāzī (Tehran 1312 H).

Ed. M. Khājavī with the *scholia* of ʿAlī Nūrī (Tehran 1363 Sh/1984). The edition, yet another uncritical one, is based on the lithograph and 2 manuscripts: MS Malik 1128 and a private MS of Sayyid Lājvardī Qummī. The editor also prefaces the edition with a good summary of the text in Arabic.

Khājavī has also translated the text into Persian and published it from Tehran in 1984.

A new Arabic uncritical edition by Muḥammad Khalīl al-Labūn (Beirut 1999).

It was lithographed along with his *Sharḥ uṣūl al-Kāfī* along with the *marginalia* of Sabzavārī in Tehran 1282/1865.

See *GAL* S II: 589, and *al-Dharī*ʿ*a* IV:279, XXI:305.
The editor thinks that it was supposed to be an introduction to his Qurʾānic exegesis and was completed in 1042/1632, when he was sixty-three years old (492). In it, he mentions many of his earlier works including the *Tafsīr* (635), *al-Mabdaʾ* (106, 266, 421), and *al-Shawāhid* (repeatedly). The work comprises his Qurʾānic hermeneutics and its relation to his metaphilosophy. It is divided into twenty keys on the relation of philosophy and the Qurʾān, divine authorial intent in the text, the nature of knowledge, inner revelation, proof for the existence of God, divine actions and their subjects, the temporal creation of the universe, the nature of man, his soul, bodily resurrection and the return to the One, and spiritual exercises. The text demonstrates how, for Mullā Ṣadrā, philosophy as a way of life, spiritual exercises, and scriptural understanding and reasoning based on spiritual experience and philosophical insight amount to a holistic hermeneutics.

MSS:
Kirmān Collection 164 (naskhī, 1207 H), 212 (naskhī, 1250 H), 387.
Tehran University Central Library 1302 (247ff, naskhī of Muḥammad Bāqir, 1203 H), 2285 (246ff, naskhī, 1260 H).
Tehran University Faculty of Law 80 beh.
Millī 1067 (118ff, naskhī, 1070 H), 1341 (230ff, nastaʿlīq, 1247 H).
Majlis-i Shūrā 132 (212ff, shikaste, 1246 H), 4308 (338ff, nastaʿlīq, 13th century H), 4942 (56r–61v, portion of first chapter, shikaste, 11th century H).
Mashhad University Faculty of Theology 1342[20863/4] (nastaʿlīq, 1204 H)).
Āstān-i Quds-i Raḍavī 910 (244ff, naskhī of Zayn al-ʿĀbidīn, 1230 H), 911 (240ff, naskhī, waqf date 1183 H), 13386 (naskhī of Muḥammad Ḥasan, 1260 H).
Malik 466 (178ff, shikaste, 13th century H), **1128 (234ff, naskhī, 1086 H Kāshān)**, 2711 (276ff, naskhī of Mīr Ṣādiq a student of the philosopher, Hādī Sabzavārī, 1206 H Sabzavar).
Madrasa-yi Sulṭānī (Kāshān) 276/3 (naskhī, 1069 H).
Indian Institute (Bodleian Library, Oxford) Arab 20 (130ff, nastaʿlīq of Mīr ʿAlī Naqī b. Nūr al-Dīn Gīlānī, Rabīʿ II 1085 H).
Personal copy of Sayyid Lājvardī Qummī.

3) *Tafsīr.*
Tafsīr al-Qurʾān al-Karīm.

Commentary on the Glorious Qur'an.[189]
Ed. M. Khājavī (7 vols, Qum 1366 Sh/1987). The editor has made a useful attempt in the introduction to construct a chronology of the works of Mullā Ṣadrā. The early sections are based on MS Masjid-i Aʿẓam (Qum) 1916; the commentary on the throne verse is based on the lithograph and MS Malik 5420 (dated 1297 H); the commentary on *Yāsīn* and *al-Aʿlā* is based on the lithograph and MS Sipahsālār 2002 and MS Malik 773; the commentary on *Jumʿa* and *al-Ṭāriq* is based on the holograph in the private collection of Sayyid Muṣṭafā Fayḍī a descendent of Fayḍ Kāshānī, and *Ḥadīd* is based on MS Malik 5420; the commentary on *al-Wāqiʿa* and *al-Zilzāl* is based on MS Majlis-i Shūrā 1719.
A 'new' edition by Muḥammad Jaʿfar Shams al-Dīn (6 vols, Beirut 1998) is basically the same (a pirated version?) as the Khājavī edition.
It was lithographed in Tehran in 1320–2 H by Aḥmad Shīrāzī.
See *al-Dharīʿa* IV:198, 282, 340–3; *GAL S* II: 588–9, and Kintūrī (Calcutta 1330 H), 128.
Most of the manuscripts include the commentaries on the two special verses. The complete exegesis includes commentaries on the following chapters and verses:

Āyat al-nūr 24: 35 [completed Rabīʿ II 1030/1621].[190]
This is an extensive commentary on this popular verse that summarises a number of exegetical glosses from a philosophical and mystical perspective. After an introductory discourse on the nature of light, the text comprises seven chapters (*fuṣūl*) and a testament. Important issues including a discussion of the spiritual hierarchy of the soul, the nature of the Perfect Man as the perfect light and manifestation of the One and his role in the cosmos as the microcosmic face of the One.
MSS:
Tehran University Central Library 2290 (118v–145r, shikaste, 1269 H), 2931 (70–94ff, nastaʿlīq, 1234 H).

---

[189] There is one important but brief study of his commentary and hermeneutics: S. H. Nasr, 'The Qur'anic commentaries of Mullā Ṣadrā', in S. J. Ashtiyani et al (eds), *Consciousness and Reality: Studies in Memory of Toshihiko Izutsu* (Islamic Philosophy, Theology and Science Texts and Studies vol. XXXVIII, Leiden 2000), 45–58.
[190] There are two studies of this commentary: Mohsen M. Saleh, 'The verse of Light: A Study of Mullā Ṣadrā's philosophical Qur'ān exegesis', unpublished Ph.D. dissertation (Temple University 1994) – this includes a complete translation of the text into English; and Latimah Peerwani, *On the Hermeneutics of the Light Verse* (London 2003).

Tehran University Faculty of Arts 189/2 (incomplete, naskhī of ʿAbd al-Wāḥid Shīrāzī, 1094–5 H), 112 (68r–70r, naskhī, 1100 H).
Sipahsālār 7524
Majlis-i Shūrā 1842 (1–32ff, naskhī, 13th century H), 1917 (162–225ff, shikaste, 12th century H), 2760 (107–75ff, shikaste, 1091 H).
Majlis-i Sīnā (Tehran) 369 (608–55ff, nastaʿlīq possibly autograph, Rabīʿ II 1030 H).
Mashhad University Faculty of Theology 663 (106ff, nastaʿlīq, 1298 H).
Āstān-i Quds-i Raḍavī 1467 (naskhī, 1262 H), 1469 (nastaʿlīq, 1262 H), 6124, 7508, 8209 (39ff, nastaʿlīq, 13th century H), 8238 (nastaʿlīq, 19th century), 11572 (mixed script, 1239 H), 14451 (naskhī, 1229 H).
Marʿashī 7716 (1v–36r, nastaʿlīq, author's hand dated Rajab 1030 H), 12151/1 (6ff, nastaʿlīq, 13th century H).

Āyat al-kursī 2: 256 [ca. 1022 H/1613, Qum] and see *al-Dharīʿa* XV:252 for a citation of a Persian translation of this text by the author entitled *al-ʿUrwa al-wuthqā.*
The text is divided into an introduction and 20 chapters on a range of issues beginning with God as the ontological ground of all that exists to the existential import of intercession and the role of the Imams in the process.
MSS:
Tehran University Central Library 884 (92ff, shikaste, 1201 H), 2290 (1v–116v, shikaste, 1269 H), 6429 (172ff, naskhī, 1292 H).
Tehran University Faculty of Arts 189/2 (incomplete, naskhī of ʿAbd al-Wāḥid Shīrāzī, 1094–5 H).
Madrasa-yi Marvī 556 (13th century H).
Sipahsālār 139, 1993, 5239 (Arabic).
Majlis-i Shūrā 3802 (1–15ff, nastaʿlīq, 12th century H), 3825 (143ff, naskhī, 1294 H), **4336 (42r–48r, nastaʿlīq, 12th century H).**
Āstān-i Quds-i Raḍavī 14451 (naskhī, 1229 H).
Mashhad University Faculty of Theology 227/16 (naskhī of Sulṭān Maḥmūd Ḥusaynī, 16 Jumāda I 1083 H Shāhjahānābād-Delhi).
Marʿashī 6376 (83ff, nastaʿlīq of ʿAlī Akbar Marāghī, 1202 H).
Raza Library (Rampur) 589 (95ff, nastaʿlīq, 1246/1830, *Rawḍat al-anwār*).

Surat al-fātiḥa 1 [completed before 1041–4 H/1631–4].

An extensive commentary that establishes the relationship between his philosophical approach and his exgesis, it includes a discussion of the existential significance of divine mercy and the advent of substantial motion.

MSS:

Tehran University Faculty of Arts 189/2 (incomplete, naskhī of ʿAbd al-Wāḥid Shīrāzī, 1094–5 H).

Majlis-i Shūrā 1217/1 (naskhī of Muḥammad Taqī Hamadānī, 1254 H), 9061 (350ff, nastaʿlīq, n.d.).

Āstān-i Quds-i Raḍavī 1479 (naskhī of Zayn al-ʿĀbidīn, 1284 H), 1480 (shikaste of ʿAbd Allāh, 1256 H), 9988 (naskhī, 1304 H).

Kitābkhāna-yi Farhang (Mashhad) 31 ba (130ff, shikaste of Aḥmad Shīrāzī, 1274 H).

Marʿashī 4170 (95v–106r, naskhī, 1241 H), 5904.

Masjid-i Aʿẓam (Qum) 851 (naskhī, 11th century H).

Surat al-baqara 2 [incomplete work 1041–4 H/1631–4].

He only comments on the first 65 verses. Of particular importance is his discussion of the disjointed letters (*ḥurūf muqaṭṭaʿa*) at the beginning of the chapter.

MSS:

Tehran University Central Library 3105 (156ff, shikaste, 13th century H), 6421 (181ff, naskhī, 12th century H).

Tehran University Faculty of Arts 189/2 (incomplete, naskhī of ʿAbd al-Wāḥid Shīrāzī, 1094–5 H).

Sipahsālār 5135.

Majlis-i Shūrā 1217/1 (naskhī of Muḥammad Taqī Hamadānī, 1254 H), 9061 (350ff, nastaʿlīq, n.d.).

Malik 305 (402ff, naskhī, 12th century H).

Masjid-i Aʿẓam (Qum) 1916 (copy of autograph).

Surat al-sajda 32.

Comprising nine chapters, this is a mystical commentary on the hierarchy of spiritual psychology.

MSS:

Tehran University Faculty of Arts 189/2 (incomplete, naskhī of ʿAbd al-Wāḥid Shīrāzī, 1094–5 H).

Āstān-i Quds-i Raḍavī 14450 (naskhī, 1187 H), 14451 (naskhī, 1229 H).

Princeton (Yahuda) 1027 (1v–69r, naskhī of Muḥammad Ṣafar, 1050 H).
Princeton (Arabic New Series) 621 (163r–170v, 13th century H, incomplete).
Marʿashī 12151/2 (nastaʿlīq, fol. 6–22, 13th century H).
Maktabat Amīr al-Muʾminīn 835 (Kāẓimiyya Dhuʾl-Qaʿda 1215 H).

Surat al-Yāsīn 36 [completed 1030 H].
His discussion of resurrection is particularly significant.
MSS:
Tehran University Faculty of Arts 189/2 (incomplete, naskhī of ʿAbd al-Wāḥid Shīrāzī, 1094-95 H), 232.
Sipahsālār 2002 (122ff, naskhī, 1271 H).
Majlis-i Shūrā 1842 (33–70ff, naskhī, 13th century H, incomplete), 1916 (250–3ff, naskhī, 13th century H).
Āstān-i Quds-i Raḍavī 1254 (189ff, nastaʿlīq, 11th century H, waqf 1145 H), 14450 (naskhī, 1187 H).
Marʿashī 4210 (1v–47r, naskhī, 1266 H).

Surat al-wāqiʿa 56.
Ed./tr. into Persian by M. Khājavī (Tehran 1363 Sh/1984).
MSS:
Tehran University Central Library 2931 (94–116ff, nastaʿlīq, 1234 H).
Millī 2697 (30-71ff, nastaʿlīq, 1230 H).
Majlis-i Shūrā 1719 (272-303ff, naskhī, 13th century H), **2760 (176–268ff, shikaste, 1091 H).**
Āstān-i Quds-i Raḍavī 1478 (naskhī, 1305 H), 9646 (mixed script, 1296 H), 10788 (nastaʿlīq, 19th century).
Malik 6222/8 (99v–136r, shikaste of Muḥammad Bāqir b. Zayn al-ʿĀbidīn Maqṣūd-ʿAlī, 1034 H).
Āstāna-yi Shāh-i Chirāgh 303.
Marʿashī 4660/4 (94v–133v, nastaʿlīq, 1257 H), 12151/6 (nastaʿlīq, fol. 101–29, 13th century H).
Maktabat Amīr al-Muʾminīn 983 (naskhī, Sayyid Raḥīm Ḥusaynī, 12th century H).
Sālār Jung 905 (68ff, naskhī, 13th century H).

Surat al-Ḥadīd 57.

MSS:

Tehran University Faculty of Arts 189/2 (incomplete, naskhī of ʿAbd al-Wāḥid Shīrāzī, 1094-95 H).

Tehran University Faculty of Theology 846 (142ff, nastaʿlīq, 1135 H).

Sipahsālār 6522 (104–50ff, naskhī).

Majlis-i Shūrā 4840 (181–343ff, nastaʿlīq, 1305 H).

Majlis-i Sīnā (Tehran) 369 (536-607ff, nastaʿlīq, 1083 H).

Āstān-i Quds-i Raḍavī 1476 (naskhī, n.d.), 14451 (naskhī, 1229 H).

Malik 185 (133ff, nastaʿlīq, 12th century H), 281 (101ff, shikaste, 13th century H).

Āstāna-yi Shāh-i Chirāgh 303.

Marʿashī 9993/3 (43r–127r, naskhī, 1303 H), 12151/4 (nastaʿlīq, fol. 29–91, 13th century H), 12737 (nastaʿlīq, fol. 1–66, 1234 H).

Maktabat Amīr al-Muʾminīn *majmūʿa* 1117 (nastaʿlīq, Muḥammad Riḍā Tabrīzī, 1232 H), 983 (naskhī, Sayyid Raḥīm Ḥusaynī, 12th century H).

Princeton (Yahuda) 1027 (1v–69r, naskhī of Muḥammad Ṣafar, 1050 H).

Surat al-jumʿa 62 [between 1041–4 H].

Divided into an introduction, 12 places of dawn (*maṭlaʿ*) and a conclusion, it includes a discussion of Avicennan radical contingency.

MSS:

Tehran University Law Faculty 22 (2v–77v, nastaʿlīq, 1298 H).

Majlis-i Shūrā 1842 (105–114ff, naskhī, 13th century H), 1916 (275–6ff, naskhī, 13th century H), 1917 (226–300ff, shikaste, 12th century H), **2760 (1–105ff, shikaste, 1091 H)**, 4840 (344–49ff, nastaʿlīq, 1305 H).

Āstān-i Quds-i Raḍavī 14451 (naskhī, 1229 H), 12851 (naskhī, 1126 H).

Marʿashī 497 (100v–105r, naskhī, 1117 H), **7716 (57v–116v, nastaʿlīq, Rajab 1030 H in author's hand)** - both as *al-maṭāliʿ waʾl-ishrāqāt*, 12151/7 (nastaʿlīq, fol. 129–63, 13th century H).

Maktabat Amīr al-Muʾminīn *majmūʿa* 1117 (nastaʿlīq, Muḥammad Riḍā Tabrīzī, 1232 H).

Surat al-Ṭāriq 86 [completed Rajab 1030 H].

Ed./tr. into Persian by M. Khājavī with commentaries on *Sūra-hā-yi Aʿlā va zilzāl* (Tehran 1363 Sh/1984).

MSS:

Sipahsālār 7533.

Majlis-i Shūrā 1842 (76–107ff, naskhī, 13th century H), 1916 (2–11ff, nastaʿlīq, 19th century), **2760 (271—307ff, shikaste of Rafīʿ al-Dīn Muḥammad Maʿṣūm, 1091 H)**, 4840 (452–96ff, nastaʿlīq, 1305 H).

Majlis-i Sīnā (Tehran) 369 (655–80ff, nastaʿlīq, 1083 H).

Āstān-i Quds-i Raḍavī 1480 (nastaʿlīq, 1256 H), 14451 (nastaʿlīq, 1229 H).

Marʿashī 4660 (134v–146v, nastaʿlīq, 1257 H), **7716 (37v–55v, nastaʿlīq of author, 1030 H).**

Maktabat Amīr al-Muʾminīn 983 (naskhī, Sayyid Raḥīm Ḥusaynī, 12th century H).

Surat al-aʿlā 87.

Lithographed on margins of *Kashf al-fawāʾid* of Ḥillī (Tehran 1312 H).

Comprising an introduction and ten glorifications (*tasbīḥ*).

MSS:

Tehran University Faculty of Arts 189/2 (incomplete, naskhī of ʿAbd al-Wāḥid Shīrāzī, 1094–5 H).

Sipahsālār 1994, 6522 (150–9ff, nastaʿlīq, 17 Rajab 1208 H).

Majlis-i Shūrā 4840 (497–528ff, nastaʿlīq, 1305 H).

Mashhad University Faculty of Theology 1342 (nastaʿlīq, 1204 H).

Āstān-i Quds-i Raḍavī 1467 (naskhī of Aḥmad Ḥusayn, 26 Dhuʾl-Qaʿda 1158 H).

Maktabat al-Imām al-Ḥakīm (Najaf) 218 mīm (16ff, 1241 H)

Maktabat Amīr al-Muʾminīn *majmūʿa* 1117 (nastaʿlīq, Muḥammad Riḍā Tabrīzī, 1232 H).

Princeton (Yahuda) 1027 (1v–69r, naskhī of Muḥammad Ṣafar, 1050 H).

Marʿashī 10353/3 (31v–485, nastaʿlīq of Muʿīn b. Ḥusayn Gīlānī, 1183 H), 12151/5 (nastaʿlīq, fol. 91–101, 13th century H).

Surat al-zilzāl 99.

MSS:

Majlis-i Shūrā 1917 (138–61ff, shikaste, 12th century H), 2760 (306–33ff, shikaste, 1091 H), 4840 (529–52ff, nastaʿlīq, 1305 H).

Malik 6222/8 (99v–136r, shikaste of Muḥammad Bāqir b. Zayn al-ʿĀbidīn Maqṣūd-ʿAlī, 1034 H).

Āstān-i Quds-i Raḍavī 1477 (naskhī, n.d.), 1478 (naskhī of Hidāyat Allāh Hamadānī, 1305 H), 10788 (nastaʿlīq, n.d.).

Marʿashī 9819 (10ff, naskhī), 12737 (nastaʿlīq, 49ff, 1234 H).
Maktabat Amīr al-Muʾminīn *majmūʿa* 1117 (nastaʿlīq, Muḥammad Riḍā Tabrīzī, 1232 H).
Sālār Jung 906 (11ff, naskhī, 13th century H).

Other MSS:
Kirmān Collection 38 (naskhī, 12th century H), 56 (naskhī, 1273 H), 413 (naskhī, 13th century H).
Tehran University Central Library 1696 (211ff, naskhī, 13th century H), 2544 (161ff, naskhī, 1242 H), 6217/8 (*āyat al-amāna* also 3901),[191] 6404 (150ff, naskhī, 1262 H).
Tehran University Faculty of Arts 232 (*al-Kawthar*), 253 (*āyat al-dukhān*).
Millī 1610 (portions, 1–82ff, nastaʿlīq, 1237 H)
Majlis-i Shūrā 1217 (602ff, nastaʿlīq, 1254 H, mistakes).
Mashhad University Faculty of Theology 1346 (naskhī, n.d.).
Āstān-i Quds-i Raḍavī 1468 (naskhī, 1305 H), 11633 (214ff, naskhī, 1253 H).
Malik 405 (224ff, shikaste, 1030H).
Marʿashī 951 (293ff, naskhī, contains autograph).
Madrasa-yi Fayḍiyya 38 (520ff, naskhī, 1336 H), 37 (616ff, naskhī, 1322 H).

4) *Mutashābihāt.*
Mutashābihāt al-Qurʾān.
The equivocal verses of the Qurʾān.
Rasāʾil-i falsafī, ed. S. J. Āshtiyānī (Qum 1362 Sh/1983), 75–121. The editor provides extensive annotation and introduction but no critical apparatus or details about the manuscripts used.
See *al-Dharīʿa* XIX:62.
It was completed between 1041–4/1631–4. This short treatise discusses the views of predecessors upon the nature of the equivocal or ambiguous verses of the Qurʾān, before he presents his own ideas on the nature of *tawḥīd* and correct Qurʾanic hermeneutics. It is divided into six chapters (*fuṣūl*). Chapter one lays out the different positions of commentators on the ambiguous and equivocal verses. Chapter two looks in details at some commentaries; in particular, it provides a critique of the Muʿtazilite interpretation of Abū Bakr Muḥammad b. ʿAlī al-Qaffāl al-Shāshī [d. 365/976].

[191] There is a well-known commentary on this verse by his student, Fayḍ Kāshānī that is attested in the manuscript catalogues, so this may be a case of misattribution.

Chapter three criticises an agnostic approach to interpretation and condemns those who deny attributes to God; the meaning of these verses is accessible to human intellects. Chapter four introduces the hermeneutics of the author. Chapter five follows up with corroborating evidence. The final chapter considers the possibility of interpretation based upon the inner-revelation and spiritual opening that God bestows upon the mystic.

MSS:

Tehran University Central Library 2273 (118v–126v, naskhī, 1279 H), **3638 (419–43ff, nastaʿlīq, 12th century H).**

Majlis-i Shūrā 1719 (222–54ff, naskhī, 13th century H), **4942/30 (shikaste, 11th century H)**, 5438 (incomplete, 50v–61v, naskhī, 1237 H).

Marʿashī 7577 (173r–181v, nastaʿlīq of ʿAbd al-Malik Bawānatī, 1129 H).

IV Mystical Works

1) *Īqāẓ.*
Īqāẓ al-nāʾimīn.
The awakening of the dormant.
Ed. M. Muʾayyadī (Tehran 1982).
A short work which parallels sections of the second *safar* of the *Asfār*. It is divided into two parts, the first on (the unity of) being according to the school of Ibn ʿArabī, and the second, a discussion of man and his place in the cosmos. It was discovered only a few decades ago and the manuscripts known are very late, both of which question its authenticity. Furthermore, the ideas are more akin to Sufi thought than philosophy and Ṣadrā is quoted by name with his works, a practice of self-reference in the third person that one does not find in other texts by him. If it is authentic, then it ought to post-date the *Asfār*, which is mentioned on pages 4 and 16. The edition contains numerous errors, as do the manuscripts (20–21). The editor claims that the text was authenticated by Corbin and Dānishpazhūh (19–20). There is a forthcoming translation in French by Cécile Bonmariage.

MSS:

L'Institut Français des recherches en Iran, Tehran (112ff, naskhī, 1273 H).

Private belonging to editor (94ff, naskhī, 1281 H).

2) *Kasr.*

Kasr aṣnām al-jāhiliyya fī dhamm al-mutaṣawwifīn.

Breaking the idols of ignorance in admonition of the soi-disant Sufis.

Ed. M. T. Dānishpazhūh (Tehran 1961). A good critical edition based on MSS Malik 4653, Majlis-i Shūrā 1480 and the personal MS of Javād Tārā.

A new critical edition prepared by Muḥsin Jahāngīrī (Tehran 1381 Sh/2002).

Translated into Persian by M. Shafīʿīhā (Tehran 1405/1984). A better translation is *ʿIrfān va ʿārif-numāyān*, tr. Muḥsin Bīdārfar (Tehran 1366 Sh/1987).

See *GAL* II: 544 and *al-Dharīʿa* XVII:293.

It was completed by Shaʿbān 1027/1618.

It constitutes an attack on false Sufis of the Safavid period and a defence of true knowledge and the spiritual path. The work comprises an introduction and four chapters on the science of theology, aims of knowledge, the attributes of the pious, and some homiletic advice. It stresses the importance of virtue and spiritual exercises on the true Sufi path. He draws on a number of Sufi sources such as al-Ghazālī [d. 1111] and philosophers such as the Ikhwān al-Ṣafā who share he stress upon the complementarity of knowledge and action.

The introduction discusses four essentials that one ought to know: humanity has a luminous, spiritual nature as well as a tenebrous corporeal nature; perfection arises from knowledge coupled with righteous action; true knowledge is the recognition of God and of the soul; and the perfection of knowledge arises through spiritual exercises and purification of the soul. He then expands on the obstacles to true knowledge and the spiritual life.

Chapter one examines the nature of the true knower, the gnostic and is divided into three *fuṣūl*: on the need for spiritual exercises, to be wary of ecstatic utterances and to understand reality through spiritual and intellectual training.

The second chapter is on the pursuit of true knowledge and is divided into nine *fuṣūl*: knowledge is the goal of the existence of humanity; purification of the soul allows for knowledge to arise; on the knowledge that is bestowed through inner-revelation; on inner-revelation; on spiritual states; on the nature of moral acts; on the true state of the true knower; on the reasons for the wretchedness in the afterlife; and a description of the true lovers of God.

The third chapter develops on the nature of virtue and the virtuous and is divided into a further nine *fuṣūl*: how to reach the station of virtue; on love and desire; on the love of God as a means to virtue; on true worship and gnosis; how to treat the soul; on the health and infirmity of the soul; on the need for obedience to God; on wretchedness in the afterlife as a result of bad moral acts; and on the problems that arise from a lack of distinction between good and evil.

The final chapter is mainly a collection of homiletic advice from God, the Prophet and Imams and the philosophers. Particularly striking is the long quotation from the Pythagorean *Golden Verses* that seem to have been influential among philosophers of the Safavid period. The conclusion returns to the problem of obstacles to true knowledge and refers the seeker for knowledge back to his major philosophical work the *Asfār* and to the Qurʾān and the sayings of the Prophet and the Imams for guidance on moral action.

MSS:
Majlis-i Shūrā 1480 (83ff, naskhī of ʿAlī Kirmānshāhī, 1222 H), 4565 (49r–83v, naskhī, 1242 H).
Mashhad University Faculty of Theology 1342[20863/2] (nastaʿlīq, 12th century H).
Āstān-i Quds-i Raḍavī 11038 (102ff, nastaʿlīq, 1273 H).
Malik 4653 (113v–168r, nastaʿlīq, 1258–60 H).
Marʿashī 880 (57v–129r, nastaʿlīq, 1292 H), 11478/3 (fol. 10–196, naskhī, Muḥarram 1222 H).
Personal MS of Javād Tārā (41ff, shikaste of Muḥammad ʿAlī b. ʿAbd al-Wahhāb).

3) *Maẓāhir.*
al-Maẓāhir al-ilāhiyya fī asrār al-ʿulūm al-kamāliyya.
Divine manifestations on the secrets of the perfect knowledge.
Ed. S. J. Āshtiyānī (Mashhad 1961, rpt, Qum 1377 Sh/1998). An uncritical edition with editorial notes.
A new edition with a lengthy introduction on the history of Sadrian philosophy by Sayyid Muḥammad Khāminihī (Tehran 1378 Sh/1999). The edition is based on the lithograph and the following manuscripts: a private one in the collection of Sayyid Muṣṭafā Fayḍī, MS Tehran University Central Library 1030, 209, MS Malik 4651, and Āstān-i Quds-i Raḍavī 7683. The best available manuscripts have been used judiciously and there is a good critical apparatus.
See *al-Dharīʿa* XXI:162.
Lithographed 1314/1897 on margins of *al-Mabdaʾ waʾl-maʿād*, 232–337.
The work comprises an introduction defining philosophy as intellectual perfection and practice, and two *fann*-s. The first fann discusses the origin of creation, ontology and God. It is divided into eight *maẓhar*-s (manifestations or proofs). The first discusses

the aims of philosophy. The second provides proofs for the existence of God. The third discusses divine unicity and necessity. The fourth is an inquiry into the divine names and attributes. The fifth is a discussion of divine knowledge. The sixth considers divine speech and the nature of the Qur'ān. The seventh is a proof for the temporal incipience of the world. The final *maẓhar* of this section deals with the return, the arcs of ascent and descent and the nature of the theological problem of *bada'*.

The second *fann* deals with the resurrection and the return to the One, and comprises eight *maẓhar*-s. The first provides a philosophical proof for bodily resurrection. The second discusses man and his faculties. The third is on the nature of death. The fourth describes the grave and the punishment in it. The fifth deals with resurrection. The sixth discusses judgement, and aspects of space-time that are relevant. The seventh describes the bridge (*ṣirāṭ*). The final *maẓhar* discusses the nature of scriptures and the lesser and greater Resurrections.

MSS:

Tehran University Central Library 209 (97ff, naskhī, 1177 H), **1030 (154ff, naskhī of Muḥammad Mu'min, 1094 H)**.

Tehran University Theology Faculty 663 (54ff, naskhī, 1274 H).

Āstān-i Quds-i Raḍavī 7683 (107ff, naskhī, 1264 H).

Malik 4651 (48ff, shikaste, Ṣafar 1099 H).

Majlis-i Shūrā 3812 (209–60ff, shikaste, 1275 H).

4) *Aṣl.*

Risāla-yi Sih aṣl.

The three principles.

Ed. S. H. Nasr (Tehran 1961, rpt, 1377 Sh/1998). The edition is based on MSS Majlis-i Shūrā 103, 1430, Āstān-i Quds 595 and the personal MSS of Javād Tārā and Mudarris-i Raḍavī.

A new edition by M. Khājavī (Tehran 1376 Sh/1997). This edition builds upon the earlier, slightly rushed one, and draws upon 2 further manuscripts: MS Tehran University Central Library 3857 and MS Majlis-i Shūrā 2992. The editor has a good introduction to the text and provides full critical apparatus and appendices.

See *al-Dharī'a* XII:261.

This work was probably completed sometime in the early 1030s H. It is his main Persian work, an attack on the exoteric scholars who reject philosophy and mysticism.

It is a homiletic and mystically inclined text upon ethics and matters of faith divided, significantly for a Twelver Shiʿi, into fourteen chapters. The three principles discusses concern obstacles to true self-knowledge and a sound psychology of the soul: the problems of ignorance of the soul and the resulting disaster, love of the world and inclination to the carnal self that helps man to forget himself, and the whisperings of the carnal self.

MSS:

British Museum Add. 16832 (incomplete 86–105ff, naskhī, 1165/1751, as *Ṭaʿn bar mujtahidīn*).

Tehran University Central Library 3857 (naskhī, n.d.).

Tehran University Central Library Microfilm collection 1439/7 (80ff, naskhī, 1091 H).

Majlis-i Shūrā 2991 (3-150ff, nastaʿlīq, 1232 H), 2992 (shikaste of Ibrāhīm Mushtarī-yi Ṭūsī, 1294 H), 1430 (nastaʿlīq, incomplete, *Sih Faṣl*), **3262 (86–160ff, nastaʿlīq, 1132 H).**

Mashhad University Faculty of Theology 1686 (naskhī, 1227 H).

Āstān-i Quds-i Raḍavī 595 (114ff, naskhī, 1281 H, incomplete, *Radd bar munkarīn-i ḥikmat*).

Personal MS of Javād Tārā copied in 1339 H from a MS in Najaf.

Personal MS of Mudarris-i Raḍavī (fol. 44-85, 1090H in hand of a student of Fayḍ Kāshānī).

V Philosophical, literary and theological works

1) *Dīwān.*

Dīwān.

Sections are edited by Nasr in his edition of *Sih Aṣl.*

Mathnawī-yi Mullā Ṣadrā, ed. Muṣṭafā Fayḍī (Qum 1376 Sh/1997). An edition of a famous Persian poem that was previously edited and published by Nasr.

Khājavī has edited a selection of his poems (Tehran 1377 Sh/1998). The edition is based on the following manuscripts: MS Majlis-i Shūrā 2992 and Tehran University Faculty of Theology 322

See *al-Dharīʿa* IX:600 citing a manuscript in Kirmanshāh.

MSS:

Tehran University Central Library 254, 849.

Tehran University Faculty of Theology 238 (1–3ff, nastaʿlīq, 11 Dhuʾl-Qaʿda 1075 H), 322 (2v–42r, naskhī).

Majlis-i Shūrā 1206, 2992 (shikaste, 1294 H).

2) *Manṭiq.*

al-Lamaʿāt al-mashriqiyya fīʾl-funūn al-manṭiqiyya

Flashes of inspiration in the logical arts.

Ed. ʿA. Mishkāt al-dīnī as *Manṭiq-i nuvīn* (Tehran 1347 Sh/1968).

It is the same text as *Risālat al-tanqīḥ* mentioned below.

3) *Letters.*

Letters to Mīr Dāmād:

1) in Āsh. 225–8, and in *Nāma-yi Āstān-i quds* 9: 59–62.

MS: Āstān-i Quds-i Raḍavī 590 (incomplete).

2) ed. M. T. Dānishpazhūh in *Rāhnuma-yi Kitāb* V, 8–9 (1341 Sh/1962), 757–65

3) and 4) ed. M. T. Dānishpazhūh in *Farhang-i Īrān zamīn* 13, 1–4 (1966), 84–95 and 95-8. The complete text of the last letter is in MSS British Museum Or. 2852 (90r–92r, Persian, 1293 H), and Tehran University Central Library 132.

4) *Ḥudūth.*

R. fī ḥudūth al-ʿālam.

On the temporal incipience of the world.

Rasāʾil (Tehran lithograph 1885), 2–109.

Ed./tr. into Persian as *Kitāb āfarīnish-i jahān* by M. Khājavī (Tehran 1377 Sh/1998).

A new critical edition by Sayyid Ḥusayn Mūsavīyān (Tehran 1378 Sh/1999). An excellent and well-annotated edition with full critical apparatus, the text has been established on the basis of the following seven manuscripts: MS Majlis-i Shūrā 1081, MS Tehran University Central Library 2602 and 2608/6, MS Malik 4652/7 (dated between 1051 and 1080 H), MS Marʿashī 497 and 686, and MS Tehran University Faculty of Theology 242/33.

A German translation by Sayyed Bagher Talgharizadeh as *Die Abhandlung über die Entstehung* (Berlin 2000).

See *GAL* II: 544, *GAL S* II: 588, and *al-Dharīʿa* II:279, VI:295.

It was probably completed in the early eleventh century and reworked by 1034/1624–5, and corresponds to *Asfār* V: 205–46. In this text, he examines the reasons for the (temporal) incipience of the world through a discussion of the metaphysics of contingency and potentiality, and substantial motion. Significantly he provides a historical assessment of the problem beginning with the Presocratics, Plato and his commentators through to Islamic thinkers. This cosmogonical text is divided into twelve chapters (significant for an Imāmī author), a conclusion and an epilogue. Chapter one deals with modalities and the relationship between necessity and contingency in the context of creation. Chapter two discusses potentiality and actuality. The next five chapters deal with the problems of motion and its innate relationship with nature. The eighth chapter discusses the reality of time and its proofs, while the following chapter explains how only God precedes time. The tenth chapter summarises the previous discussions of space, time and motion. The final two chapters deal with the connexion between the eternal and the incipient and the mediation of agent intellects. The conclusion and epilogue recap the opinions of previous thinkers on this issue and proffer concluding remarks.

MSS:

Tehran University Central Library 2602 (autograph written for Mullā Shamsā Gīlānī, 68ff, nastaʿlīq), 2608 (153–237ff, naskhī, 1301 H), 2812 (46v–78v, nastaʿlīq, 1233 H).

Tehran University Faculty of Theology 242/33 (106–21ff, shikaste of Farīd al-Dīn b. Muḥammad, 1057–61 H).

Millī 1881 (42–65ff, nastaʿlīq, 1276 H).

Majlis-i Shūrā 1081 (255ff, naskhī, 1083 H), 1802 (106–69ff, naskhī, 1244 H).

Āstān-i Quds-i Raḍavī 578 (shikaste, 1292 H), 579, 9020 (83ff, naskhī, n.d.).

Marʿashī 497 (48v–99r, naskhī, 1117 H), 686 (13r–51v, nastaʿlīq, 11th century H), 974 (21v–81r, nastaʿlīq, 1282 H).

Maktabat Amīr al-Muʾminīn *majmūʿa* 1117 (nastaʿlīq, Muḥammad Riḍā Tabrīzī, 1232 H).

Princeton (Arabic New Series) 28 (76ff, naskhī, 1072 H), 527 (32ff, 13th century), 2003 (51v–101r, naskhī, completion date of 1034 H given).

5) *Iksīr.*

R. Iksīr al-ʿārifīn fī maʿrifat ṭarīq al-ḥaqq waʾl-yaqīn.

The elixir of the gnostics on the knowledge of the way of Truth and certainty.

Rasāʾil (Tehran lithograph 1885), 278–340.

Ed./tr. in Japanese by Shigeru Kamada (Tokyo 1984).

An English translation by William Chittick as *The Elixir of the Gnostics* (Islamic Translations Series, Provo, UH 2003). An excellent rendition with some good annotation based on the Kamada edition and proofs of the forthcoming edition of Yaḥyā Yathribī (Tehran 1374 Sh/2006).

See *GAL* S II: 589, III: 1300, and *al-Dharīʿa* II:279.

It was completed by 1031/1621.

Chittick has demonstrated successfully that this is a revision and adaptation of the Persian work *Jāvīdān-nāma* of Afḍal al-Dīn Kāshānī [d. 1214]. In this mystical text that is distinguished by the articulation of the ideas and lexicon of the school of Ibn ʿArabī, he discusses some of the noble aporiai of philosophy according to the people of God and the true philosophers (*ahl Allāh waʾl-ḥukamāʾ al-ṣādiqīn*).

The text is divided into four *abwāb*. The first is further divided into five *fuṣūl* discussing a rather Sufi-oriented division and classification of the sciences. Sciences either relate to this world or to the afterlife. Those relating to this realm are of three types: sciences of statements, of actions, and of (spiritual and intellectual) states. These range from music theory and prosody to mathematics and logic. Sciences of the afterlife concern man's pursuit of fulfilment and felicity in the next realm and are the knowledge of God, His attributes, His scriptures, prophets and the nature of the resurrection and the afterlife. The first *bāb* closely follows the *Jāvīdān-nāma* with additional material on knowledge of the afterlife.

The second *bāb* is a detailed discussion of the psychology of the soul, divided into ten chapters. They concern the need for self-knowledge and self-purification of the true realisation of the self and portray a psychic cosmology that is characteristic of Sufi metaphysics. It summarises much of the section of the *Jāvīdān-nāma* and drops some parts.

The third *bāb*, which is divided into ten chapters, is an account of preliminary concepts that a person needs to find familiar, and they rage from logical issues of the nature of priority, intension and extension, through to the nature of angels and devils. This section contains much revision of the *Jāvīdān-nāma*, especially omitting sections about the way of the Sunnis.

The fourth *bāb* follows on with a discussion of goals and *teloi*, and also comprises ten chapters. In the, he discusses the destination of the soul, the nature of death, and the pursuit of a good afterlife within the parameters of his psychology and his doctrine of substantial motion. Much of this section has been revised from the *Jāvīdān-nāma*.

MSS:

Tehran University Central Library 2608 (99r–153r, naskhī, 1301 H), 3322 (84–92ff, nastaʿlīq, late 12th century H).

Madrasa-yi Marvī 651 (1279 H).

Majlis-i Shūrā 79 (mixed script, 13th century H), **1688 (autograph dated 1031/1621)**, 1719 (304–7ff, naskhī, 13th century H), 5083 (142ff, naskhī, 1309 H), 5333 (57v–86v, nastaʿlīq, n.d.).

Āstān-i Quds-i Raḍavī 337 (nastaʿlīq, 1264 H), 338 (nastaʿlīq, 1313 H), **10819 (naskhī of Muḥammad Ḥusayn, 1102 H)**, 12163 (naskhī 1212 H).

Marʿashī 3629 (101ff, naskhī, 1263 H).

Maktabat al-Imām al-Ḥakīm 1142 (53ff).

Maktabat Amīr al-Muʾminīn 1117 (nastaʿlīq of Muḥammad Riḍā Tabrīzī, 1232 H).

Princeton (Arabic New Series) 2003 (8v–36r, 1034 H).

Private - Dānishpazhūh (nastaʿlīq of author, 1031 H).

6) *Ittiṣāf.*

R. fī ittiṣāf al-māhiyya biʾl-wujūd.

On the qualification of quiddity by being.

Rasāʾil (Tehran lithograph 1885), 110–9.

It was also lithographed on the margins of Ḥillī, *al-Jawhar al-naḍīd* (Tehran 1311 H lithograph), 1–23.

See *GAL* S II: 589, and *al-Dharīʿa* I:82.

Pace Nasr, it is not a youthful treatise expressing views he later changed since he quotes the *Asfār* and affirms his famous doctrine of *aṣālat al-wujūd*. It is a critique of the views of Davānī on predication, accidental relations and the sense and reference of being. He analyses the connection between these two concepts in three ways. The first affirms the priority of being over quiddity and rejects the theory that describes being morphologically as a name of second imposition. The second approach affirms the reality of the relationship in the light of the doctrine of the subordination rule (*qāʿida farʿiyya*). The third discusses being as self-individuating and obtaining independently of anything else in reality. He concludes with a discussion of the different senses of being, of which the real and concrete existence is primary.

MSS:

Tehran University Central Library 870 (43–50ff, taʿlīq), 2273 (127v–131v, naskhī, 1279 H), 2608 (70r–77v, naskhī, 1301 H), **3638 (285–95ff, nastaʿlīq, 12th century H)**, 6275/5.

Majlis-i Shūrā 1719 (195–200ff, naskhī, 13th century H), 1866 (3–46ff, naskhī, 13th century H), **4942 (85v–88r, shikaste, 11th century H)**, 5438 (45r–50r, naskhī, 1237 H).

Āstān-i Quds-i Raḍavī 6408 (4ff, nastaʿlīq of Aḥmad Ḥusaynī, 1216 H).

Marʿashī 6717 (1v–5v, nastaʿlīq, 1279 H), 7577 (119v–124r, nastaʿlīq, 1128 H).

Maktabat al-Imām al-Ḥakīm 900 mīm (2 ff, 1263 H).

Raza Library (Rampur) 1027 (nastaʿlīq of Muḥammad Ṣādiq Gīlānī in Isfahan, 151r–156r, 18th century), 574 (naskhī, 42r–66v, 1146/1733).

7) *Tashakhkhuṣ.*

R. fīʾl-tashakhkhuṣ.

On individuation.

Rasāʾil (Tehran lithograph 1885), 120–32.

See *GAL* S II: 589, and *al-Dharīʿa* II:589.

The treatise discusses the reality of the self-individuation of being, its independence from the thing and from quiddity. He deals with objections and closely criticises the views of Ghiyāth al-Dīn Manṣūr Dashtakī, who wrote a work adjudicating between the views of his father and Davānī.

MSS:

Tehran University Central Library 2608 (78r–86v, naskhī, 1301 H), 3638 (375–88ff, nastaʿlīq, 12th century H).

Sipahsālār 7453 (1v–6v, naskhī, 13th century H), 7545 (92r–99v, naskhī, 13th century H).

Majlis-i Shūrā 1719 (210–1ff, naskhī, 13th century H), 1866 (46–50ff, naskhī, 13th century H), **4942 (82v–85v, shikaste, 11th century H)**, 5438 (38v–45r, naskhī, 1237 H).

Marʿashī 7577 (155v–161v, nastaʿlīq of ʿAbd al-Malik Bawānatī, 1128 H).

Raza Library (Rampur) 1027 (nastaʿlīq of Muḥammad Ṣādiq Gīlānī in Isfahan, 145r–151r, 18th century).

8) *Sarayān.*

R. fī sarayān wujūd al-Ḥaqq (or Ṭarḥ al-kawnayn).

On the flow of the True Being.

Rasāʾil (Tehran lithograph 1885), 132–48.

Ed. Khadīja Muqaddas-zāda as *Kayfiyyat maʿiyyat al-Wājib biʾl-mawjūdāt* in *Ganjīna-yi Bahāristān: Ḥikmat I*, gen. ed. ʿAlī Awjabī (Tehran 1379 Sh/2000), 281–99.

See *al-Dharīʿa* VI:138, and *GAL S* II: 588-9.

Also known as *Maʿiyyat al-wājib biʾl-mawjūdāt* and *Sarayān Nūr al-Ḥaqq*. It was written in his youth (before 1600) as an affirmation of the ontological principality of quiddity (*aṣālat al-māhiyya*) following the investigative method of Davānī known as *dhawq al-taʾalluh*. It asserts (135) that God's creative activity is related to quiddities (*majʿūliyyat al-māhiyya*). It also suggests (138) that the notion of being is ambiguous (i.e. the term is a pure equivocal) while such a position is rejected later in the *Asfār* I: 35.

Iṣfahānī (*Majmūʿa*, pānzdah) says that this is identical to the versions known as *Risāla fīʾl-maʿiyya* (*al-Dharīʿa*, XII:178). He also argues that this cannot be the work of Ṣadrā because it upholds the doctrine of the ontological priority of quiddity that he rejected, and because the text directly criticises his views. He concludes that the real author of the work is another student of Mīr Dāmād, Niẓām al-Dīn Aḥmad Dashtakī.[192] However, Ṣadrā tells us in the *Asfār* (I: 52) that he held this view in his youth, following his teacher Mīr Dāmād but was later guided to the truth by God. Muẓaffar (*Asfār* I: qāf) considers this to be *Ṭarḥ al-kawnayn*.

MSS:

Tehran University Central Library 2608 (87r–99r, naskh, 1301 H), 3238 (88–102ff, nastaʿlīq, 1241 H).

Millī 1384 (39-50ff, naskhī of ʿAbd al-Qādir Urdūbādī, Muḥarram 1034 H), 1853 (110–124ff, naskhī and nastaʿlīq, 11th century H).

Majlis-i Shūrā 79 (mixed script, 13th century H), 3812 (141–83ff, shikaste, 1275 H).

Āstān-i Quds-i Raḍavī shīn 599 (12ff, naskhī, 19th century), ḍād 9201 (nastaʿlīq, 1111 H).

Marʿashī 286 (71v–74v, nastaʿlīq, 1072 H), 11528/1 (fol. 1–21, naskhī of ʿAbd Allāh b. Mubārak b. ʿAlī b. Ḥumaydān al-Aḥsāʾī in Najaf, 1276 H).

Raza Library (Rampur) 1923 (nastaʿlīq, 7ff, 19th century).

[192] He may also have been the author of the *Riṣāla fīʾl-wujūd* mentioned below. See MS Princeton Arabic New Series 2000 for both.

9) *Qaḍāʾ.*
R. fīʾl-qaḍāʾ waʾl-qadar.
On the divine decree and will.
Rasāʾil (Tehran lithograph 1885), 148–237.
See *al-Dharʿa* XVII:49, and *GAL S* II: 588. Cf. *Asfār* VI: 369 passim.
In its order and style, this treatise mirrors the work on the same topic by the famous Shiʿi Sufi ʿAbd al-Razzāq Kāshānī [d. 1336].[193] It contains six chapters on the meaning of providential decree and will, on the locus of the divine decree, on the world created as the best of all possible worlds, on the nature of our free will, and on the benefits of obedience and supplication.

MSS:
Tehran University Central Library 849 (61r–174r, taʿlīq, 1300 H), 2608 (237r–243r, naskhī, 1301 H), 2812 (2v–45, nastaʿlīq, 1233 H), **5898 (naskhī of Zayn al-ʿĀbidīn, Shawwāl 1127 H)**, 6217 (nastaʿlīq, 13th century H).
Majlis-i Shūrā 1719 (163–87ff, naskhī, 13th century H), 1802 (51–105ff, naskhī, 1244 H), 1816 (122–274ff, nastaʿlīq, 19th century), 1934 (1–46ff, shikaste, end of 11th century H), 1935 (1–193ff, nastaʿlīq, 13th century H), 5333 (15r–55r, nastaʿlīq, n.d.).
Āstān-i Quds-i Raḍavī 7043.
Marʿashī 1430 (70v–107r, nastaʿlīq, 1222 H), 1999 (177v–228r, naskhī, 1262 H).
Sālār Jung 84 (132ff, nastaʿlīq, n.d.).
Raza Library 1027 (nastaʿlīq of Muḥammad Ṣādiq Gīlānī, 2v–48v, 18th century).
Princeton (Arabic New Series) 33 (145r–173v, 13th century H).

10) *Wāridāt.*
R. fīʾl-wāridāt al-qalbiyya fī maʿrifat al-rubūbiyya.
Insights in the heart about knowledge of the divine.
Rasāʾil (Tehran lithograph 1885), 238–77.
Ed. A. Shafīʿīhā (Tehran 1979). This careful critical edition is based on the following MSS: Tehran University Central Library 252, 279, 884, Majlis-i Shūrā 592, 9019, 4969, British Museum Add. 16832, Millī 827 and 225.
See *GAL* S II: 589, and *al-Dharīʿa* XXV:10.
It is a short mystical text composed in rhyming prose (*sajʿ*) dated Dhuʾl-Qaʿda 1023/1614. The treatise focuses upon the notion of the One as pure good emanating

[193] *Majmūʿa-yi rasāʾil va muṣannafāt*, ed. M. Hādīzāda (Tehran, 1380 Sh/2001), 566–93.

good to the cosmos. It is divided into forty sections each called a *fayḍ*. The work begins with a discussion of the pure being of the true One and develops the descent of being drawing upon the terminology of the school of Ibn ʿArabī and Islamic Neoplatonism. From *fayḍ* seventeen, it shifts to humanity as the microcosm and examines the reality of humanity and its culmination the *walī*. This final section contains a critique of court scholars who support unjust rulers.

MSS:

British Museum Add. 7529 (168v–80r, naskhī, incomplete, 18th century), Add. 16832 (105–33ff, naskhī, 1169 H/1756).

Kirmān Collection 279 (nastaʿlīq, 1188 H)

Madrasa-yi Marvī 856 (1119 H).

Majlis-i Shūrā 79 (mixed script, 13th century H), 592 (22ff, nastaʿlīq, Jumāda II 124 H), 4969 (43ff, naskhī, 12th century H), 9019 (45ff, nastaʿlīq, n.d.).

Millī 827 ʿayn (61ff, taʿlīq, 19th CE), 225 (51–69ff, shikaste, Shawwāl 1149 H).

Tehran University Central Library 22 (347v–56r, naskhī of Nūr al-Dīn Muḥammad Kāshī, Jumāda II 1115 H), 279 jīm (26ff, taʿlīq, 1188H), 884 (98v–119v, naskhī of Ismāʿīl b. Ibrāhīm, Ṣafar 1200 H)

Shrine of Shāh ʿAbd al-ʿAẓīm (Rayy) 157/1 (naskhī of Ḥusayn b. Muḥammad Mahdī, Dhu'l-Qaʿda 1033 H).

Āstān-i Quds-i Raḍavī 957 (39ff, nastaʿlīq of Muṣṭafā-qulī, 1306 H Shiraz), **958 (37ff, nastaʿlīq of Naṣīr b. Muḥammad Mashhadī, 1088 H)**, 11892 (naskhī, early 12th century H), **ḍād 13568 (shikaste of Muḥammad Amīn Tabrīzī, 1078 H)**.

Kitābkhāna-yi Gawharshād 877/10 (as *al-tasbīḥāt al-qalbiyya*, 118ff, nastaʿlīq, 12th century H).

Malik 1676 (35ff, shikaste, 13th century H).

Marʿashī 497 (1v–47r, naskhī of Muḥammad Rafīʿ, Jumāda I 1117 H), 5829 (42ff, [copied from?] naskhī of ʿAlam al-Hudā b. Fayḍ Kāshānī, 1336 H[waqf date?]).

Asiatic Society of Bengal 801 (naskhī)

11) *Ḥashr*.

R. fī'l-ḥashr.

On the resurrection.

Rasā'il (Tehran lithograph 1885), 341–71.

Ed./tr. in Persian by M. Khājavī as *Rastākhīz-i jahān* (Tehran 1366 Sh/1987). The edition is based on the following manuscripts: MS Majlis-i Shūrā 1719 and a private copy belonging to the editor.
It was lithographed on the margins of *al-Mabdaʾ*, 184–231, and of *Kashf al-fawāʾid* of al-Ḥillī, calligraphed by Muḥammad al-Ḥusaynī (Tehran 1305/1888, 94–140).
A French translation by Christian Jambet as *Se rendre immortel* (Paris 2000).
See *GAL* S II: 544, and *al-Dharīʿa* VII:279.
It is mentioned in *Asfār* IX: 198. It was completed on 22 Rajab 1032/22 May 1623. According to Āsh (255), this is the *Risāla ṭarḥ al-kawnayn*. In this text composed of eight chapters, five categories of beings are described in descending order in their vertical hierarchy: separable intellects, higher souls, lower souls, vegetative souls and bodies. He then deals with the resurrection of each class of being. His defence of the resurrection of the physical faculties and bodies provides an argument for corporal resurrection. Overall the text displays a marked Neoplatonic interpretation of the body-soul relationship.

MSS:
Tehran University Central Library 1030 (100–115ff, taʿlīq of Muḥammad Muʾmin, 1094 H), 2812 (79r–89r, nastaʿlīq, 1233 H), 3638 (247–285ff, nastaʿlīq, 12th century H, *Ṭarḥ al-kawnayn fī ḥashr al-ʿālamīn*).
Millī 1853 (126–47ff, naskhī /nastaʿlīq, 11th century H).
Majlis-i Shūrā 1719 (259–81ff, naskhī, 13th century H), **4942 (38v–47v, shikaste, 11th century H)**.
Āstān-i Quds-i Raḍavī 9948 (naskhī of Muḥammad Rafīʿ Mashhadī, 1150 H), 11358 (nastaʿlīq, 13th century H).
Marʿashī 974 (1v–20v, nastaʿlīq, 1282 H), 1786 (29ff, naskhī, copied from autograph), 3666 (1v–31r, naskhī, Shaʿbān 1287 H), 7577 (104v–119v, nastaʿlīq of ʿAbd al-Malik Bawānatī, 1128 H).
Raza Library 1924 (nastaʿlīq, 13ff, 19th century).
Cambridge University Library Browne Collection N. 5 (fol. 72–111, naskhī, n.d.)

12) *Qudsiyya.*
Al-Masāʾil al-qudsiyya fīʾl-ḥikma al-mutaʿāliya (or Al-qawāʿid al-malakūtiyya).
Sacred issues of transcendent philosophy.
Rasāʾil-i falsafī, ed. S. J. Āshtiyānī (Qum 1362 Sh/1983), 3–72. This is not a critical edition.

See *al-Dharīʿa* XX:362, which suggests that it is the same as *Ṭarḥ al-kawnayn*.

The text is incomplete and the final draft is dated 1034/1624. It is a summary of Sadrian doctrines on three issues: being, necessity of being, and proof for mental being and he refers to the *Asfār* for further details of the arguments. The work contains three chapters and a few appendices on objections to his ideas. The first chapter deals with the nature of philosophy, its subject-matter as well as some elementary aspects of his ontology. The second chapter discusses his notions of modality of necessity and its relationship to contingency. The third chapter is a detailed discussion of the proof for mental being with a consideration of five objections.

MSS:

Tehran University Central Library 1030 taʿlīq of Muḥammad Muʾmin, 1094 H), 9112 (54–93ff, naskhī, 1209 H).

Majlis-i Shūrā (Tehran) 1806 (121–78ff, shikaste, 12th century H).

Āstān-i Quds-i Raḍavī 11088 (naskhī, 13th century H)

Malik 6222/4 (33v–56r, shikaste of Muḥammad Bāqir b. Zayn al-ʿĀbidīn, 1034 H Qazwin).

13) *Khillān.*

Ajwibat al-masāʾil aw jawāb masāʾil baʿḍ al-khillān.

Answers to questions of a friend (student).

Rasāʾil-i falsafī, ed. S. J. Āshtiyānī, 125–98 .

See *GAL* S II: 589, and *al-Dharīʿa* V:228.

It is mentioned in his *Sharḥ al-hidāya* (182). The text comprises answers to philosophical questions posed to our philosopher probably by one of his students. There are five questions. The first concerns the nature of divine will and desire, and their relationship to divine knowledge. The second question is a logical inquiry into the nature of substance acting as a genus for substantial species. The third question asks what the nature of *hyle* is and discusses its relationship with body. The fourth poses the question whether accidents have matter through which they are composed. The final question concerns the nature of aspects or haeccities. Does the multiplicity of aspects of a substance *qua* its various properties infer that that substance is a universal?

Bonmariage (II: 3) following Corbin (28) says that this is the same text as the answers to Kāshānī, which is quite incorrect.

MSS:
Majlis-i Shūrā 1719 (335–6ff, naskhī, 13th century H).

14) *Gīlānī.*
Ajwibat masā'il Mullā Shamsā Gīlānī [d. 1081/1670].
Answers to the questions of Mullā Shamsā Gīlānī.
Majmū'a-yi Rasā'il-i falsafī-yi Ṣadr al-muta'allihīn, ed. Ḥāmid Nājī Iṣfahānī (Tehran 1996), 107–21.[194] The edition is based on two manuscripts: MS Āstān-i Quds-i Raḍavī 304 and MS Tehran University Central Library 1030.
See *GAL* S III: 1300.
It was lithographed on margins of *al-Mabda'* (Tehran 1311 H), 340–59.
It was completed on 19 Jumāda II 1034/ 28 March 1625 in Qum according to a manuscript in the hand of Fayyāḍ-i Lāhījī. In it, he describes Gīlānī, a student of Mīr Dāmād, as 'one of our dearest brothers and precious scholars, foremost in the science of *ḥadīth* and gnosis (*'irfān*)'. It contains five questions. The first concerns the correct categories in which motion falls and which undergo change. The second asks about the vegetative part of the soul and the incorporeality of the soul. The third considers the nature of intellectual conception, mental existence and knowledge. The fourth concerns the distinction between the perception of animals and of men and whether animals are resurrected. The fifth questions the pre-existence or creation of souls.

MSS:
Tehran University Central Library 1030 (95–100ff, ta'līq of Muḥammad Mu'min, 1094 H), 2608 (includes a letter addressed to him prefacing his answer).
Majlis-i Shūrā 1719 (308–21ff, naskhī, 13th century H).
Āstān-i Quds-i Raḍavī 304 (24ff, shikaste from autograph, 1292 H).
Malik 6222/1 (shikaste of 'Abd al-Razzāq Gīlānī the son-in-law, 19 Jumāda II, 1034 H).
Raza Library (Rampur) 3600 (nasta'līq, 13ff, 19th century).

15) *Kāshānī.*
Ajwibat masā'il Mullā Muẓaffar Ḥusayn Kāshānī.
Answers to questions of Kāshānī.

---

194 This collection was pirated by Dār Iḥyā' al-turāth al-'Arabī (Beirut 2000), with the addition of a pirated version of *Risāla fī'l-taṣawwur wa'l-taṣdīq.*

Majmūʿa-yi Rasāʾil, 125–60. The edition is based on MS Tehran University Central Library 1030 and MS Āstān-i Quds-i Raḍavī 1632.
It comprises answers to five questions on the nature of the human soul, animal sense perception, and the faculties of the tripartite soul.

MSS:
Tehran University Central Library 1030 (80–94ff, taʿlīq of Muḥammad Muʾmin, 1094 H).
Majlis-i Shūrā 3812 (172–208ff, shikaste, 1275 H)
Āstān-i Quds-i Raḍavī 1632.
Raza Library (Rampur) 384 D (nastaʿlīq, 16ff, 19th century).
Princeton (Arabic New Series) 2003 (37v–50r, naskhī, 1034 H).

16) *Naṣīriyya.*
Ajwibat masāʾil-i Naṣīriyya.
Answers to questions posed by Ṭūsī.
Majmūʿa-yi Rasāʾil, 163–77. The edition is based on MS Tehran University Central Library 1030 and MS Marʿashī 1948.
See *GAL* S III: 1300.
It was lithographed on the margins of *Sharḥ al-Hidāya*, 383–93, and *al-Mabdaʾ waʾl-maʿād*, 372–91.
It contains questions that Ṭūsī had asked of ʿAbd al-Ḥamīd Khusrawshāhī [d. 1254] but remained unanswered. The issues concern motion as the cause of time, privation and contingency of souls, and the emanation of the many from a single cause.[195] The answer to the second question is also discussed in *Asfār* VIII: 390, and *Taʿlīqa ʿalāʾl-ilāhiyyāt al-Shifāʾ* (1303 H, 170).

MSS:
Tehran University Central Library 1030 (74–80ff, taʿlīq of Muḥammad Muʾmin, 1094 H).
Majlis-i Shūrā 3812 (73–82ff, shikaste, 1275 H)
Āstān-i Quds-i Raḍavī 1632, 6124 (nastaʿlīq, 1292 H).

---

[195] There is a good translation and discussion of this text in Ghulāmḥusayn Ibrāhīmī-yi Dīnānī, *Qawāʿid-i kullī-yi falsafī* (Tehran 1365 Sh/1986).

17) *Dībāja.*

Dībāja ʿarsh al-taqdīs.

Preface to the Throne of Sanctification.

Majmūʿa-yi Rasāʾil, 265–7.

See *al-Dharīʿa* XV:244 that cites a manuscript of the text of Dāmād in the hand of Ṣadrā in Tehran University Central Library. The *ʿArsh al-Taqdīs* or *al-Taqdīsāt* is a text of Dāmād on philosophical theology and one of the early manuscripts of it in the hand of Ṣadrā has this short preface.[196]

MSS:

Tehran University Central Library 299.

18) *Aṣālat.*

R. aṣālat jaʿl al-wujūd.

On the principality of the instauration of being.

Majmūʿa-yi Rasāʾil, 181–91. The edition is based on the sole Tehran University Central Library manuscript.

See *al-Dharīʿa* II:118.

In it, fifteen proofs are provided for the principality of being and its existentiation. He discusses three views: the primacy of quiddity, the conjunction of quiddity and existence in the Peripatetic school (the famous existence-essence distinction in Avicennan metaphysics) and his own famous doctrine. As such, the text is an excellent summary of arguments ranged over extended textual debates in his other works.

MS:

Tehran University Central Library 9112 (46v–49v, Nastaʿlīq, 1205 H)

19) *Ḥashriyya.*

R. al-Ḥashriyya.

Treatise on the resurrection.

Majmūʿa-yi Rasāʾil, 239–62. The edition is based on MSS Tehran University Central Library 7400 and Majlis-i Shūrā 1802.

---

[196] *Muṣannafāt Mīr Dāmād*, vol. 1, ed. ʿAbd Allāh Nūrānī (Tehran 1381 Sh/2002), 113–4.

It comprises nine chapters on the nature of the states of the grave, the resurrection and the judgement and its result in the afterlife. It is probably an epitome culled from his other works and may more reasonably be attributed to a student.

MSS:
Tehran University Central Library 7400 (*Adhāb al-qabr*, naskhī, 1201 H).
Majlis-i Shūrā 5003/2 (29r–30r, naskhī, Ramaḍān 1092 H), 1802 (190–202ff, naskhī, 1244 H).

20) *Ittiḥād.*
R. fī ittiḥād al-ʿāqil waʾl-maʿqūl.
On the union of the intellecting agent and the intellected.
Majmūʿa-yi Rasāʾil, 63–103. The edition is based on MS Āstān-i Quds-i Raḍavī 7068, MS Malik 4653, and MS Tehran University Central Library Microfilm collection 1744.
Edited and translated by Ḥasanzāda Āmulī (Tehran 1404/1984).
An English translation and commentary by Ibrahim Kalin (Karachi 2007).
See *al-Dharīʿa* I:81.
This critical work on his notion of knowledge is an extended defence of Porphyry. The first section discusses the topic head on and is divided into six chapters which trace the hierarchy of the intellect through Alexander of Aphrodisias and Neoplatonic sources, the nature of God's knowledge, and refutation of Avicenna's attack on this doctrine. The second section affirms the doctrine of the simple reality and intellect encompasses all realities and intellects. It comprises three chapters on the knowing soul, naming the source of the doctrine in the *Theologia Aristotelis* and criticising the views of Avicenna. It reads like a summary of the relevant section of *Asfār* VI.

MSS:
Sipahsālār 2992 (38v–44r).
Āstān-i Quds-i Raḍavī 7068 (nastaʿlīq, 1263 H).
Malik 4646 (incomplete, naskhī, 11th century H), 4653 (shikaste, 1258 H).
Personal MS of Āyatullāh Sayyid ʿIzz al-Dīn Zanjānī.
Personal MS of Sayyed Jalālodīn Āshtiyānī (Āsh, 251).
Marʿashī 1948 (1v–7r, naskhī), 4763/9 (174v–76v, naskhī, 12th century H).

21) *Khalq*.

R. fī khalq al-aʿmāl.

On the creation of acts or on free-will and determinism.

Rasāʾil (Tehran lithograph 1885), 371–7.

Majmūʿa-yi Rasāʾil, 271–9. The editor has supplemented previous editions with readings from MS Āstān-i Quds-i Raḍavī 7065.

Ed./tr. M. A. Rawḍātī as *Risāla-yi jabr wa tafwīḍ maʿrūf bi-khalq al-aʿmāl* (Isfahan 1340 Sh/1961).

Ed. Yāsīn al-Sayyid Muḥsin (Baghdad 1978).

See *GAL* S II: 589; *al-Dharīʿa* V:84, VII:242; and Kintūrī (Calcutta 1330 H), 261.

It was lithographed on margins of Ḥillī's *Kashf al-fawāʾid*, 146–58.

This short treatise assesses the doctrine of four different schools of thought and then provides his judgement. The first position associated with the Muʿtazila advocates absolute freedom (*tafwīḍ*). The second position advocates absolute determinism precluding the possibility of any secondary causality and is associated with the *Jabariyya*, most probably one of the pejorative terms for the extreme Ḥanābila or some of the early Shiʿi extremists. The Ashʿarite position of soft determinism that considers God to be the source cause whose actions are acquired (*muktasib*) by human agents is the third position, better than the two extremes but still inadequate. The final position that he himself endorses is that of those rooted in knowledge and expresses Imāmī doctrine drawing upon proof texts from the narrations of the Imams.

MSS:

Tehran University Central Library 3322 (69–79ff, nastaʿlīq, late 12th century H), 7154 (naskhī, 1111 H).

Madrasa-yi Marvī 651 (1279 H).

Majlis-i Shūrā 1824 (243–54ff, nastaʿlīq, 12th century H), 3320 (498–500ff, nastaʿlīq, 12th century H), **3321 (naskhī of Ḥakīm Muʾmin Tunkābūnī, 11th century H)**, 5201 (41v–47v, nastaʿlīq, 1260 H).

Āstān-i Quds-i Raḍavī 7065 (nastaʿlīq, 1263 H).

Marʿashī 4349/37 (169v–71v, naskhī/nastaʿlīq of Muḥammad Mahdī Ḥusaynī Qummī, 1084–1107 H), 4763 (171r–173v, naskhī, 12th century H), 6824 (13ff, nastaʿlīq, 13th century H), 8373 (171r–73v, naskhī, 12th century H), 10353/2 (25v–29r, nastaʿlīq of Muʿīn b. Ḥusayn Gīlānī, 1183 H).

Maktabat Amīr al-Muʾminīn 1547/6 (as *al-jabr waʾl-tafwīḍ*, naskhī of al-Sayyid al-Ḥasan al-Taqawī al-Shīrāzī al-Ṭihrānī, 1284 H).

22) *Khulsa.*
R. al-Khulsa.
The fleeting moment.
Majmūʿa-yi Rasāʾil, 265–7. The edition is based on the unicum.
This short text is an account of a dream in which the author saw the Prophet on the last night of Ramaḍān in 1028 H, and is related on the authority of his son, Ibrāhīm dated Shawwāl 1114 H.

MS:
Tehran University Central Library 8231 (naskhī, Shawwāl 1114 H).

23) *Limmiyyat.*
R. limmiyyat ikhtiṣāṣ al-minṭaqa [or al-Quṭb waʾl-manṭiqa].
On astronomy and motion of the heavens.
Majmūʿa-yi Rasāʾil, 365–8. The edition is based on MSS Tehran University Central Library 5908 and Āstan-i Quds-i Raḍavī 8760.
Eds. Ḥasanzāda Āmulī and ʿA. Shakība (Tehran 1378 Sh/1999). This is a more reliable if uncritical edition by a major contemporary traditional philosopher with astronomical interest.
This short treatise is concerned with the heavenly location of the zodiac and other bodies in relation to the emanating chain of intellects. It discusses three metaphysical principles that may solve problems of celestial motion, and argues for the emanation of the spheres from the angelic world.

MSS:
Tehran University Central Library 5908 (2–7ff, nastaʿlīq, 13th century H).
Majlis-i Shūrā 1721 (144–8ff, naskhī of Muḥammad Bāqir b. Ismāʿīl, 1091 H).
Āstan-i Quds-i Raḍavī 8760.

24) *Mizāj.*
R. al-mizāj.
On temperament.
Majmūʿa-yi Rasāʾil, 371–92. The edition is based on the unicum.
This text discusses the nature of substance and accident, and the nature of the faculties of perception and comprises five chapters. See the relevant passage in *Asfār* V, 320–42.

MS:

Āstan-i Quds-i Raḍavī 634 (10ff, nastaʿlīq, 19th century).

25) *Rubūbiyya.*

R. al-Shawāhid al-rubūbiyya.

Witnessing the divine.

Majmūʿa-yi Rasāʾil, 283–341. The edition is based on MSS Sipahsālār 6319, Marʿashī 1948 and Āstan-i Quds-i Raḍavī 304.

This is essentially a list of metaphysical *aporiai* and may well be an alternative contents list of the longer text of the same name.

MSS:

Sipahsālār 6319.

Marʿashī 1948 (7r–57r, naskhī).

Āstan-i Quds-i Raḍavī 304

Uppsala Arabic 63.

26) *Tanqīḥ.*

R. al-tanqīḥ fīʾl-manṭiq.

An examination of logic.

Majmūʿa-yi Rasāʾil, 195–236. The edition is based on MSS Majlis-i Shūrā 1719 and 1721.

(1362 Sh/1983), *al-Lamaʿāt al-mashriqiyya fī funūn al-manṭiqiyya* in *Manṭiq-i nuvīn*, ed. ʿA. Mishkāt al-Dīnī (Tehran 1362 Sh/1983).

A new edition by G. Yāsīpūr (Tehran 1379 Sh/2000. A rigorous edition that builds on previous ones and has a coherent account of Sadrian logic in the introduction, it is based on MSS Majlis-i Shūrā 1711 and 1720.

See *al-Dharīʿa* XVIII:436.

The text is divided into nine illuminations comprising an Illuminationist Organon. They are on the *Isagoge* and the imposition of names, on declarative statements, on the *De Interpretatione*, on propositions, on syllogisms, on non-categorical syllogisms, on induction and analogy, on demonstration and on fallacies. In actuality, there is little here that distinguishes it from Avicennan logic that dominated the medieval schools.

MSS:

Majlis-i Shūrā 1711 (73–103ff, naskhī, 19th century), 1720 (268–79ff, nastaʿlīq, 12th century H), 1719 (73–103ff, *naskhī*, 1091 H), **1721 (1–100ff, naskhī of Muḥammad Bāqir b. Ismāʿīl, 1091 H)**.
Tehran University Theology Faculty dāl 776 (incomplete, *naskhī*).
Marʿashī 11294/6 (fol. 20–36, nastaʿlīq of Żiyāʾ al-Dīn Ḥadāʾiqī Shīrāzī, 13 Ṣafar 1350 at Madrasa-yi Sipahsālār in Tehran).

27) *Tawḥīd.*
Tafsīr sūrat al-tawḥīd I and II.
Commentary upon the chapter of Unity.
Majmūʿa-yi Rasāʾil, 395–449. The edition is only based on MS Majlis-i Shūrā 1719. The latter is a brief discussion of unity and some traditions on it. The former is a detailed consideration of unity, monorealism and the mystical vision of being divided into six *fawāʾid* (helpful points). This may also be an unsafe attribution.

MSS:

Sipahsālār 1994 (75v-76v, 13th century H).
Majlis-i Shūrā 1719 (naskhī, 13th century H).
Āstan-i Quds-i Raḍavī 8991.

28) *Maʿād.*
R. fīʾl-maʿād al-jismānī.
On corporeal resurrection.
[Probably the same as *Zād al-musāfirīn*].

29) *Taṣawwur.*
R. fīʾl-taṣawwur waʾl-taṣdīq.
On conception and judgement.
Translated into Persian and annotated by M. Ḥāʾirī as *Āgāhī va gavāhī* (Tehran 1980).
It was lithographed on the margins of al-Ḥillī's *al-Jawhar al-naḍīd.*
Ed. Mahdī Sharīʿatī in *Risālatān fīʾl-taṣawwur waʾl-taṣdīq* (Qum 1995). The editor says that he used 6 manuscripts with MS Madrasa-yi Fayḍiyya 1370 (dated 1245 H) as the basis; the others are MS Madrasa-yi Fayḍiyya 1330 (dated 1239 H), MS Mashhad University Faculty of Arts 335 (dated 1263 H), MS Kitābkhāna-yi Imām Jumʿa (Zanjān), and MS Majlis-i Shūrā 1802.

See *GAL* S II: 589, and *al-Dharīʿa* IV:198.
It mentions the *Asfār* (312), which would suggest that it is posterior to it. However, the earliest manuscript copy which is possibly an autograph is dated 999 H – that would make him rather precocious.

MSS:
British Library Add. 16839 (352v–60r, nastaʿlīq, early 18th century).
Sipahsālār 6656 (67ff, nastaʿlīq, Rabīʿ I 1288 H).
Majlis-i Shūrā 1802 (170–80ff, naskhī, 1244 H).
Āstān-i Quds-i Raḍavī 12145/5 (autograph, 999 H), 12158 (nastaʿlīq, 1264 H), 15041.
Jāmiʿ-yi Gawharshād 912 (70ff, naskhī, 1215 H).
Princeton (Arabic New Series) 1042 (136v–156v, 13th century H).
Marʿashī 8746/5 (109v–122v, naskhī, 12th century H), 12158/10 (nastaʿlīq, fol. 108–116, 1264 H).

30) *Wujūdiyya.*
R. al-wujūdiyya.
The treatise of existentials.
The texts according to Anvār (1979, 10: 402–3) discusses the identity of existents with Being, and deals with issues of predication, creation, reference and sense of being, the qualification of properties and quiddites by being, and the realtionship between the mental and extra-mental realms of being.

MS:
Millī 1820 (1–38ff, nastaʿlīq, 12th century H).

31) *Zād.*
Zād al-musāfirīn.
Provisions for the travellers [from this world to the next].
Ed. K. Mudīr Shānachī, *Nashriyya-yi dānishkada-yi ilāhiyyāt va maʿārif-i islāmī dānishgāh-i Mashhad* 2 (1351 Sh/1972), 134–44.
Edited with an extensive Persian commentary by S. J. Āshtiyānī as *Maʿād-i jismānī, sharḥ bar Zād al-musāfir-i Mullā Ṣadrā*, 2nd printing (Tehran 1980).
The text itself is rather brief. It is actually a treatise comprising twelve arguments in defence of the theological doctrine of the bodily resurrection. This demonstrates

Mullā Ṣadrā's commitment to the use of philosophical argumentation to defend theological doctrine.

MSS:

Millī 1853 (100–9ff, naskhī/nastaʿlīq of ʿAlam al-Hudā b. Fayḍ Kāshānī, 11th century H).

Mashhad University Faculty of Theology 607 (147–151ff, shikaste).

Marʿashī 4763 (168r–170v, naskhī, 12th century H).

VI Suspect works attributed to Mullā Ṣadrā

[Dānishpazhūh, *SCV*, 119–20; Nasr, 50; Corbin, 41.]

Common sources of confusion include the homonymy of the name Ṣadr al-Dīn. But given the subject matter, there is often an overlap with the works of another famous Shīrāzī family the Dashtakīs. In a separate paper, I have argued that some key works like the *Risāla fi'l-wujūd* were in fact composed by his contemporary Niẓām al-Dīn Dashtakī. For many of these short treatises, examine them against MS Princeton Arabic New Series 2000 a collection of the work of Niẓām al-Dīn Dashtakī.

Ādāb al-baḥth wa'l-munāẓara [*GAL S* II: 589].

The etiquette of argument and disputation.

A treatise on this popular topic; most probably the commentary by Ghiyāth ad-Dīn Manṣūr the son of his namesake Ṣadr al-Dīn Shīrāzī/Dashtakī on the famous treatise on the subject by Aḍud al-Dīn al-Ījī [d. 756/1355] (see *al-Dharīʿa* I:14).[197]

Ajwibat al-as'ila [*GAL S* II: 589].

Answers to questions.

It is unclear whether this is another work or just one of the series of answers that he presented to questions posed to him. A number of the manuscripts of these answers do not specify in their given title to which collection they pertain.

al-Fawā'id.

Includes:

[197] Cf. Barakat, 114.

R. fī kayfiyyat tarkīb al-mādda wa'l-ṣūra (On the nature of the composition of matter and form).
R. radd al-shubahāt al-iblīsiyya (Refutation of satanic doubts).
Dhayl āyat al-amāna wa'l-mawādd al-thalātha (Appendix to the commentary upon the verse of trust and the three modalities).
Sharḥ ḥadīth kuntu kanzan makhfiyyan (Commentary upon the hidden treasure saying).
Majmūʿa-yi Rasā'il (Tehran 1996), 345–61.
Despite the edition, these do not seem to be his work. The third of these texts is probably not his (it is probably the work of Fayḍ Kāshānī) and the fourth one is almost definitely a misattribution, probably being a work of the school of Ibn ʿArabī.[198] There is little internal evidence in these short works that points towards the sound possibility of attribution to Mullā Ṣadrā.
MSS:
Tehran University Central Library 2830 (70ff, nastaʿlīq, 1279 H).
Majlis-i Shūrā 1804, 1822.

Al-Qudsiyyāt fī asrār al-nuqṭa al-ḥissiyya, on margins of *al-Mabda'* lithograph.
Sacred issues on the secrets of the sensible point.
It is attributed to Sayyid ʿAlī Hamadānī in *al-Dharīʿa* XVII:50 and on the colophon of MS Āstān-i Quds-i Raḍavī 8428. Cf. *al-Dharīʿa* XII:170, XIII:52. The attribution to Mullā Ṣadrā is suspect although given his interest in astronomy attested by the works in his library it is not improbable.
MSS:
Malik 3542 (19ff, nastaʿlīq, 13th century H).
Dār al-Kutub 20252 (89–116ff, mixed script).
Bibliothèque Nationale 2348.

R. fī ithbāt wājib al-wujūd [*GAL S* II: 589].
On the proof of the necessary existent.
In fact, it is by Ṣadr al-Dīn Dashtakī (Āsh, 266; *al-Dharīʿa*, I:108).[199] Although this genre of texts was popular in the late Timurid and Safavid periods, Mullā Ṣadrā never

---

[198] It has been published in the name of the Andalusian Sufi edited by Fāṭima Fanā in Sayyid Mahdī Jaḥrumī (ed.), *Ganjīna-yi Bahāristān I: ʿUlūm Qur'ānī va ravā'ī* (Tehran 1380 Sh/2001), 267–9.
[199] Barakat, 17–18.

wrote one that is extant; he did, however, discuss other works on the genre within his proofs for the existence of God in *al-Asfār*, VI, 11–118.

R. fī baḥth al-mughāliṭāt [*GAL S* II: 589].
Discussion of sophistics.
This is a mis-rendition of *R. fī baḥth al-mughāliṭā al-mashhūra bi-jadhr al-aṣamm* a work of Ṣadr al-Dīn Dashtakī, cited below, on the Liar's Paradox (*al-Dharīʿa* V:92).[200]

R. badʾ wujūd al-insān.
On the inception of human existence.
[*GAL S* II: 589, *al-Dharīʿa* III:51 and is referred in *Sih aṣl*; in fact, it is the fifth chapter of *Iksīr al-ʿārifīn*.]

R. ḥal shubhat al-jadhr al-aṣamm.
On the Liar's Paradox.
Majmūʿa-yi Rasāʾil (Tehran 1996), 467–78.
It is not clear why Iṣfahānī includes this work on a collection of the works of Ṣadrā since it is clearly the work of Ṣadr al-Dīn Dashtakī.[201]
R. fīʾl-ḥikma.
On wisdom.
This may well be a work of Ṣadr al-Dīn or Niẓām al-Dīn Dashtakī to whom such a titled work is attributed. It is probably the work of the latter. The British Library (MS Delhi Arabic 865) also has a manuscript entitled *Ri fīʾl-ḥikma* or *Daqīq al-ḥikam* attributed to a Ṣadr al-Dīn b. Ibrāhīm Shīrāzī.
MSS:
Āstān-i Quds-i Raḍavī 11911, 15057.
British Library Delhi Arabic 865 (19th century, naskhī, 58ff).

R. fī tajrīd maqālāt Arasṭū.
A summary of the works of Aristotle.
[*GAL S* II: 589].

---

200 Barakat, 26–7.
201 Cf. Aḥmad Farāmarz Qarāmalakī, 'Mukātaba-yi Davānī va Dashtakī dar ḥall shubhat jadhr aṣamm', *Ṣadrā* 8 and 9 (1376 Sh/1997), 95–101.

If this were genuine and available, it would have a considerable bearing upon our interpretation of his concept of the modulation of being. It is unclear whether this is supposed to be a work on the categories or a doxographical summary of Aristotelian philosophy. From his library, we know that he owned a copy of the *Categories* and *De Anima.*

R. fī'l-alwāḥ al-ma'ādiyya.
Treatise on the tablets of the Return.
This is probably the same as *Zād al-musāfirīn*; or a short epitome of *al-Alwāḥ al-ʿImādiyya* of Suhrawardī that may be a spurious attribution - we know that he owned the latter. There is no evidence linking a work of this title to Mullā Ṣadrā.

R. fī'l-ḥaraka al-jawhariyya.
On substantial motion.
This is probably just an excerpt from his exposition on the subject in the *Asfār.*

R. fī'l-imāma.
On the Imamate.
See *al-Dharīʿa* II:333.
SCV (120) considers it suspect though Corbin (33) suggests that it is authentic. Perhaps it is an extract from some other work of his such as *Sharḥ Uṣūl al-Kāfī.*
MS:
Majlis-i Sīnā 280/2 (shikaste, 1191 H).

R. fī'l-kufr wa'l-īmān.
On faith and infidelity.
[*GAL S* II: 589]
MS:
Marʿashī 7577 (161v–173r, nastaʿlīq, 1128 H).
Raza Library (Rampur) 3924 M (nastaʿlīq, 140r–141r, 18th century).

R. fī'l-mabāḥith al-iʿtiqādiyya [*GAL* II: 413].
A *kalām* work of which there is a copy in the Āṣafiya Library (now the Andhra Pradesh Oriental Manuscripts Library) in Hyderabad, India.

R. al-wujūd.
On being.
Majmūʿa-yi Rasāʾil (Tehran 1996), 453–63.
See Kintūrī (Calcutta 1330/1912), 245.
The attribution is suspect; it is almost definitely by Niẓām al-Dīn Dashtakī.
MS:
Majlis-i Shūrā 4942 (34v–36r, shikaste, 11th century H) [compare Princeton Arabic New Series 2000].

Sharḥ al-najāt of Avicenna, according to *al-Dharīʿa* XXIV:56, citing a copy belonging to ʿAlī b. Zayn al-ʿĀbidīn Māzandarānī. We know that he owned a copy of the Avicennian text.

Sharḥ Ḥikmat al-ʿayn of Najm al-Dīn Dabīrān al-Kātibī al-Qazwīnī [d. 675/1276].
Commentary upon the Wisdom of the Eye.
This work is a commentary on a Peripatetic encyclopaedia popular in India and Central Asia. It is probable that this attribution is incorrect. The work is almost definitely the *marginalia* upon the commentary of Shams al-Dīn Muḥammad b. Mīrak Bukhārī by Mīr Ṣadr al-Dīn Shīrāzī/Dashtakī [d. 1497], a common mistake (see *al-Dharīʿa* XI:196).[202]
MS:
Ẓāhiriyya/Maktabat al-Asad (Damascus) 3126 (*ḥikma* 76, 506–82ff, naskhī, 13th century H).

Ḥāshiya ʿalā tajrīd al-iʿtiqād of Naṣīr al-Dīn al-Ṭūsī [d. 672/1274].
Probably the work of Dashtakī (Āsh, 267; *al-Dharīʿa* VI:214).[203] He wrote two *marginalia*, an earlier one criticising Davānī and a later one setting out his own position, as well as a short gloss on the logic section of the text.

Ḥāshiya ʿalāʾl-rawḍa al-bahiyya fī sharḥ al-lumʿa al-dimashqiyya.
[Dānishpazhūh, *SCV*, 120 says that it is by his son.]

---

202 Barakat, 29.
203 Barakat, 19–23, 28–9.

Ḥāshiya ʿalāʾl-sharḥ al-jadīd liʾl-Qūshjī ʿalā Tajrīd al-iʿtiqād.

A work of this name (or rather a supergloss on the gloss of Khafarī) is attributed to his son Ibrāhīm (*al-Dharīʿa* VI:64). All these manuscripts of the work confirm this.

MSS:

Sipahsālār 1455 (attributed to his son).

Majlis-i Shūrā 1736 (text of Muḥammad Qāsim Iṣfahānī includes the *marginalia*, 145ff, shikaste, 1090 H), 1737 (texts of Muḥammad Fasāʾī includes it, 344ff, naskhī, 12th century H).

Marʿashī 617 (62v–109r, nastaʿlīq, 4 Ṣafar 1098 H), 4640 (97ff, naskhī, 17 Shaʿbān 1186 H), 5084 (1v–24v, nastaʿlīq, 12th century H), 7158 (45v–64v, nastaʿlīq, 12th century H).

Jāmiʿ-yi Gawharshād 1339 (nastaʿlīq, 1035 H).

Ḥāshiya mabḥath al-mushtarak fīʾl-Shamsiyya.

Marginalia on homonyms in the Shamsiyya of Kātibī.

Iṣfahānī says that a microfilm 1039 in Tehran University Library attributes this work to him but in fact it is appended to a treatise of his namesake Dashtakī – *al-Dharīʿa* VI:37. It is most likely to be the *marginalia* of Dashtakī on a section of the commentary by Quṭb al-Dīn Shīrāzī on this famous logic school-text.[204] Again he had a copy of the text but since it was a common school-text, it does not mean that the attribution is sound.

Ḥāshiya ʿalāʾl-Qabasāt of Dāmād, according to *al-Dharīʿa* that cites a manuscript in the hand of the author with *marginalia* dated 1034 H.

Ḥāshiya ʿalāʾl-Ṭabīʿiyyāt min al-Shifāʾ.

[Iṣfahānī, *Majmūʿa*, says that in the manuscript catalogue for MS Majlis-i Shūrā 4778 (nastaʿlīq, 1070 H) it is attributed to him; it is, in fact, the section on physics from *al-Muḥākamāt* of Quṭb al-Dīn Shīrāzī.]

Taʿlīqa ʿalā Anwār al-tanzīl of al-Bayḍāwī.

Such *scholia* were very popular in this period (his teachers Shaykh Bahāʾī and Mīr Dāmād both authored such works) but there is no evidence that he wrote one. This may be another probable case of him being confused with Dashtakī.

---

[204] Barakat, 23–4.

Appendix IV
The Personal Library of Mullā Ṣadrā

A valuable codex preserved in the Kitābkhāna-yi Madrasa-yi Imām-i ʿAṣr in Shiraz contains autograph copies of some works of Mullā Ṣadrā. In it are notes (*yāddāsht-hā*) copied from various works and a list of works that he possessed in his personal library. Muḥammad Barakat has produced an edition of the notes and details of his library.[205] He surmises, based on internal evidence of works and individuals cited, that the codex must date from between 1014 and 1030 H.[206] A study of his library can help us understand both the curriculum that he underwent (and later may have taught) and the influences upon his philosophical, exegetical and theological writings. A number of legal and jurisprudential works in the list also suggest his strong training in *fiqh* and *uṣūl al-fiqh* and may suggest that he played a role as a jurist in his home town. As far as the dating of the library list and notes are concerned, I would venture a dating of around the early 1020s H. The notes betray the *aide-mémoire* of a young scholar and the need to pen them and a list of his works may reflect his experience as a young scholar, recently established in Shiraz as a teacher.
In what follows I reproduce the list of codices in the order that they are given in the manuscript and provide an annotated description of them.[207]

1. and 2. Copies of the Qurʾān.
One would expect a scholar to have copies of the scripture, especially an exegete like Mullā Ṣadrā.
3. and 4. *Majmaʿ al-bayān.*

---

205 Muḥammad Barakat, *Yāddāsht-hā-yi Mullā Ṣadrā* (Qum 1377 Sh/1998).
206 Barakat, *Yāddāsht-hā-yi Mullā Ṣadrā*, 8.
207 Barkat, *Yāddāsht-hā-yi Mullā Ṣadrā*, 65–73. For an excellent study of a medieval library and its use for discerning sources, see Etan Kohlberg, *A Medieval Muslim Scholar at Work: Ibn Ṭāwūs and his Library* (Islamic Philosophy, Theology and Science Texts and Studies vol. XII, Leiden 1992).

This is the famous Qur'ānic exegesis of the Imāmī Shiʿi theologian Amīn al-Islām Abū ʿAlī al-Faḍl b. al-Ḥasan al-Ṭabrisī [d. 548/1154],[208] and perhaps the major classical commentary from a Muʿtazilī rationalist method in the Imāmī Shiʿi tradition.[209] An extensive work that signals its debt to the earlier commentary of the Imāmī Shiʿi (and Muʿtazilī) theologian Abū Jaʿfar Muḥammad b. al-Ḥasan al-Ṭūsī [d. 460/1067], it contains traditional material from Sunnī and Shiʿi sources as well as discussions in rational theology, and was completed in Dhu'l-Qaʿda 534/July 1140 in Mashhad for al-Sharīf Jalāl al-Dīn Abū Manṣūr Muḥammad Ḥusaynī al-Zubārī [d. 539/1145]. See *al-Dharīʿa* II:24.

5. The first half of *Jāmiʿ al-jawāmiʿ*.

This is another, more succinct Qur'ānic exegesis completed by al-Ṭabrisī for his son al-Ḥasan in Muḥarram 543/June 1168.[210] See *al-Dharīʿa* V:248.

6. A quarter of the *Tafsīr* of al-Nasafī.

This is the Qur'ānic exegesis entitled *Madārik al-tanzīl wa-ḥaqā'iq al-ta'wīl* of the Transoxanian Sunnī theologian, Ḥanafī jurist and grammarian Ḥāfiẓ al-Dīn Abu'l-Barakāt ʿAbd Allāh b. Aḥmad al-Nasafī [d. 710/1310].[211] See *Kashf* 2:1640.

7. A half of a *Tafsīr* whose author is unknown.

It is unclear which commentary this is and it seems that even Mullā Ṣadrā did not know.

8. A part of the *Tafsīr* of al-Bayḍāwī with some other texts.

This is the famous commentary entitled *Anwār al-tanzīl wa-asrār al-ta'wīl* of the Sunnī Ashʿarī theologian Nāṣir al-Dīn Abu'l-Khayr ʿAbd Allāh b. ʿUmar al-Bayḍāwī [d. 685/1286].[212] Because it is a correction of the much used Muʿtazilī lexicographical commentary of al-Zamakhsharī, it was popular as a teaching text in the Persianate world, and despite being a Sunnī work was much commented upon by Safavid

---

[208] LB 346–8; RU IV, 340–59; *Aʿyān*, VIII, 398–401; E. Kohlberg, 'al-Ṭabrisī', *EI*² X, 40–1.

[209] This has been published many times in 20 parts (or 10 volumes) mostly with an introduction by al-Sayyid Muḥsin al-Amīn al-ʿĀmilī by Mu'assasat al-Aʿlamī in Beirut. Cf. Ḥusayn Karīmān, *Ṭabrisī va majmaʿ al-bayān* (2 vols, Tehran 1360 Sh/1981); *GAL* I, 513–4, S I, 708–9 ; Musa A. O. Abdul, *The Qur'ān : Shaykh Ṭabarsī's Commentary* (Lahore 1977); M. H. Maʿrifat, *al-Tafsīr wa'l-mufassirūn* (Mashhad 1998), II, 382–90.

[210] This was published in 4 volumes (Qum 1998).

[211] It has been published many times in 3 volumes, most recently edited by Yūsuf Badīwī (Beirut 1998). Cf. *GAL* II, 197, S II, 267–8; W. Heffening, 'al-Nasafī', *EI*² VII, 969; Maʿrifat, *al-Tafsīr wa'l-mufassirūn*, II, 433–4.

[212] It was most recently published in 3 volumes (Beirut 2000). Cf. *GAL* I, 416, S I, 738; Maʿrifat, *al-Tafsīr wa'l-mufassirūn*, 430–3; E. Kohlberg, 'al-Bayḍāwī', *EIr* IV, 15–7.

scholars as attested by the number of manuscripts and commentaries. See *Kashf* 1:168.

9. *Qawāʿid al-aḥkām.*

This is the legal *fiqhī* manual entitled *Qawāʿid al-aḥkām fī masāʾil al-ḥalāl waʾl-ḥarām* of the foremost classical Imāmī Shiʿi jurist and theologian al-ʿAllāma Jamāl al-Dīn al-Ḥasan b. Yūsuf Ibn al-Muṭahhar al-Ḥillī [d. 726/1325].[213] Al-Ḥillī had studied Shāfiʿī *fiqh* with Shams al-Dīn Muḥammad al-Kīshī [d. 695/1296] at the Niẓāmiyya in Baghdad,[214] and his work *Qawāʿid al-aḥkām* embroiled him in disputations with the Ḥanbalī jurist Taqī al-Dīn ʿAbd Allāh al-Zarīrātī [d. 729/1329] and the Shāfiʿī jurist ʿAbd Allāh b. ʿUmar al-Bayḍāwī. It was the main legal textbook of the Safavid seminary. Devin Stewart has argued that the *qawāʿid* genre became popular in Sunnī jurisprudence in the twelfth/thirteenth century whence it influenced developments in Shiʿi jurisprudence of which this text is an early exemplar.[215] See *al-Dharīʿa* XVII:930; MT 73–4.

10. *Sharāʾiʿ al-islām.*

This is a *fiqh* manual authored by Najm al-Dīn Abuʾl-Qāsim Jaʿfar b. al-Ḥasan al-Ḥillī [d. 676/1277] known as al-Muḥaqqiq.[216] It was a popular school text in the Safavid period as attested by ʿAlī b. Muḥammad al-ʿĀmilī [d. 1103/1692] describing the education of his son al-Ḥusayn in the 1660s.[217] See *al-Dharīʿa* XIII:47; MT 67–70.

11. *Kitāb al-Irshād.*

This is probably the legal *fiqhī* text entitled *Irshād al-adhhān ilā aḥkām al-īmān* of al-ʿAllāma al-Ḥillī.[218] See *al-Dharīʿa* I:510; MT 71–2.

12. *Ḥāshiya ʿalāʾl-Sharāʾiʿ.*

---

[213] As the basic legal textbook of the Shiʿi seminary, it has been published and translated on numerous occasions, most recently in 1998 by the seminary in Qum. For a biography and study of al-Ḥillī, see Sabine Schmitdke, *The Theology of al-ʿAllāma al-Ḥillī (d. 726/1325)* (Berlin 1991); eadem, 'Ḥellī, Ḥasan', *EIr* XII, 164–9; *Aʿyān*, V, 396—408. For a useful discussion of the library of al-Ḥillī and the transmission of his works into Safavid Iran, see al-Sayyid ʿAbd al-ʿAzīz Ṭabāṭabāʾī, *Maktabat al-ʿAllāma al-Ḥillī* (Qum 1416/1996).

[214] Al-Ḥillī, *al-Ijāza al-kabīra* in *Biḥār*, CVII, 65–6. On al-Kīshī, see Ṣalāḥ al-Dīn Khalīl b. Aybak al-Ṣafadī, *al-Wāfī biʾl-wafayāt*, ed. S. Dedering (Leipzig/Istanbul 1949), II, 141 (no. 143).

[215] Devin Stewart, *Islamic Legal Orthodoxy: Twelver Shiite Responses to the Sunni Legal System* (Salt Lake City, UH 1998), 16.

[216] *Aʿyān*, IV, 89–93; cf. E. Kohlberg, 'Ḥellī, Najm-al-dīn', *EIr* XII, 169–70. As a major legal school text, it has been published on numerous occasions not least with the glosses of the contemporary jurist al-Sayyid al-Ṣādiq al-Shīrāzī (Beirut 1983).

[217] ʿAlī al-ʿĀmilī, *al-Durr al-manthūr min al-maʾthūr wa-ghayr al-maʾthūr* (Qum 1978), II, 246.

[218] It was edited by Fāris al-Ḥassūn (2 vols, Qum 1990).

It is unclear which gloss upon this legal text, *Sharāʾiʿ al-islām*, this is. Perhaps the most famous gloss is by the Imāmī Shiʿi jurist and martyr (hence al-Shahīd al-Thānī) Zayn al-Dīn b. ʿAlī al-ʿĀmilī [d. 965/1558] entitled *Masālik al-afhām ilā sharḥ Sharāʾiʿ al-Islām.*[219] See *al-Dharīʿa* VI:248; MT 68.

13. *Tanqīḥ sharḥ al-Sharāʾiʿ* and *al-Khiṣāl* of Ibn Bābawayh.

The first text is a legal work most likely to be *al-Tanqīḥ al-rāʾiʿ li-Mukhtaṣar al-Sharāʾiʿ*, a super-commentary by the Imāmī Shiʿi jurist Miqdād b. ʿAbd Allāh al-Siyūrī [d. 826/1423] upon *al-Mukhtaṣar al-Nāfiʿ* (see below).[220] See *al-Dharīʿa* IV:463; MT 78.

The second text is a homiletic collection of *ḥadīth* compiled by the early Imāmī Shiʿi tradent Ibn Bābawayh known as al-Shaykh al-Ṣadūq [d. 381/991].[221] See *al-Dharīʿa* VII:162.

14. *Sharḥ mukhtaṣar al-ʿAḍudī.*

This is a Sunnī text of *uṣūl al-fiqh*, a commentary by the Shāfiʿī jurist (and Sunnī theologian) ʿAḍud al-Dīn ʿAbd al-Raḥmān b. Aḥmad al-Ījī [d. 756/1355][222] on the *Mukhtaṣar* of the Mālikī jurist and grammarian Ibn Ḥājib [d. 646/1248].[223] The *Mukhtaṣar*, Ibn Ḥājib's abridgment of his own *Muntahā al-sūl waʾl-amal fī ʿilmayy al-uṣūl waʾl-jadal*, was a popular Sunnī text.[224] Along with the later *Tahdhīb al-wuṣūl* of al-ʿAllāma al-Ḥillī, *al-Sharḥ al-ʿAḍudī* was the main text in legal theory studied in the seminary; in fact the text of al-Ḥillī is based on the *Mukhtaṣar*. Stewart discusses the significance of the work in the Shiʿi seminary.[225] See *Kashf* 2: 1625, 1853.

15. *Sharḥ al-Sharḥ li-ʿAllāma al-Taftazānī.*

Since the list has previously mentioned legal and jurisprudential works, this may be *Sharḥ al-talwīḥ ʿalāʾl-tawḍīḥ li-matn al-Tanqīḥ fī uṣūl al-fiqh* a legal commentary by the Sunnī theologian Saʿd al-Dīn Masʿūd b. ʿUmar al-Taftazānī [d. 792/1389][226] on

---

[219] Cf. E. Kohlberg, 'Shahīd Thānī', *EI²* IX, 209–10; *GAL* II, 425, S II, 449–50. This text has been published most recently (Qum 1380 Sh/2001).

[220] This text was edited by al-Sayyid ʿAbd al-Laṭīf al-Kuhkāmaraʾī (Qum 1984).

[221] A. Fyzee, 'Ibn Bābawayh', *EI²* III, 726–7; M. McDermott, 'Ebn Bābawayh', *EIr* VIII, 2–4; *GAL* I, 187, S I 187–8; M. I. Marcinkowski, 'Twelver Shīʿite scholars and Buyid domination: a glance at the life and times of Ibn Bābūya al-Shaykh al-Ṣadūq', *Islamic Quarterly* 45 (2001), 199–222. This is published in Najaf in 1971 in an edition prepared by al-Sayyid Muḥammad Mahdī al-Kharsān.

[222] J. van Ess, 'Īdjī', *EI²* III, 1022; *GAL* II, 267, S II, 287; van Ess, *Die Erkenntnislehre des ʿAḍudaddīn al-Īcī* (Wisebaden 1966).

[223] W. Fleisch, 'Ibn Ḥādjib, *EI²* III, 781; *GAL* I, 303, S I, 531.

[224] It remains so. Edited by Shaʿbān Muḥammad Ismāʿīl, it was published at al-Azhar in 2 volumes in 1974.

[225] Stewart, *Islamic Legal Orthodoxy*, 97–100.

[226] W. Madelung, 'al-Taftazānī', *EI²* X, 88–9; *GAL* II, 278–80, S II, 301–4.

the manual on jurisprudence of the Ḥanafī ʿUbayd Allāh b. Masʿūd al-Maḥbūbī al-Bukhārī [d. 747/1347].[227]

16. and 17. Copies of *Kitāb al-muṭawwal.*

This work was the main seminary text on rhetoric, a long commentary by al-Taftazānī on the abridgment, *al-Talkhīṣ*, by al-Khaṭīb al-Qazwīnī [d. 739/1338] on the *Miftāḥ al-ʿulūm* of al-Sakkākī [d. 626/1229].[228] The work was written for the ruler of Herat, Muʿizz al-Dīn Kark in 748/1347, but it was presented much later to Timur. See *Kashf* 1:473 and 2:1762.

18. *Sharḥ al-miftāḥ.*

This is probably the abridged commentary, also known as the *Mukhtaṣar*, of the Sunnī theologian al-Taftazānī on the *Miftāḥ al-ʿulūm*, a work on logic and rhetoric by al-Sakkākī.[229] See *Kashf* 2:1762.

19. The ontology section (*umūr ʿāmma*) of the *Sharḥ al-Tajrīd.*

Al-Tajrīd fīʾl-iʿtiqād was a succinct work of systematic theology written by the Imāmī Shiʿi theologian Naṣīr al-Dīn al-Ṭūsī [d. 672/1274].[230] The logic section was usually considered to be a separate text. The main text is divided into six goals (*maqāṣid*), the first of which is the preliminary on ontology. The earliest most significant commentary was *Kashf al-murād* written by al-ʿAllāma al-Ḥillī, a student of al-Ṭūsī.[231] A number of commentaries, super-commentaries and glosses were later written on it. The two most famous commentaries, known respectively as the old and the new commentaries were *Tasdīd al-qawāʿid fī sharḥ Tajrīd al-ʿaqāʾid* of Shams al-Dīn Maḥmūd b. ʿAbd al-Raḥmān al-Iṣfahānī [d. 749/1349] and the work of the Ottoman savant ʿAlāʾ al-Dīn ʿAlī b. Muḥammad al-Qūshjī [d. 879/1474], which was particularly popular in the sixteenth and seventeenth centuries. The work in Mullā Ṣadrā's library is probably the latter commentary.

20. *Al-Ḥāshiya al-qadīma* of al-ʿAllāma al-Dawānī.

---

[227] This text was edited by Zakariyyā ʿUmayrāt (2 vols, Beirut 1996).

[228] As a school text, it is rarely out of print and was reprinted in Beirut in 2001 in one large volume.

[229] The most recent edition of the text was published in Tyre in 2003. On al-Sakkākī, see W. Heinrichs, 'al-Sakkākī', *EI²* VIII, 893–4; *GAL* I, 244, S I, 515; W. Smyth, 'The making of a textbook', *SI* 78 (1993), 99–115; A. Maṭlūb, *al-Qazwīnī wa-shurūḥ al-Talkhīṣ* (Baghdad 1967).

[230] H. Daiber and J. Ragep, 'al-Ṭūsī', *EI²* X, 746–52; *GAL* I, 670–6, S I, 924–33; M. T. Mudarris Raḍavī, *Aḥwāl va āthār-i Naṣīr al-Dīn* (Tehran 1354 Sh/1975). On the *Tajrīd* and its commentaries and glosses, see Sayyid Aḥmad Tuysirkānī, 'Shurūḥ va ḥavāshī bar kitāb *Tajrīd al-iʿtiqād*, in S. A. Tuysirkānī (ed.), *Sabʿ rasāʾil* (Tehran 1381 Sh/2002), 287–304.

[231] A useful edition of this text was produced with annotation by Ḥasanzāda Āmulī and published by the seminary in Qum in 1988.

This is the first *marginalia* that the famous philosopher of Shiraz, Jalāl al-Dīn Muḥammad b. Asʿad Davānī [d. 908/1502] wrote on the later commentary on *al-Tajrīd*.[232] It was originally written for the Āq-Quyunlū ruler Sulṭān Yaʿqūb [d. 896/1490] but later presented to the Ottoman Sultan Bayezid II [d. 918/1512]. See *al-Dharīʿa* VI:116.

21. *Al-Ḥāshiya al-jadīda al-Tajrīdīya* of al-Sayyid al-Sanad [Ṣadr al-Dīn Dashtakī Shīrāzī] and the *Ḥāshiya* of al-Sayyid al-Sammākī on *Sharḥ al-hidāya*.

The first text is also a *marginalia* written by another Shīrāzī philosopher al-Sayyid Ṣadr al-Dīn Muḥammad Dashtakī [d. 903/1497], popularly known as al-Sayyid al-Sanad, in response to Davānī's earlier *marginalia* on the later commentary on *al-Tajrīd*. See *al-Dharīʿa* VI:117.

The second text is a *marginalia* that was written by Mīr Fakhr al-Dīn Sammākī, who was Mīr Dāmād's teacher in philosophy, upon the famous commentary by Mīr Ḥusayn Maybudī [d. 910/1504] upon *al-Hidāya* of Athīr al-Dīn al-Abharī [d. 663/1264].[233] See *al-Dharīʿa* VI:139. Mullā Ṣadrā himself wrote a commentary on *al-Hidāya* that became the standard one (see above).

22. *Ḥāshiya Sharḥ al-tajrīd* of al-Fāḍil al-Ardabīlī.

This is another *marginalia* upon the later commentary on *al-Tajrīd* written by the Imāmī Shiʿi jurist Aḥmad b. Muḥammad al-Ardabīlī known as al-Muqaddas [d. 993/1585].[234] He had studied law with al-Shahīd II and philosophy with Jamāl al-Dīn Maḥmūd Shīrāzī. He wrote it for his son Abuʾl-Ṣalāḥ Muḥammad and completed it on 13 Rabīʿ I 986/21 May 1578. It begins with the ontology and finishes at the end with the resurrection. See *al-Dharīʿa* VI:113.

23. *Ḥāshiya Sharḥ al-mukhtaṣar* of al-Sayyid al-Jurjānī.

This is a *marginalia* written by the Timurid thinker and Shāfiʿī jurist al-Sayyid ʿAlī al-Jurjānī [d. 816/1413] on the commentary of al-Ījī above on *uṣūl al-fiqh*.[235] See *Kashf* 2:1854.

24. *Ḥāshiya Sharḥ al-tajrīd* of al-Allāma al-Shīrāzī (*mīm nūn*).

---

[232] Tuysirkānī, 'Shurūḥ va ḥavāshī bar kitāb *Tajrīd al-iʿtiqād*', in *Sabʿ rasāʾil*, 297. On Dawānī, see A. Lambton, 'al-Dawānī', *EI²* II, 173–4; W. Chittick, 'Dawwānī', *EIr* VII, 132–3; ʿAlī Davānī, *Sharḥ-i Zindigānī-yi Mullā Jalāl al-Dīn Davānī* (Qum 1956).

[233] An excellent copy of al-Sammākī's *marginalia* is available in MS Princeton Arabic New Series 948, fol. 1v–80r. Cf. Barakat, 214–6. On al-Abharī, see G. Anawati, 'al-Abharī', *EIr* I, 216–7; *GAL* I, 608, S I, 839–44.

[234] W. Madelung, 'Ardabīlī', *EIr* II, 368–70; AA II, 23; LB 148–50; *Rawḍāt*, I, 88–94. This text has been recently edited by Aḥmad al-ʿĀbidī (Qum 1377 Sh/1998).

[235] A. S. Tritton, 'al-Djurdjānī', *EI²* II, 602; *GAL* II, 216, S II, 305.

This is another *marginalia* upon the later commentary on *al-Tajrīd* written by the Imāmī Shiʿi philosopher and scion of the famous Dashtakī family of Shiraz, Ghiyāth al-Dīn Manṣūr b. Ṣadr al-Dīn Muḥammad [d. 948/1542].[236] It is an attempt to adjudicate between the works of his father and Davānī. See *al-Dharīʿa* VI:67.

25. *Sharḥ tahdhīb al-uṣūl* of al-ʿAmīdī.

This is the commentary on the famous *uṣūl al-fiqh* text of al-ʿAllāma al-Ḥillī entitled *Tahdhīb ṭarīq al-wuṣūl ilā ʿilm al-uṣūl* by the sixteenth century Imāmī Shiʿi jurist al-Sayyid Ḥusayn al-ʿAmīdī al-Najafī,[237] the main teacher of the prominent Safavid jurist al-Sayyid Ḥusayn al-Karakī [d. 1001/1592].[238] See *al-Dharīʿa* IV:511.

26. and 27. 2 copies of *Sharḥ al-ishārāt* of al-Ṭūsī.

A major philosophical influence on Mullā Ṣadrā, this is the commentary by Naṣīr al-Dīn al-Ṭūsī on *al-Ishārāt wa'l-tanbīhāt* of Avicenna. See *al-Dharīʿa* VII:75.

28. *Al-Ishārāt* and *al-Adwiya al-qalbiyya* and some other texts of al-Shaykh al-Ra'īs.

These are both works of the famous philosopher Avicenna [Ibn Sīnā].[239] The first is his major late encyclopaedia *al-Ishārāt wa'l-tanbīhāt* that was particularly popular in the Islamic East [See *al-Dharīʿa* II:96; Mahdavi 27], and the second is a medical text. See Mahdavi 14.

29. The *Metaphysics* (*al-ilāhiyyāt*) of *al-Shifā'*, the *De Anima* (*fi'l-nafs*) of Aristotle, and the *liber de Pomo* (*al-Tuffāḥa*) of (ps-)Aristotle.

The first text is the section of the early encyclopaedia of Avicenna upon which Mullā Ṣadrā wrote a commentary (see above). See Mahdavi 84.

The second text was quite popular and a major starting point on the theory of the soul and intellect from Avicenna onwards. The translation of Isḥāq b. Ḥunayn was available in a Persian version by Afḍal al-Dīn Kāshānī [d. 610/1213–4].[240]

The third text is a pseudoepigraphic work attributed to Aristotle that describes his death-bed *waṣiyya*.[241] It was also available in a Persian version by Afḍal al-Dīn Kāshānī.[242]

---

[236] Tuysirkānī, 'Shurūḥ va ḥavāshī bar kitāb *Tajrīd al-iʿtiqād*', in *Sabʿ rasā'il*, 297.

[237] RU II, 50.

[238] RU II, 88.

[239] See various, 'Avicenna', *EIr* III, 66–110; Dimitri Gutas, *Avicenna and the Aristotelian Tradition* (Islamic Philosophy, Theology and Science Texts and Studies vol. IV, Leiden 1988).

[240] F. E. Peters, *Aristoteles Arabus* (Leiden 1968), 43; the Arabic text is *Fī'l-Nafs*, ed. ʿA. Badawī (Beirut 1980), 3–88. The Persian text is in *Muṣannafāt-i Bābā Afḍal Kāshānī*, eds. M. Mīnuvī and Y. Mahdavī (Tehran 1331 Sh/1952), 389–458. For an excerpt of the Persian translation of the text rendered into English, see William Chittick, *The Heart of Islamic Philosophy* (New York/Oxford 2001), 106–7.

[241] See J. Kraemer, 'Das arabische Original des Liber de Pomo', in *Studi Orientali in onore de G. Levi della Vida* (Rome 1956), I, 484–506; D. S. Margoliouth, 'The Book of the Apple ascribed to Aristotle' edited in

30. *Al-Taʿlīqāt* of al-Shaykh al-Raʾīs.

Mullā Ṣadrā used this work of Avicenna extensively and may well have had an alternative recension of the text that has not survived in manuscript form.[243] See Mahdavi 49.

31. *Kitāb al-Najāt* of al-Shaykh.

Another major philosophical work of Avicenna, this epitome of *al-Shifāʾ* is often cited by Mullā Ṣadrā. See Mahdavi 118.

32. *Sharḥ al-Hayākil* of al-Muḥaqqiq al-Dawānī.

A philosophical work of Davānī, *Shawākil al-ḥūr fī sharḥ Hayākil al-nūr* is a commentary on *Hayākil al-nūr* of Suhrawardī.[244] See *al-Dharīʿa* XIV:177.

33. Commentaries on *al-Hayākil* including *al-Ḥāshiya al-Manṣūriyya.*

This codex probably contained a few commentaries on the text of Suhrawardī including *Ishrāq hayākil al-nūr fī [or li-kashf] ẓulamāt shawākil al-ghurūr*, a hostile refutation of Davānī by Manṣūr Dashtakī.[245] See *al-Dharīʿa* II:103.

34. *Rasāʾil* of al-Shaykh al-Raʾīs including *al-Miʿrājiyya.*

It is difficult to know which works of Avicenna may have been in this codex. However, the *Miʿrājiyya* which is probably only an Arabic title for the Persian work, *Miʿrājnāma*, has been incorrectly ascribed to Avicenna as Mahdavi says in his entry no. 227.[246] Cf. *al-Dharīʿa* XXI:230.

35. *Majmūʿa rasāʾil* including *al-Fuṣūṣ* of al-Fārābī.

The attribution of *al-Fuṣūṣ fīʾl-ḥikma* to the early philosopher Abū Naṣr al-Fārābī [d. 339/950] is not entirely sound.[247] The text was popular in the philosophical curriculum of the Islamic East, especially in Safavid Iran.[248] See *al-Dharīʿa* XVI:235.

Persian and translated into English, *JRAS* (1895) 187ff; Maroun Aouad, 'Aristote: *de Pomo*', in R. Goulet (ed.), *Dictionnaire des philosophes antiques* (Paris 1989), I, 537–41.

[242] *Muṣannafāt-i Bābā Afḍal Kāshānī*, 113–44.

[243] See Jules Janssens, 'Mullā Ṣadrā's use of Ibn Sīnā's *al-Taʿlīqāt* in the *Asfār*', *JIS* 13 (2002), 1–13; the text itself has been edited by ʿAbd al-Raḥmān Badawī (Cairo 1973).

[244] The original text by Suhrawardī has been critically edited by Muḥammad Karīmī Zanjānī-Aṣl (Tehran 1379 Sh/2000). The commentary was edited by al-Sayyid Aḥmad Tuysirkānī (Mashhad 1411/1991), 105–256.

[245] This text has now been edited by ʿAlī Awjabī (Tehran 1382 Sh/2003). Cf. Barakat, 117–8.

[246] Peter Heath, on the other hand, considers it to be authentic and provides an English translation – see his *Allegory and Philosophy in Avicenna: with a Translation of the Book of the Prophet Muhammad's Ascent to heaven* (Philadelphia, PA 1992).

[247] See Shlomo Pines, 'Ibn Sīnā et l'auteur de *Risālat al-Fuṣūṣ fī-l-ḥikma*', reprinted in his *Studies in the History of Arabic Philosophy* (Jerusalem 1996), 297–300. On the author, see various, 'Fārābi', *EIr* IX, 208–29.

36. *Majmūʿa rasāʾil* including *Ithbāt al-wājib.*
This collection includes one of the famous treatises demonstrating the existence of God as the Necessary Being by the Safavid philosopher Shams al-Dīn Muḥammad b. Aḥmad al-Khafarī [d. 957/1550].[249] See *al-Dharīʿa* I:106.
37. *Majmūʿa rasāʾil* including sections of the *Iḥyāʾ al-ʿulūm.*
This collection includes sections of the major work of the Sunnī theologian and Sufi Abū Ḥāmid Muḥammad Ghazālī [d. 555/1111].[250] See *Kashf* 1:23.
38. *Majmūʿa rasāʾil* including *Asrār al-ṣalāt* of al-Shaykh al-Raʾīs.
This collection includes a short treatise by Avicenna on the secrets or true nature of the ritual prayer. See Mahdavi 85; *al-Dharīʿa* II:48.
39. *Majmūʿa rasāʾil* including *al-Zawrāʾ.*
This short treatise is a philosophical disquisition on the existence and knowledge of God by Davānī and he himself wrote a commentary upon it. It has been published recently.[251]
40. *ʿAwārif al-maʿārif* and *Minhāj al-ʿābidīn.*
These are both Sufi texts on the comportment of the noviate. The first is a major manual written for the resident members of *khānaqāh*-s by the eponymous founder of the Suhrawardī order, Abū Ḥafṣ ʿUmar al-Suhrawardī [d. 632/1234].[252] The text was completed in 612/1215–6. See *Kashf* 2:1177.
The second is a short Sufi treatise by the famous Ghazālī.[253]
41. *Sharḥ al-mūjaz.*
This is a medical text. The *Mūjaz* is an epitome of the *Canon* of Avicenna by ʿAlāʾ al-Dīn ʿAlī al-Qurashī known as Ibn al-Nafīs al-Dimashqī [d. 687/1288][254] and the

---

[248] The text has recently been edited critically with the *marginalia* of Mīr Dāmād by ʿAlī Awjabī and published in Tehran by the Institute for Cultural Works (*Anjuman-i āthār va mafākhir-i farhangī*) in 2003.

[249] On the five treatises by him on the metaphysics of the Necessary Being extant, see Fīrūza Sāʿatchīyān, 'Maʿarrifī-yi panj risāla-yi Khafarī dar ilāhiyyāt va ithbāt-i wājib al-wujūd', *Maʿārif* 59 (1372 Sh/2003), 98–111; Barakat, 172–8.

[250] For an introduction to this important thinker, see various, 'Ġazālī', *EIr* X, 358–77.

[251] In a collection of treatises of Davānī entitled *Sabʿ rasāʾil*, ed. S. A. Tuysirkānī (Tehran 1381 Sh/2002), 173–84.

[252] As a much used handbook, it is constantly in print. A recent edition was prepared by Muḥammad Kamdānī (Mecca 2001). There are a number of English renditions including an old British print at the Calcutta Press of the Government of India by Col. H. Wilberforce Clarke in 1891. On the text, see W. Chittick, 'ʿAwārif al-maʿārif', *EIr* III, 114–5; A. Hartmann, 'Suhrawardī', *EI²* IX, 778–82; *GAL* I, 440, S I, 788.

[253] The most recent edition is by ʿAbd al-Azīz al-Sayrawān (Damascus 1996).

[254] Max Meyerhof [J. Schacht], 'Ibn al-Nafīs', *EI²* III, 897–8; *GAL* I, 649, S I, 899; cf. M. Ullmann, *Islamic Medicine* (Edinburgh 1997), 48, 68–9 (on pulmonary circulation); Max Meyerhof, 'Ibn an-Nafīs und seine

commentary is by Burhān al-Dīn Nafīs b. ʿIwaḍ al-Kirmānī [d. 853/1449]. The text is also known as *al-Sharḥ al-Nafīsī.* See *Kashf* 2:1899.

42. *Al-Qawāʿid* of al-Shahīd al-Thānī.

The *Tamhīd al-qawāʿid* or *Fawāʾid al-qawāʿid* is a commentary by al-Shahīd II on the legal text of al-ʿAllāma al-Ḥillī mentioned above. See *al-Dharīʿa* IV:452; MT 80.

43. *Al-Mabāḥith al-mashriqiyya* of Fakhr al-Dīn al-Rāzī.

This is a philosophical encyclopaedia written fairly early in his career by the famous Transoxanian Ashʿarī theologian and exegete Fakhr al-Dīn al-Rāzī [d. 606/1210].[255] See *Kashf* 2:1577.

44. *Jāmiʿ al-lughatayn.*

It seems that this is a lexicon probably of the Persian language. There does not seem to be a known text of this exact name. Two possibilities come to mind: *Jāmiʿ al-lughghāt* of Niyāzī Ḥijāzī – see *al-Dharīʿa* V:69 or *Jāmiʿ al-lugha* of al-Sayyid Muḥammad b. al-Ḥasan – see *Kashf* 5:72. Both are fifteenth century Timurid works.

45. *Al-Tuḥfa al-Shāhiyya* of al-ʿAllāma al-Shīrāzī.

This is a work on astronomy written for the Saljuq prince Amīr Shāh Muḥammad b. Tāj al-Dīn in 684/1285 by the scientist and philosopher Quṭb al-Dīn Maḥmūd b. Masʿūd al-Shīrāzī [d. 710/1311].[256] See *al-Dharīʿa* III:443.

46. *Tahdhīb al-uṣūl* of al-ʿAllāma al-Ḥillī.

This is the famous school text in Imāmī Shiʿi *uṣūl al-fiqh* entitled *Tahdhīb ṭarīq al-wuṣūl ilā ʿilm al-uṣūl* of al-ʿAllāma al-Ḥillī. See *al-Dharīʿa* V:511.

47. *Al-Ufuq al-mubīn* of al-Sayyid Dāmād (may God preserve his blessings upon us).

This is a work of philosophical theology, on time and existence in the God-world relationship that was particularly popular in India written by the famous philosopher and teacher of Mullā Ṣadrā, Mīr Dāmād.[257] It was written probably in the early 1020s. See *al-Dharīʿa* II:261.

Theorie des Lungenkreislaufs', *Quellen und Studien zur Geschichte der Naturwissenschaften und Medizin* 3 (1935), 37–88; Ullmann, *Die Medizin im Islam* (Leiden 1970), 173–6; E. Savage-Smith, 'Medicine', in R. Rashed (ed.), *Encyclopaedia of Arabic Science* (London 1996), 902–62, especially 932–3; Seyyed Hossein Nasr, *Science and Civilisation in Islam* (Cambridge 1987), 212–14.

[255] A recent edition is by Muḥammad al-Baghdādī (2 vols, Beirut 1990).

[256] On this eminent scientist and Illuminationist philosopher, see John Walbridge, *The Science of Mystic Lights: Quṭb al-Dīn Shīrāzī and the Illuminationist Tradition in Islamic Philosophy* (Cambridge, MA 1992); cf. George Saliba, 'Arabic planetary theories', in R. Rashed (ed.), *Encyclopaedia of Arabic Science*, 98–9. There is another text of the same name by Manṣūr Dashtakī on astronomy (*al-Dharīʿa* III, 443); however, the title of the author indicates that my identification is correct.

[257] Sayyid ʿAlī Mūsawī Bihbahānī, *Ḥakīm-i Astarābād* (3rd edn, Tehran 1377Sh/1998), 119.

48. *Al-Ṣirāṭ al-mustaqīm* of al-Sayyid Dāmād (may God preserve his blessings upon us).

This is another work of philosophical theology that focuses on divine attributes and the nature of divine timelessness in relation to the incipience of creation.[258] See *al-Dharīʿa* XV:35.

49. *Al-Taqdīsāt* and *al-īmāḍāt* al-Sayyid Dāmād (may God preserve his blessings upon us).

These are both texts of philosophical theology.[259] The full title of the second is *al-Imāḍāt wa'l-tashrīqāt* and it is a study of time and creation. See *al-Dharīʿa* IV:364 and II:509.

50. *Ithbāt al-jadīd* of al-ʿAllāma al-Dawānī and some others treatises.

This first text is *al-Risāla al-jadīda li-Ithbāt al-wājib* of Davānī, the second treatise that he wrote on the topic of the Necessary Being.[260] See *al-Dharīʿa* I:107.

51. The second half of *al-Kashshāf*.

This is the famous lexicographical Qur'ānic commentary of the Muʿtazilī theologian Abu'l-Qāsim Jār Allāh Maḥmūd b. ʿUmar al-Zamakhsharī [d. 538/1144]. It was the subject of numerous *marginalia* in the Shiʿi tradition (both Imāmī and Zaydī) and generally in the Timurid and Safavid periods.[261] See *Kashf* 2:1475.

52. *Sharḥ kullīyāt al-mūjaz* of al-Nafīsī.

This is probably a shortened version of the commentary on the epitome of the *Canon* of Avicenna by al-Nafīsī mentioned above.

53. *Sharḥ al-Shāfiya* of al-Jāribirdī.

This is a text in the morphology of the Arabic language and was the main school text for the subject in the Safavid period. The original text *al-Shāfiya* is by Ibn Ḥājib [d. 646/1249] and the commentary is by Aḥmad b. al-Ḥasan al-Jāribirdī [d. 746/1345]. See *Kashf* 2:1020.

54. *Al-Mukhtaṣar al-Nāfiʿ*.

This is an Imāmī Shiʿi legal school text by al-Muḥaqqiq al-Ḥillī [d. 676/1277], an epitome of his *Sharāʾiʿ al-Islām*, and remained a major seminary text until the nineteenth century. See MT 65–6; *al-Dharīʿa* XX:1213.

---

[258] It had been edited by ʿAlī Awjabī (Tehran 2002). Cf. Bihbahānī, *Ḥakīm-i Astarābād*, 157–8.

[259] Bihbahānī, *Ḥakīm-i Astarābād*, 123, 126. Uncritical editions of the texts (transcriptions of a single manuscript copy) have been prepared by ʿAbd Allāh Nūrānī (ed.), *Muṣannafāt-i Mīr Dāmād Volume 1* (Tehran 1381 Sh/2002).

[260] *Sabʿ rasāʾil*, 117–70.

[261] This text is always in print and popular throughout the Muslim world in scholarly circles although still awaiting a critical edition.

55. *Majmūʿa rasāʾil* including parts of *al-Ḥikma al-mashriqiyya* of al-Shaykh al-Raʾīs.
This collection contains parts (not identified) of one of the most (in)famous texts of Avicenna. Supposedly a later endorsement of a mystical approach to philosophy, only part of the logic is extant and is the focus of an academic debate.[262] See Mahdavi 63.
56. *Majmūʿa rasāʾil* including some works of al-Shaykh al-Raʾīs.
Again we are not told what these works of Avicenna are. But it is significant that he owned most of the Avicennan corpus in terms of influence and borrowings and citations in his work.
57. *Majmūʿa rasāʾil* including *al-Risāla al-tahlīliyya* of al-Dawānī.
This treatise is a commentary on the phrase *lā ilāha illā Allāh* by the Shīrāzī philosopher.[263] See *al-Dharīʿa* IV:516.
58. *Majmūʿa rasāʾil* including the *Categories* of Aristotle.
A commentary on the *Categories* is attributed to him but this cannot be corroborated merely by the fact that he owned a copy of it.
59. *Majmūʿa rasāʾil* including *al-Arbaʿūna ḥadīthan* of al-Shaykh al-Bahāʾī (may his shadow remain over us).
This collection contains a famous, mainly legal-moral collection of Prophetic and Imamic sayings collated by the teacher of Mullā Ṣadrā, Shaykh Bahāʾī.[264] See *al-Dharīʿa* I:425.
60. *Ḥāshiya al-Jaghmīnī* of al-Bīrjandī and *Ḥāshiya ʿalāʾl-ilāhiyyāt* of al-Khafarī.
The first text is a work of astronomy. Maḥmūd b. ʿUmar Jaghmīnī [d. 744/1344] wrote the *Mulakhkhaṣ fīʾl-hayʾa* on astronomy for the famous patron Ulugh Beg. There are two famous *marginalia* on it: the first is by ʿAbd ʿAlī b. Muḥammad al-Bīrjandī [d. 934/1527] and the second by the thinker al-Sharīf al-Jurjānī. The text is the former gloss. See *Kashf* 2:1819.
The second text is a renowned *marginalia* on the ontology section of the later commentary on *al-Tajrīd* by the Shirazi philosopher al-Khafarī.[265] See *al-Dharīʿa* VI:116.
61. *Majmūʿa rasāʾil* including *Awṣāf-i Ashrāf* of al-Ṭūsī.
This collection contains the most openly Sufi work of the philosopher Naṣīr al-Dīn al-Ṭūsī, probably from the period when he was Ismāʿīlī.[266] See *al-Dharīʿa* II:477.

---

[262] See Dimitri Gutas, 'Avicenna's Eastern ("Oriental") philosophy', *Arabic Sciences and Philosophy* 10 (2000), 159–80.
[263] It was edited by Firishta Farīdūnī (Tehran 1373 Sh/1994).
[264] It was published by the seminary in Qum in 1994.
[265] This has been edited by Fīrūza Sāʿatchīyān (Tehran 1383 Sh/2004).

62. *Majmūʿa rasāʾil* including parts of *al-Futūḥāt.*
This collection contains one of the most influential works of later Islamic thought and a work that is often cited by Mullā Ṣadrā, *al-Futūḥāt al-Makkiyya* of the Andalusian Sufi Ibn ʿArabī [d. 638/1240].[267] A massive compendium of Sufi lore and commentary, it appears throughout the text of the *Asfār*, in particular the sections on the nature of the soul at the end.[268] See *Kashf* 2:1237.
63. *Majmūʿa rasāʾil* including *al-Risāla [illegible]* of al-ʿAllāma al-Shīrāzī.
This may refer to the earlier treatise on the nature of the Necessary Being or some other work of Manṣūr Dashtakī.
64. *Majmūʿa rasāʾil* including *Risālat al-qirāʾāt.*
The author is not named and it could be one of a number of works written on the recitations and modes of the text of the Qurʾān.
65. *Majmūʿa rasāʾil* including *Ḥāshiya ʿalāʾl-Ishārāt* of al-ʿAllāma al-Dawānī.
This is quite interesting. Bibliographies do not record a *marginalia* by Davānī on this text of Avicenna. However, a gloss upon the adjudication between the two famous commentaries on the text (namely of al-Rāzī and al-Ṭūsī) by Quṭb al-Dīn Rāzī Taḥtānī [d. 765/1365] is mentioned. See *al-Dharīʿa* VI:32.
66. Selections from *Sharḥ al-dīwān* of al-Fāḍil al-Maybudī.
This is a popular Timurid mystical and philosophical commentary on the *dīwān* attributed to Imam ʿAlī b. Abī Ṭālib written by the philosopher Mīr Ḥusayn Maybudī.[269] See *al-Dharīʿa* XIII:266.
67. *Majmūʿa rasāʾil* including *al-Mabdaʾ waʾl-maʿād* of al-Shaykh al-Raʾīs.
This is an early philosophical text of particular significance for the theory of the afterlife of the soul. Mullā Ṣadrā wrote a version that closely follows the text of Avicenna. See Mahdavi 106.
68. *Majmūʿa rasāʾil* including *Risāla al-qaḍāʾ waʾl-qadar* of al-Qāshānī.
This collection includes a treatise on divine determinism of human acts written by the Shiʿi Sufi ʿAbd al-Razzāq Kāshānī [d. 736/1336].[270] See *al-Dharīʿa* XVII:148.

---

[266] The text was edited by Īraj Gulsurkhī (Tehran 1376 Sh/1997).
[267] W. Chittick, 'Ebn ʿArabī', *EIr* VII, 664–70; idem, *The Sufi Path of Knowledge: Ibn ʿArabī's Metaphysics of Imagination* (Albany, NY 1989); idem, *Ibn ʿArabī* (The Makers of the Muslim World Series, Oxford 2006); James Morris, Introduction to *The Meccan Revelations*, trs. W. Chittick and J. Morris (rpt, New York 2002), 3–26.
[268] The old Būlāq edition remains the choice for references, although there is an incomplete critical edition by the late Osman Yahia.
[269] The text was edited by Ḥasan Raḥmānī et al (Tehran 1379 Sh/2000).

69. *Majmūʿa rasāʾil* including *al-Alwāḥ* of Shaykh al-Ishrāq.

This is an early philosophical text of the philosopher Shihāb al-Dīn Yaḥyā Suhrawardī [d. 587/1191] entitled *al-Alwāḥ al-ʿImādiyya* that he wrote for ʿImād al-Dīn Abū Bakr, the Qārākhānid prince of Khartpert.[271] See *Kashf* 1:159.

70. *Majmūʿa rasāʾil* including *Ithbāt al-wājib* of al-Khafarī.

Another copy [or another treatise] on the Necessary being written by this early Safavid philosopher is found in this codex.

71. *Majmūʿa rasāʾil* including *al-ghurba al-gharbiyya* [sic!] of Ṣāḥib al-Ishrāq.

This codex includes a short treatise of Suhrawardī entitled *Qiṣṣat al-ghurba al-gharbiyya.* The treatise is extant in an Arabic and a Persian recension. It is a short mystical treatise of the return to the true self from the alienation of the world. See *al-Dharīʿa* XVI:33.

72. *Majmūʿa rasāʾil* including *Uthūlūjīya* of Aristotle.

This text is the famous *Theologia Aristotelis*, an Arabic recension of a (probably Greek original) paraphrase of selections from *Enneads* IV–VI of Plotinus.[272] The text had a great impact on the origins of Islamic Neoplatonism and enjoyed a revival in the Safavid period and is cited on numerous occasions by Mullā Ṣadrā.

73. *Majmūʿa rasāʾil* including *Anmūzaj al-ʿulūm* of al-Dawānī.

This codex includes a well known work of Davānī on the logic, methodology and classification of knowledge.[273] See *al-Dharīʿa* II:406.

74. *Majmūʿa rasāʾil* including *Sharḥ tahdhīb al-manṭiq.*

The commentary may in fact be the popular *marginalia* and seminary text of Mullā Shihāb al-Dīn ʿAbd Allāh b. al-Ḥusayn Yazdī [d. 981/1573]. This logical text is still studied in the seminary. The original *Tahdhīb al-manṭiq* was written by al-Taftazānī.

75. *Majmūʿa rasāʾil* including *Risālat al-fuṣūl* of al-Ṭūsī.

This collection included a short theological treatise in Persian of the Shiʿi philosopher Naṣīr al-Dīn al-Ṭūsī. See *al-Dharīʿa* XVI:246.

76. *Majmūʿa rasāʾil* including *al-Shāfiya.*

This collection probably included logical works such as this important grammatical work of Ibn Ḥājib. See *Kashf* 2:1020.

---

[270] The treatise has been edited by Majīd Hādīzāda in *Majmūʿa-yi Rasāʾil va muṣannafāt-i Shaykh Kamāl al-Dīn ʿAbd al-Razzāq Kāshānī* (Tehran 1379 Sh/2000).

[271] See Naṣr Allāh Pūrjavādī, 'Shaykh-i Ishrāq va taʾlīf-i *Alwāḥ-i ʿImādī*', in Sayyid ʿAlī Dāvūd (ed.), *Nāma-yi Iqbāl* (Tehran 1997), 1–11.

[272] On the text, see Peter Adamson, *The Arabic Plotinus* (London 2002).

[273] The text has been edited by Sayyid Aḥmad Tuysirkānī in *Thalāth rasāʾil* (Mashhad 1411/1991), 271–333.

77. *Majmūʿa rasāʾil* including *Asrār al-Nujūm* of Aristotle.

Perhaps a codex of astronomical works, it is unclear whether this is an authentic work of Aristotle.

78. *Sharḥ al-tadhkira fīʾl-hayʾa* of al-ʿAllāma al-Khafarī.

The *al-Tadhkira fī ʿilm al-hayʾa* is a famous memoir on astronomy by Naṣīr al-Dīn al-Ṭūsī. This commentary, also known as *al-Takmila*, is by the Safavid philosopher and scientist al-Khafarī.[274] See *al-Dharīʿa* XIII:144 and IV:409.

79. *Majmūʿa* of commentaries on *al-Hidāya*.

This codex contained a collection of commentaries on the philosophical encyclopaedia of al-Abharī.

80. *Majmūʿa* of commentaries on verses of the mystic Shaykh Ibn Fāriḍ.

The Egyptian Sufi poet Abuʾl-Qāsim ʿUmar Ibn al-Fāriḍ [d. 632/1235] wrote mystical verse that remains popular.[275] His famous ode known simply as the *Tāʾiyya* because of its rhyme sequence was the subject of many Sufi commentaries. See *Kashf* 1:265.

81. *Taḥrīr Kitāb al-Uqlīdus* of the philosopher (*al-Ḥakīm*) al-Ṭūsī.

This is a recension of the translation made by the early translator and scientist äābit b. Qurra of the arithmetic and geometric work of Euclid prepared by the philosopher and scientist Naṣīr al-Dīn al-Ṭūsī. It was the most important school text in the subject in the seminary. Mathematics was a key aspect of the training of a philosopher going back at least to Middle Platonism.[276] See *al-Dharīʿa* III:379.

82. *Taḥrīr al-Uqlīdus* of other than the philosopher al-Ṭūsī.

This codex contains writings of other famous scientists on the recension of Euclid.

83. *Majmūʿa rasāʾil* including *al-Taḥṣīl* of Bahmanyār.

This text is the famous epitome of *al-Shifāʾ* by Bahmanyār b. Marzubān [d. 458/1066], the most eminent student of Avicenna.[277] It was an influential philosophical text and often the doctrines of Avicenna are cited by Mullā Ṣadrā from this work. See *al-Dharīʿa* III:395.

84. *Majmūʿa rasāʾil* including *al-Talwīḥāt* of Ṣāḥib al-Ishrāq.

This text is an earlier critique of Avicennan philosophy by Suhrawardī divided into three parts of logic, metaphysics and physics. It was a key text of the Illuminationist tradition and many commentaries were written on it. See *Kashf* 1:482.

---

[274] Barakat, 180–2. The original text has been edited by ʿAbbās Sulaymān (Kuwait 1993). It has also been translated and studied by F. J. Ragep (New York 1993).

[275] On him and his verse, see Th. Emil Homerin, *From Arab Poet to Muslim Saint* (rpt, Cairo 2001).

[276] See D. J. O'Meara, *Pythagoras Revived: Mathematics and Philosophy in Late Antiquity* (Oxford 1989).

[277] H. Daiber, 'Bahmanyār', *EIr* III, 501–3. It was edited by Murtaḍā Muṭahharī (Tehran 1978).

85. *Majmūʿa rasāʾil* including *al-Lamaḥāt* of Ṣāḥib al-Ishrāq.
This is another early philosophical work of Suhrawardī on the Avicennan model entitled *al-Lamaḥāt fīʾl-ḥaqāʾiq.*[278] See *Kashf* 2:1560.
86. The second quarter of *Iḥyāʾ al-ʿulūm.*
This *magnum opus*, *Iḥyāʾ ʿulūm al-Dīn*, of Ghazālī is divided into four sections. The second quarter comprises the ten chapters on social comportment and etiquette.
87. *Tāj al-maʾāthir.*
It is unclear what this is. However, bibliographies record a work of Persian history by Ṣadr al-Dīn Ḥasan b. Muḥammad Niẓāmī. See *Kashf* 1:269; *al-Dharīʿa* III:207.
88. *Sharḥ al-qawāʿid* of al-ʿAllāma Fakhr al-Dīn.
This is the *Īḍāḥ al-fawāʾid* (or *Īḍāḥ al-maqāṣid*), a commentary by Fakhr al-Dīn Muḥammad b. al-Ḥasan al-Ḥillī [d. 771/1370] on the legal text of his father, al-ʿAllāma al-Ḥillī. See *al-Dharīʿa* II:496; MT 76.
89. *Sharḥ al-Shamsiyya.*
The *Risāla Shamsiyya* by the logician Najm al-Dīn ʿAlī b. ʿUmar Kātibī Qazwīnī known as Dabīrān [d. 675/1276] was the most popular logic text of the seminary and usually studied with this commentary known as *Taḥrīr al-qawāʿid al-manṭiqiyya* by the philosopher Quṭb al-Dīn Muḥammad Rāzī Taḥtānī [d. 765/1365]. See *Kashf* 2:1063.
90. *Ḥāshiya* of al-Jurjānī on *al-Shamsiyya.*
The philosopher al-Jurjānī wrote a *marginalia* on this logical text that was often studied alongside the commentary of Taḥtānī. See *Kashf* 2:1062; *al-Dharīʿa* VI:73.
91. *Ḥāshiya al-Sharīfiyya* on *Sharḥ al-maṭāliʿ.*
This is probably the logical *marginalia* of al-Jurjānī. The original text is *Maṭāliʿ al-anwār* of Sirāj al-Dīn Maḥmūd b. Abī Bakr al-Urmawī [d. 682/1283] is a compendium of logic and philosophy upon which ʿAḍud al-Dīn al-Ījī [d. 756/1355] wrote a commentary.[279] However, the *marginalia* is probably on the logical commentary by Quṭb al-Dīn al-Taḥtānī. See *Kashf* 2:1715; *al-Dharīʿa* VI:76.
92. *Majmūʿa rasāʾil* including *Risālat al-ḥall* of al-Khafarī.

[278] There are a number of editions of this text including: Emile Maalouf (Beirut 1991); Najafqulī Ḥabībī (Tehran 1977); Muḥammad Abū Rayyān (Alexandria 1988).

[279] There is an excellent translation and study of the work: *Nature, Man and God in Medieval Islam*, eds./trs. E. E. Caverley and James W. Pollock (2 vols, Islamic Philosophy, Theology and Science Texts and Studies vol. XL, Leiden 2002).

This may have been another logical codex. The treatise is a solution to the Liar's paradox entitled *ʿIbrat al-fuḍalāʾ fī ḥall shubhat jadhr al-aṣamm* by the Safavid philosopher al-Khafarī.[280] See *al-Dharīʿa* VII:13 and 67.

93. *Majmūʿa rasāʾil* including *Ḥāshiyat al-tahdhīb* of al-Dawānī and 2 other *risāla*-s.

This logical codex includes the *marginalia* of Davānī on probably the commentary on the logical text by Taḥtānī. See *al-Dharīʿa* VI:54.

94. *Ḥāshiyat al-Sayyid Amīr Abuʾl-Fatḥ* on *Ḥāshiyat al-tahdhīb.*

This is a *marginalia* on the *marginalia* of Davānī, the previous text, by al-Sayyid Amīr Abuʾl-Fatḥ better known as Mīr Makhdūm Shīrāzī [d. 995/1586], a Sunnī theologian who was briefly *ṣadr* under Shah Ismāʿīl II [d. 985/1577] and then fled Safavid lands for the safety of the Ottoman court.[281] See *al-Dharīʿa* VI:59.

95. *Al-Miftāḥ.*

This is probably the original text on logic and methodology by al-Sakkākī.

96. The second and third quarters of *al-Kashshāf.*

This codex contains more parts of the famous commentary of al-Zamakhsharī.

97. *Majmūʿa rasāʾil* including *Tahāfut al-falāsifa* of al-Ghazālī and *al-Siyāsa al-madaniyya* of al-Fārābī.

The first text is the famous attack on philosophy in particular citing three philosophical doctrines that are heretical.[282] It was written by the famous theologian al-Ghazālī. See *Kashf* 1:509.

The second text is a work of metaphysics by the early philosopher al-Fārābī.[283] See *Kashf* 2:1011.

98. *Fuṣūṣ al-ḥikam* of Shaykh Muḥyī al-Dīn Ibn ʿArabī.

This is one of the most influential works of Sufi metaphysics written by Ibn ʿArabī and a major influence upon Mullā Ṣadrā.[284] See *Kashf* 2:1261.

99. *Jawāmiʿ al-ḥisāb* of al-Ṭūsī.

---

[280] Barakat, 189–90. The text has been edited: A. Qarāmalakī, 'Muʿammāʾ-yi jadhr aṣamm dar ḥawza-yi falsafī-yi Shīrāz', *Ṣadrā* 4 (1375 Sh/1996), 86–90.

[281] IBM I, 148–9; Rosemary Stanfield Johnson, 'Sunni survival in Safavid Iran: Anti-Sunni activities during the reign of Tahmasp I', *IS* 27 (1994), 123–33; Shohreh Gholsorkhi, 'Ismail II and Mirza Makhdum Sharifi: an interlude in Safavid history', *IJMES* 26 (1994), 477–88.

[282] There is an excellent edition and English translation by Michael Marmura (Islamic Translations Series, Provo, UH 1998).

[283] It was edited and translated by Fawzi Najjar (Beirut 1964).

[284] It was edited by Abuʾl-Aʿlā ʿAfīfī with annotation (Cairo 1946). The best known English translation is by Ralph Austin (New York 1981); a recent rendition is by Caner Dagli (Chicago 2004).

This is another mathematical text, a work on arithmetic by the philosopher and scientist Naṣīr al-Dīn al-Ṭūsī. See *al-Dharīʿa* V:249.

100. *Sharḥ al-asṭarlāb* of al-Birjandī.

This is an astronomical commentary on a work by Naṣīr al-Dīn al-Ṭūsī on the astrolabe by Niẓām al-Dīn ʿAbd al-ʿAlī al-Bīrjandī. See *al-Dharīʿa* XIII:130.

101. *Majmūʿa rasāʾil* including *al-asṭarlāb waʾl-nujūm* in an old hand (*khaṭṭ qadīm*).

This is probably a codex of astronomical works including that of Naṣīr al-Dīn al-Ṭūsī.

102. *Taḥrīr al-aḥkām fīʾl-fiqh* of al-Ḥillī.

This is another legal work by al-ʿAllāma al-Ḥillī also called *Taḥrīr al-aḥkām al-Sharʿiyya.* See *al-Dharīʿa* III:378.

103. *Al-Miṣbāḥ al-ṣaghīr.*

This is a collection of Imāmī Shiʿi supplications and litanies collected by the jurist, theologian and *muḥaddith* Abū Jaʿfar Muḥammad b. al-Ḥasan al-Ṭūsī [d. 460/1067] entitled *al-Miṣbāḥ al-mutahajjid.* See *al-Dharīʿa* XXI:118.

104. *Al-Ṣaḥīfa al-kāmila.*

This is the collection of supplications attributed to the fourth Shiʿi Imam ʿAlī b. al-Ḥusayn Zayn al-ʿĀbidīn that was popularised in the Safavid period and the teachers of Mullā Ṣadrā wrote significant *marginalia* on it.[285] See *al-Dharīʿa* XV:18.

105. and 106. and 107. Collections of supplications (*al-daʿwāt*).

These are further codices of supplications. Their presence in his library signals his devotional practice and interest in these texts.

108. *Man lā yaḥḍuruhu l-Faqīh.*

This is one of the four books of early Imāmī Shiʿi *ḥadīth* compiled by al-Shaykh al-Ṣadūq. Traditions were popularised in the Safavid period and Mullā Ṣadrā himself wrote a commentary on another famous collection.[286] See *al-Dharīʿa* XXII:232.

109. Part I of *al-Tahdhīb* of *ḥadīth* of al-Ṭūsī.

This is another collection of early Imāmī Shiʿi *ḥadīth* known as *Tahdhīb al-aḥkām* compiled by al-Ṭūsī [d. 460/1067].[287] See *al-Dharīʿa* IV:504.

110. The first volume of *Sharḥ al-qawāʿid* of al-Shaykh ʿAlī.

---

[285] For an excellent study of the text, its recensions and its manuscript tradition, see al-Sayyid Muḥammad Ḥusayn Jalālī, *Dirāsa ḥawl al-Ṣaḥīfa al-Sajjādīya* (Beirut 2000). The collection has been translated into English by William Chittick as *The Psalms of Islam* (London 1988).

[286] There are numerous editions and printings of the text usually in 4 volumes.

[287] There are numerous editions and printings of the text usually in 10 volumes. It is the largest of the early Imāmī Shiʿi *ḥadīth* collections.

This is an incomplete commentary on the legal text of al-ʿAllāma al-Ḥillī by the most prominent jurist of the early Safavid period and grandfather of Mīr Dāmād, Nūr al-Dīn ʿAlī b. ʿAbd ʿAlī al-Karakī [d. 940/1534]. The text is called *Jāmiʿ al-maqāṣid.* See *al-Dharīʿa* V:72; MT 8.

111. *Makārim al-akhlāq.*

This is a famous and popular compilation of spiritual, religious and social etiquette written by the Shiʿi exegete al-Ṭabrisī mentioned above. See *al-Dharīʿa* XXII:146.

Chapter 3
Sources on Safavid Intellectual History and the History of Philosophy

The aim of this chapter is to introduce discursively the sources that one can utilise for the study of philosophical traditions in the Safavid period. Before considering them and their utility, it would be useful to preface the functional part of the chapter with a methodological discussion of some issues in the study of the intellectual history of the period and the problems that arise from it.

Max Horten, the eminent German Orientalist, initiated the modern academic study of Safavid philosophy, indeed of Islamic philosophy on the whole, with two monographs (including translated excerpts) on the thought of Mullā Ṣadrā Shīrāzī in the early twentieth century.[288] Almost a half a century later, the efforts of the French orientalist and philosopher Henry Corbin [d. 1978],[289] the Iranian thinker Seyyed Hossein Nasr,[290] and the Iranian philosopher-theologian Sayyid Jalāl al-Dīn Āshtiyānī made a number of texts and studies available to the academic field of Islamic thought, not least the four volume *Anthologie des philosophes iraniens (Muntakhabātī az āthār-i ḥukamāʾ-yi ilāhī-yi Īrān).*[291] Toshihiko Izutsu and Mehdi Mohaghegh followed

---

[288] *Die Gottesbeweise bei Schirazi* (Bonn 1912) and *Das philosophische System von Schirazi* (Strassburg 1912).

[289] 'La place de Mollā Ṣadrā dans la philosophie iranienne', *SI* 18 (1962), 81–113; *En Islam Iranien* (4 tomes, Paris 1971–2); *La Philosophie iranienne islamique aux XVIIe et XVIIIe siècles* (Paris 1981); *Histoire de la philosophie islamique* (Paris 1986); for his editions, see the references in Chapter 2. On Corbin, see Daryush Shayegan, 'Corbin, Henry', *EIr* VI, 268–72; idem, *Henry Corbin: La topographie spirituelle de l'Islam iranien* (Paris 1990); C. Jambet (ed.), *Cahiers de l'Herne: Henry Corbin* (Paris 1981).

[290] *Sadra Commemoration Volume* (Tehran 1961); *Sadr al-Din Shirazi and his Transcendent Theosophy* (Tehran 1977); *The Islamic Intellectual Tradition in Persia*, ed. M. Aminrazavi (Richmond 1996).

[291] It was published by the L'Institut Français de recherches en Iran (Tehran 1972–8). This anthology was prefaced with introductions to the relevant thinkers by Henry Corbin and explanatory notes in Persian by Āshtiyānī. It collates texts, selections in some cases and complete treatises in others, both in Arabic and Persian, of twenty-five thinkers beginning with Mīr Dāmād and ending with Mullā Naẓar ʿAlī Gīlānī [fl. 1193/1779].

the line in producing studies of the metaphysics of thinkers of the period and commentaries on them from a later period, notably the significant Qajar philosophical compendium *Sharḥ ghurar al-farāʾid [Sharḥ al-manẓūma]* of Mullā Hādī Sabzavārī [d. 1289/1873].[292] It was Corbin and Nasr who coined the phrase school of Isfahan to describe philosophical inquiry in the Safavid period in particular in the age of Shah ʿAbbās I [r. 1588–1629] and this became the paradigm through which later scholars studied Safavid philosophy.[293] They perceived continuity in the later (Iranian) philosophical tradition in Islam from Suhrawardī in the twelfth century to Sabzavārī and the Shaykhiyya in the nineteenth century as thinkers engaged in the same quest for mystical understanding of the nature of reality and a thorough esoteric approach to questions of philosophy.[294] The suggestion was that the school of Isfahan was an intellectual, spiritual and cultural (and significantly apolitical) movement based in Isfahan. Newman has already successfully shown that the idea that figures involved were mystics divorced from politics and jurisprudence is a myth that cannot be sustained.[295] It certainly would be odd to argue that Shaykh Bahāʾī and Mīr Dāmād were apolitical given their roles at court and their public role as state jurists.

---

[292] They published the sections on metaphysics and theology (*al-ilāhiyyāt biʾl-maʿnā al-ʿāmm waʾl-akhaṣṣ*) in Tehran in 1969–77 published by the McGill Institute of Islamic Studies Tehran Branch. Sabzavārī played a crucial role in establishing the school of Mullā Ṣadrā as the dominant philosophical movement in the seminary. See Seyyed Hossein Nasr, 'Hādi Sabzavāri', *EIr* XI, 437–41; idem, 'The metaphysics of Ṣadr al-Dīn al-Shīrāzī and Islamic philosophy in Qajar Iran', in C. E. Bosworth and C. Hillenbrand (eds), *Qajar Iran: Political, Social and Cultural Change* (Edinburgh 1983), 177–98; idem, 'Renaissance in Iran: Mullā Hādī Sabzavārī', in M. M. Sharif (ed.), *A History of Muslim Philosophy* (Wiesbaden 1966), 1543–55; Ghulām Ḥusayn Riżā-Nizhād, *Ḥakīm-i Sabzavārī* (Tehran 1371 Sh/1992); Sajjad Rizvi, 'The revival of gnostic philosophy (*Ḥikmat-i ilāhī*) in Nineteenth Century Iran: A study of Mullā Hādī Sabzavārī (d. 1873) and his Sharḥ al-Manẓūmah', unpublished M.Phil dissertation (Oxford University 1996).

[293] One notable exception is Fazlur Rahman who in his *The Philosophy of Mullā Ṣadrā* (Albany, NY 1975), and 'Mīr Dāmād's concept of *Ḥudūth dahrī*: A contribution to the study of the God-world relationship theories in Safavid Iran', *JNES* 39 (1980), 139–51, dissents from this trend and presents a broadly Avicennian interpretation consistent with his own philosophical tastes.

[294] On the Shaykhiyya, see Corbin, *En Islam iranien*, IV, 205–300; D. MacEoin, 'Shaykhiyya', *EI²* IX, 403–5; [Steven Scholl and] Sajjad Rizvi, 'Shaykhiyya', *Encyclopaedia of Religion* 2nd edn, XII, 8307–9.

[295] Andrew Newman, 'Towards a reconsideration of the Iṣfahān school of philosophy: Shaykh Bahāʾī and the Ṣafawid ʿulamā'', *SIr* 15 (1986), 165–99; for a summary of the perceptions, see Sajjad Rizvi, 'Isfahan, the school of', *EIr* forthcoming [available at http://www.iranica.com].

Figure 2. The School of Isfahan

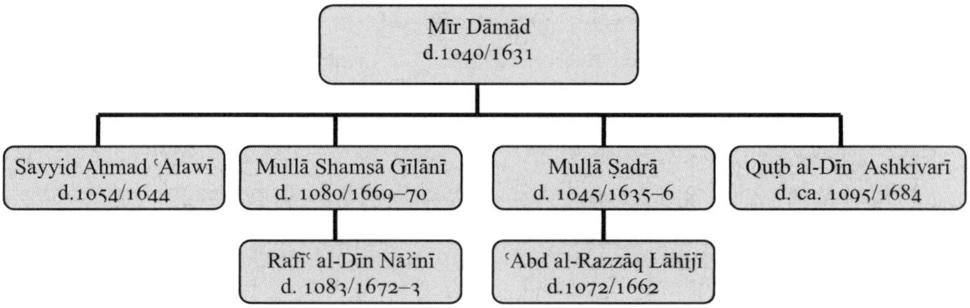

But was there ever a philosophical school? A school may be a particular institution founded by an individual, or a body of doctrines associated with a particular thinker, or an intellectual movement that comprises an interpretative community of a particular text. We may, for example, talk about the school of Plato as the Academy itself, or his followers who perpetuated his 'esoteric' teachings or the students who taught and studied his dialogues. But once we start talking about Platonism, Middle Platonism and Neoplatonism, the idea of a unified school certainly begins to break down.[296] In what sense then can we consider the Isfahan philosophers to constitute a school, especially since Nasr and Leaman used the term to designate thinkers who were not based in Isfahan such as Qāḍī Saʿīd Qummī [d. 1107/1696]?[297] There is little doubt that they did not share a central text or a central doctrine or body of doctrines. On the question of being and existence, for example, Shaykh Bahāʾī upheld the Sufi doctrine of monorealism (*waḥdat al-wujūd*), Mīr Dāmād denied the ultimate reality and reference of the term existence of all other than God, while Mullā Ṣadrā argued that the most fundamental reality true of all things including God was existence. Recognising a plurality and admitting to the multiplicity of philosophical

[296] See the comments of John Dillon, *The Heirs of Plato* (Oxford 2004), 1–29

[297] On this important thinker about whom more below, see Corbin, *En Islam iranien*, IV, 123–201; RU II, 284; *Aʿyān*, IX, 344; *Rawḍāt*, IV, 9; Tabrīzī, *Rayḥānat al-adab*, IV, 412; Sajjad Rizvi, 'Neoplatonism revived: Qāḍī Saʿīd Qummī (d. 1696) and his commentary on the *Theologia Aristotelis*', in P. Adamson (ed.), *Classical Arabic Philosophy: Sources and Reception* (London 2007); idem, 'Qāżi Saʿid Qomi', *EIr* forthcoming.

traditions in the Safavid period (essentialists, existentialists, monists, Avicennians, Illuminationists, Sadrians, etc) will enrich our understanding of the intellectual history of these crucial centuries and shift the sole emphasis away from Mullā Ṣadrā and consider the broader questions. What were the influences on his thought and who was he responding to? How did his thought emerge as an antithetical response to his teacher? How did others later respond to it?

However, we can save the appearance of a school by approaching the question through commonalities that are sometimes described as family resemblances and common contextual possibilities. Isfahan was indeed the centre of learning and practically all the thinkers had at some time studied there. They also shared some common preconceptions about the story of philosophy and wisdom and the intellectual pursuit they were undertaking. To put it simply, they considered the pursuit of knowledge to be a holistic endeavour in which the study of scripture, theology, politics, philosophy and mysticism (both theoretical and the application of experience) were harmonised. Given this common background and context, it is then the job of the intellectual historian to grasp the divergences and differences within the thinkers introduced by Corbin and Nasr and further search for those before and after them to understand their wider intellectual and cultural context.

Although the *Anthologie* has introduced a number of thinkers to us, and indeed recent editions published by Mīrāth-i Maktūb have added to these, a number of key thinkers remain unknown and their works remain unedited: one thinks in particular of major figures of the Dashtakī *sayyid* family of Shiraz such as Ghiyāth al-Dīn Manṣūr [d. 948/1542] and Niẓām al-Dīn Aḥmad [d. 1015/1606], and others such as Mīr Fakhr al-Dīn Sammākī Astarābādī [fl. 980/1572], the teacher of Mīr Dāmād.[298] One reason for the neglect has been that the school of Isfahan paradigm of study has tended to focus on the school of Mullā Ṣadrā to the exclusion of others and the need to disaggregate this approach will reveal the important of these other Avicennian, Illuminationist and essentially anti-Ṣadrian figures.

---

[298] One text of Sammākī that seems to be important given the number of manuscript copies is his marginalia (*ḥāshiya*) on the *Sharḥ al-Hidāya*, the commentary by Mīr Ḥusayn Maybudī on the original Avicennian philosophical compendium of Athīr al-Dīn al-Abharī. Here are details of three copies that I have consulted: MS Princeton Arabic New Series 948, fol. 1v–80r, good *naskhī*, dated 18 Jumāda II 1097/11 May 1686; MS Princeton Arabic New Series 1535, an acephalous copy dated 993/1585; MS Chester Beatty 4449, 104ff, *taʿlīq* dated 8 Rajab 981/3 November 1572, which may have been copied in the presence of the author. There are at least another ten copies of this text.

Figure 3. The Dashtakī family of philosophers

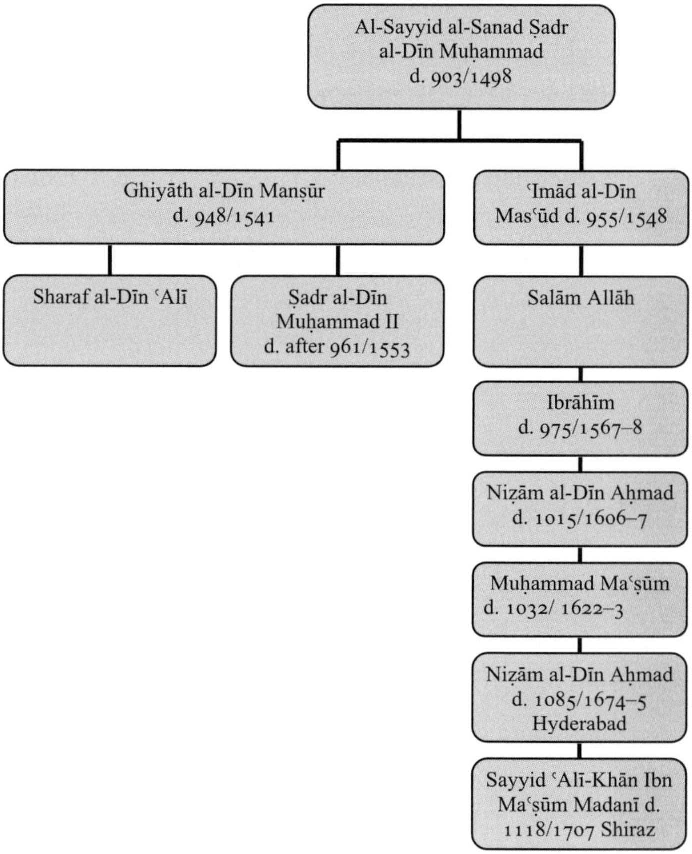

Nasr also coined the term the 'school of Shiraz' to describe the key figures of the sixteenth century and urged future research on them.[299] A number of their texts have been recently published. There are some key research aids for their study (not least the excellent editor introductions to the texts). Muḥammad Barakat has recently prepared a useful bibliography entitled *Kitābshināsī-yi maktab-i falsafī-yi Shīrāz* (Shiraz 1383 Sh/2004) which includes manuscript and publication details of the works of Ṣadr al-Dīn Muḥammad Dashtakī, Jalāl al-Dīn Davānī, Manṣūr Dashtakī, Shams

[299] Nasr, 'The place of the school of Isfahan', in L. Lewisohn (ed.), *The Heritage of Sufism III* (Oxford 1999), 5–6; idem, *Islamic Philosophy from its Origins to the* Present (Albany 2006), 193–207; Corbin, *En Islam Iranien*, IV, 61 mentions the concept but his referent is the school of Mullā Ṣadrā.

al-Dīn Muḥammad Khafarī [d. 942/1535 or 957/1550],[300] Maḥmūd b. Muḥammad Nayrīzī,[301] Jamāl al-Dīn Maḥmūd Shīrāzī, Mīr Fakhr al-Dīn Sammākī [d. 984/1576], Mīrzā-jān Ḥabīb Allāh Bāghnawī Shīrāzī [d. 994/1586], Kamāl al-Dīn Ḥusayn Ilāhī Ardabīlī [d. 950/1543–4],[302] and Ṣadr al-Dīn Muḥammad b. Manṣūr Dashtakī II. A few contemporary academics have devoted some studies to aspects of their thought considering mainly their influence on Mullā Ṣadrā as well as their contributions to philosophical logic through their discussion of the Liar's Paradox (*shubhat jadhr aṣamm*).[303]

[300] ʿAbd al-Nabī Qazwīnī, *Tatmīm Amal al-āmil*, ed. S. A. Ḥusaynī (Qum 1987), 64–5; Sayyid Nūr Allāh Shūstarī [d. 1019/1610], *Majālis al-muʾminīn*, ed. R. Malik (Tehran 1977), II, 233.

[301] He is the subject of a doctoral research project at Berlin undertaken by Reza Pourjavady, who has already edited his *Risāla dar qidam va ḥudūth-i ajsām* in *Maʿārif* 59 (1381 Sh/2002), 88–106.

[302] Cf. Muḥammad Riḍā Khāliqī, 'Sharḥ-i ḥāl va āthār-i Ilāhī Ardabīlī', *Mīrāth-i Jāvīdān* 3.1 (1374 Sh/1995), 132–40; Barakat, 234–6; RU II, 98–108 (an extensive entry that includes his licenses).

[303] Qāsim Kākāʾī, 'Āshnāʾ-yi bā maktab-i Shīrāz', *Ṣadrā* 3 (1975 Sh/1996), 82–9 (on Ṣadr al-Dīn Dashtakī), 4 (1375 Sh/1996), 71–9 (on al-Khafarī), 5 and 6 (1375 Sh/1996), 83–90 (on Manṣūr Dashtakī), 7 (1376 Sh/1997), 59–67 (also on Manṣūr Dashtakī), 11 (1377 Sh/1998), 23–32 (on the school of Manṣūr Dashtakī); A. Qarāmalakī, 'Muʿammāʾ-yi jadhr aṣamm dar ḥawza-yi falsafī-yi Shīrāz', *Ṣadrā* 4 (1375 Sh/1996), 80–90; cf. Erica Glassen, 'Shah Ismāʿīl I und die Theologen seiner Zeit', *Der Islam* 48 (1972), 254–68.

Figure 4.1. The School of Shiraz

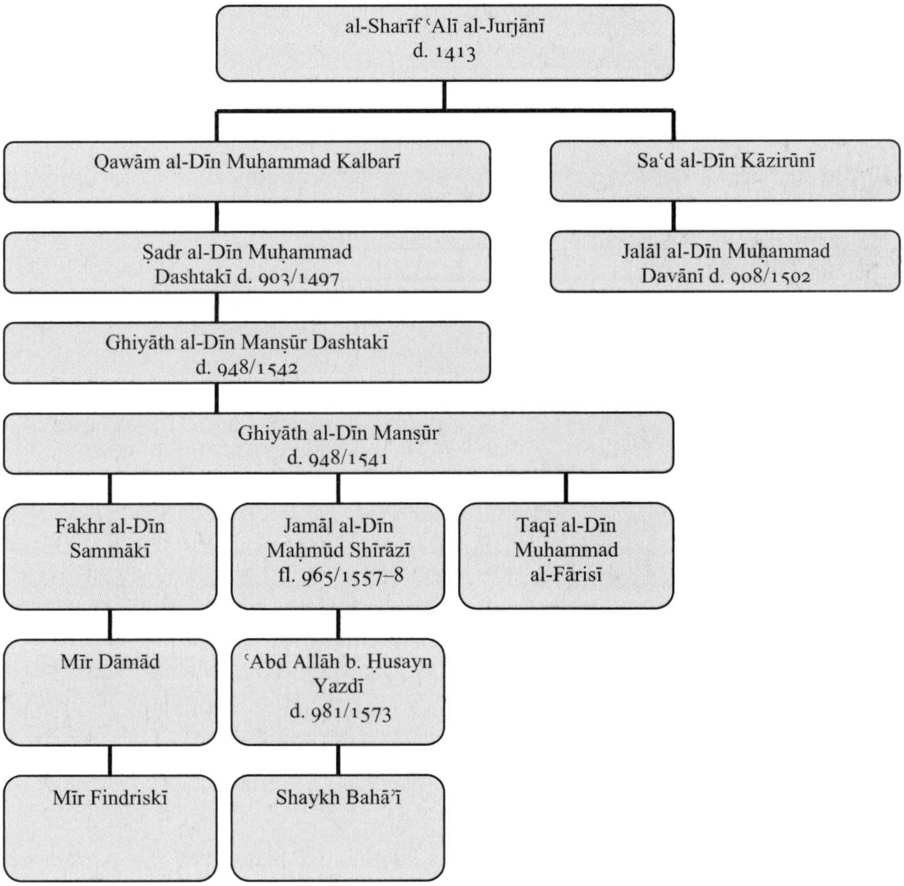

Figure 4.2 The School of Shiraz

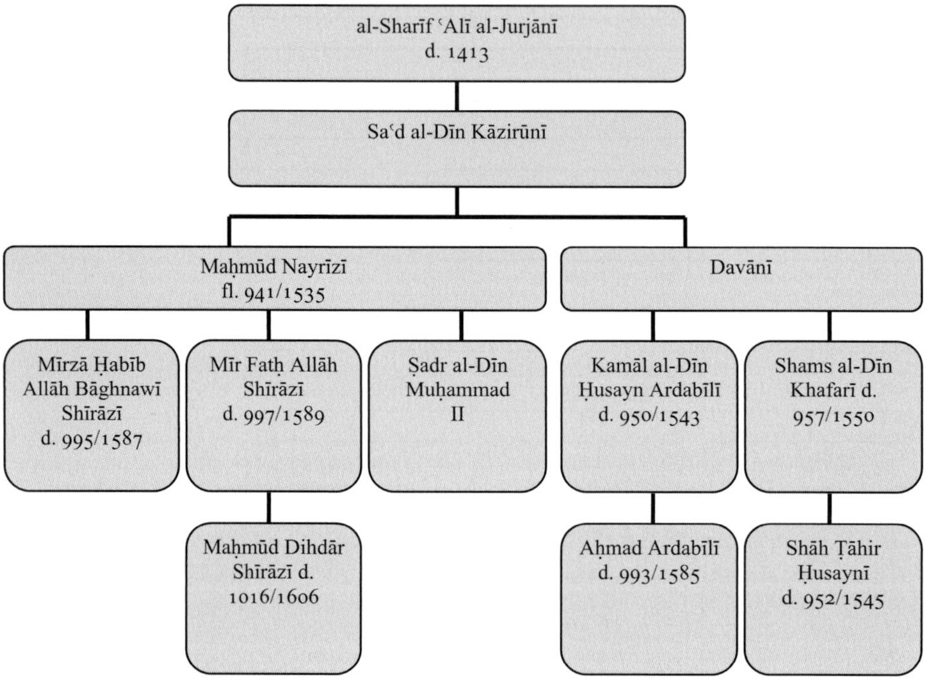

What sources can one use to construct an intellectual history of the period with particular reference to philosophical traditions?

I Works of authors themselves

Before one attempts to examine the historical and intellectual contexts and frameworks of discourse and the performativity of the texts and their intertextuality, the first place to start is the text itself. The *Anthologie* of Corbin and Āshtiyānī remains indispensable even if it does not provide critical editions of the revelant texts; in a number of cases the texts have been edited anew with *apparatus criticus*. Rarely is the manuscript that is the foundation of the edition discussed and at times the chosen manuscript is not the best one available: the *Glosses* of Qāḍī Saʿīd Qummī on the so-called *Theology of Aristotle* are edited on the basis of defective manuscripts from the

Āstān-i Quds collection in Mashhad despite the availability of an excellent and superior manuscript in Tehran (MS Tehran University Central Library 374). Nevertheless, Āshtiyānī provides a valuable and extended commentary on the texts locating them within their intellectual contexts and discussing the wider debates alluded within the texts. The very availability of the texts is another aspect of this significant contribution that he has made to Safavid intellectual history. This collection includes texts by the following thinkers:

1. Mīr Dāmād, a key figure of the Safavid renaissance, companion of Shah ʿAbbās I and teacher of Mullā Ṣadrā: selections from *al-Ṣirāṭ al-mustaqīm*,[304] his Glosses on *al-Shifāʾ*,[305] and *al-Qabasāt* on the incipience in perpetuity (*ḥudūth dahrī*) of the cosmos; [306] from *al-Qabasāt* and *al-Khulsa al-malakūtiyya* on essentialism (*aṣālat al-māhiyya*);[307] from *al-Qabasāt* on the nature of divine knowledge, [308] and from *Jadhavāt* on the intermediary ontological plane (*al-barzakh*).[309]
2. Mīr Findiriskī, an itinerant thinker, Indophile and Avicennian: extracts from his major Persian treatise *Risāla-yi Ṣināʿiyya*;[310] the complete text of his *Risāla fīʾl-ḥaraka* based on an unidentified manuscript in the Majlis-i Shūrā Library; and a short reply in Persian to a question posed by Āqā Muẓaffar Ḥusayn Kāshānī on whether quiddity (*māhiyya*) undergoes modulation (*tashkīk*) through intensification, once again based on two unidentified manuscripts in the Majlis-i Shūrā Library in Tehran.[311]
3. Mullā Ṣadrā: sixteen selections from his *al-Asfār al-arbaʿa*, *al-Mashāʿir*, *al-Mabdaʾ waʾl-maʿād*, and *al-Shawāhid al-rubūbiyya* on the fundamental status

---

[304] The selection from *al-Ṣirāṭ al-mustaqīm* is based on an unidentified manuscript in the library of the editor. The text itself has now been edited twice, once critically by ʿAlī Awjabī (Tehran 1381 Sh/2002), and in the same year an uncritical edition by ʿAbd Allāh Nūrānī in a collection of the treatises of Mīr Dāmād.

[305] The selection is based on the autograph MS Tehran University Central Library (Mishkāt Collection) 242 fol. 141r. Cf. Bihbahānī, *Ḥakīm-i Astarābād*, 133.

[306] These passages correspond to the edition of *al-Qabasāt* by M. Mohaghegh and T. Izutsu (Tehran 1977), 13–4, 53–5, 60–1.

[307] Cf. ed. Mohaghegh and Izutsu, 27, 36.

[308] Cf. ed. Mohaghegh and Izutsu, 241–2.

[309] The selection is based on a manuscript in the possession of the editor. The text is now available, edited by ʿAlī Awjabī (Tehran 1380 Sh/2001).

[310] The selections are based on 2 manuscripts in the library of the editor and correspond to the edition by ʿAlī Shihābī (Mashhad 1317 Sh/1938), 6–9, 18–21.

[311] I have not been able to identify the questioner in the biographical sources. He seems to have been a contemporary, perhaps a student also of Mullā Ṣadrā, who also wrote a response to some questions posed by him on the nature of the soul – see Chapter 2.

of existence;[312] thirteen selections from *al-Asfār al-arbaʿa*, his *Glosses* on *al-Shifāʾ* and *al-Shawāhid al-rubūbiyya* on mental existence;[313] five selections from *al-Asfār al-arbaʿa* and *al-Shawāhid al-rubūbiyya* on the proof for the existence and unicity of God;[314] three selections from *al-Asfār al-arbaʿa* modifying Aristotelian hylomorphism and presenting his own novel approach to causality;[315] nine selections from *al-Asfār al-arbaʿa* and *al-Shawāhid al-rubūbiyya* on his famous doctrine of substantial motion;[316] five selections from *al-Asfār al-arbaʿa* on the union of the intellecting subject and object, and the union of the human intellect with the active intellect;[317] three selections from *al-Asfār al-arbaʿa* on the imaginal realm and its epistemic value;[318] and four selections from *al-Asfār al-arbaʿa*, *al-shawāhid al-rubūbiyya* and his Glosses on *Sharḥ Ḥikmat al-ishrāq* on Platonic forms.[319]

4. Rajab ʿAlī Tabrīzī [d. 1080/1669–70], a student of Mīr Findiriskī and a thinker famed for his critique of the metaphysics of Mullā Ṣadrā and for advocating an apophatic approach to the questions of God and existence: the complete text of his Persian treatise affirming God based on MS Āstān-i Quds-i Raḍavī (Mashhad) 720; and eleven selections from his Arabic treatise *Aṣl al-aṣīl* or *Uṣūl al-Āṣafiyya* on the principles of metaphysics, physics and the nature of the soul based on MS Majlis-i Shūrā Library (Tehran) 4090.
5. ʿAbd al-Razzāq Lāhījī, student and son-in-law of Mullā Ṣadrā and a favourite of Shah ʿAbbās II: a selection on the extensional identity of existence and essence in extra-mental reality, critiques of the doctrine of the fundamental reality of existence and an analysis of the Sufi doctrine of monorealism from his commentary on the *Tajrīd al-iʿtiqād* of Naṣīr al-Dīn al-Ṭūsī entitled

---

[312] These correspond to the Beirut edition, I, 35–6, 37–9, 55–6; Āshtiyānī edition of *Sharḥ al-mashāʿir*, 41–3, 84–7, 226, 261–4; Āshtiyānī edition of *al-Mabdaʾ*, 10–1; Mashhad edition of *al-Shawāhid*, 47–8, 49–50, 54–5.

[313] These correspond to the Beirut edition, I, 263–5, 268; Tehran lithograph, 126–7, 128–9; Mashhad edition of *al-Shawāhid*, 24, 29–30, 31–2, 34–5, 65–6.

[314] These correspond to the Beirut edition, I, 105, 202; Mashhad edition of *al-Shawāhid*, 36–7.

[315] These correspond to the Beirut edition, II, 234–9, 286–9, 299–301, 327–9.

[316] These correspond to passages from the Beirut edition, III, 21–93; Mashhad edition of *al-Shawāhid*, 83–5, 95–7.

[317] These correspond to passages from the Beirut edition, III, 312–44.

[318] These correspond to passages from the Beirut edition, III, 475–80.

[319] These correspond to passages from the Beirut edition, I, 287–314; Mashhad edition of *al-Shawāhid*, 154–5, 160–1; Tehran lithograph, 273–4.

Shawāriq al-ilhām;[320] selections from his Persian treatise written for Shah ʿAbbās II, the *Gawhar-i murād* criticising the Sadrian doctrines of the fundamental reality of existence, the imaginal realm, substantial motion and the Sufi doctrine of the unity of existence; and selections from his Arabic *Glosses* on the *Marginalia* of al-Khafarī on *Sharḥ al-Tajrīd* based on a manuscript in the library of the editor on the proof of the existence of God.

6. Ḥusayn Khwānsārī [d. 1098/1686–7], another student of Mīr Findiriskī and a known teacher of Avicennism; selections from his Glosses on *al-Shifāʾ* based on MS Āstān-i Quds-i Raḍavī (Mashhad) 529.[321]
7. Mullā Shamsā Gīlānī [d. 1080/1669–70], a student of Mīr Dāmād and the key figure in propagating his school: the complete text of his work *Masālik al-yaqīn* on God being the only true referent of Being based on MS Tehran University Central Library (Mishkāt Collection) 436; selections from his Persian treatise *Iẓhār al-kamāl* on the same question based on an unidentified manuscript in the Majlis-i Shūrā Library; and selections from his Arabic treatise on the incipience of the cosmos (*ḥudūth al-ʿālam*) based on his autograph MS Tehran University Central Library (Mishkāt Collection) 200.
8. Sayyid Aḥmad ʿAlawī ʿĀmilī, the student and son-in-law of Mīr Dāmād: extracts from his Arabic commentary on *al-Shifāʾ* of Avicenna on the problem of resurrection and aspects of metaphysics.[322]
9. Mullā Muḥsin Fayḍ Kāshānī, the famous polymath and student of Mullā Ṣadrā: the complete text of *Uṣūl al-maʿārif*, an accessible epitome of *al-Asfār al-arbaʿa* of Mullā Ṣadrā.[323]
10. Muḥammad b. ʿAlī-Riḍā Āqājānī Māzandarānī, a student of Mullā Ṣadrā: extracts from his massive Arabic commentary on *al-Qabasāt* of Mīr Dāmād.
11. Shaykh Ḥusayn Tunikābunī, another student of Mullā Ṣadrā: two short Arabic treatises established on the basis of 'contemporary manuscripts', one on the notion of the imaginal realm and the other on the controversial doctrine of the oneness of being (*waḥdat al-wujūd*).
12. Qawām al-Dīn Muḥammad Rāzī [late 17th century], a student of Rajab ʿAlī Tabrīzī: a Persian treatise inquiring into the nature of First Philosophy.

---

320 Cf. Tehran lithograph 1307 H, II, 106–9, 284.

321 Cf. the edition of the text published by his memorial conference in Qum in 1999.

322 The edition is based on a manuscript in the collection of the editor dated 1098/1686–7.

323 This text was published separately as well with an extensive introduction by the editor in Tehran in 1975.

13. Muḥammad Rafīᶜ Pīrzāda [late 17th century], another student of Rajab ᶜAlī Tabrīzī: sections from his philosophical epitome in Arabic *al-Maᶜārif al-ilāhiyya.*
14. Muḥammad Bāqir Sabzavārī [d. 1090/1679], a famous philosopher and jurist and student of Fayḍ Kāshānī: sections from his *Glosses* (*Taᶜlīqāt*) on *al-Shifāʾ* of Avicenna.
15. Qāḍī Saᶜīd Qummī [d. 1107/1696], perhaps the most eminent and explicitly Neoplatonic student of Tabrīzī: a complete edition of his *Glosses* on the *Theology of Aristotle.*
16. Mīrzā Ḥasan b. ᶜAbd al-Razzāq Lāhījī [d. 1121/1709], the grandson of Mullā Ṣadrā: the complete text of his Arabic philosophical epitome *Zawāhir al-ḥikma.*[324]
17. Mullā Muḥammad Naᶜīmā Ṭāliqānī [d. after 1151/1738], a thinker of the late Safavid period who lived through the sack of Isfahan in 1722: the complete text of his Avicennian philosophical text *Aṣl al-uṣūl.*[325]
18. Sayyid Bahāʾ al-Dīn Muḥammad Ṭabāṭabāʾī [d. 1137/1725] known as Fāḍil-i Hindī because he was born in India: sections from his Arabic commentary on the text of Avicenna entitled *ᶜAwn ikhwān al-ṣafāʾ ᶜalā fahm Kitāb al-Shifāʾ.*[326]
19. Mullā ᶜAbd al-Raḥīm b. Muḥammad Yūnus Damāvandī Rāzī [d. before 1170/1757], a student of Muḥammad Ṣādiq Ardistānī and a Sufi: the complete text of a mystical treatise in Persian entitled *Sharḥ-i asrār-i asmāʾ-yi ḥusnā* or *Asrār-i Ḥusaynī.*
20. Mullā Muḥammad Ṣādiq Ardistānī [d. 1134/1722], perhaps the last major philosopher in Isfahan who along with Fāḍil-i Hindī died in the sack of the city by the Afghans: the complete text of an Arabic work entitled *al-Ḥikma al-Ṣādiqiyya* transcribed by his student Ḥamza Gīlānī based on his teachings.

---

[324] A critical edition of his Persian philosophical and theological treatises (*Āyīna-yi ḥikmat, Uṣūl-i dīn, Tazkīyat al-ṣuḥba, Durr-i maknūn, Sirr-i makhzūn, Hadyat al-musāfir*) has been published: *Rasāʾil-i fārsī*, ed. ᶜAlī Ṣadrāʾī-yi Khūʾī (Tehran 1375 Sh/1996).

[325] This was also published separately in Tehran in 1357 Sh/1978 by the Imperial Iranian Academy of Philosophy.

[326] *Al-Dharīᶜa* IV, n. 1868. A Persian text of his entitled *Ḥikmat-i Khāqāniyya* was published in Tehran by MM in 1377 Sh/1998. That work is divided into three sections: logic, physics and metaphysics. On his life and works, see Rasūl Jaᶜfarīyān, *Bahāʾ al-Dīn Muḥammad Iṣfahānī mashhūr bih Fāḍil-i Hindī* (Qum 1416/1996), especially 57–8 where he indicates *ᶜAwn ikhwān al-ṣafāʾ* dated 1084/1673–4 in MS Tehran University Central Library 1864 (fol. 111–162, *naskhī*).

21. Mullā Ismāʿīl Māzandarānī Khājūʾī [d. 1173/1760], a student of Fāḍil-i Hindī and Ardistānī: the complete text of an Arabic work on resurrection entitled *Thamarat al-fuʾād*, and an Arabic treatise on time (*fī ibṭāl al-zamān al-mawhūm*).[327]
22. Muḥammad Bīdābādī [d. 1198/1783], a major figure in the revival of the school of Mullā Ṣadrā: the complete text of a Persian treatise called *al-Mabdaʾ waʾl-maʿād*.
23. Mullā Muḥammad Mahdī Narāqī [d. 1209/1794–5], a major polymath and jurist who lived into the early Qajar period: the complete text of his philosophical epitome in Arabic entitled *Qurrat al-ʿuyūn*.
24. Mullā ʿAlī Nūrī [d. 1246/1831], a major figure in the revival of philosophy in Isfahan and the teacher of Mullā Hādī Sabzavārī [d. 1289/1873]: the complete text of four Arabic treatises on metaphysics and semantics – *Risāla basīṭ al-ḥaqīqa*, *Risāla waḥdat al-wujūd*, *al-Maʿānī al-ʿāmma*, and *fī anna wujūd al-mumkin zāʾidun ʿalāʾl-māhiyya*.
25. Mullā Naẓar ʿAlī Gīlānī [fl. 1193/1779], a student of Bīdābādī: the complete text of an Arabic philosophical work *Kitāb al-Tuḥfa*.

Despite the existence of this *Anthologie*, most of these thinkers have never been studied in European languages.

The editions of works by Mullā Ṣadrā have already been noted. The Sadra Islamic Philosophy Research Institute (*Bunyād-i pazhūhishī-yi ḥikmat-i islāmī-yi Ṣadrā*), a semi-official body run by Sayyid Muḥammad Khāminihī from offices in northern Tehran, has undertaken the task of producing critical editions of his work, some of which have appeared (and are noted in Chapter 2). They have also commissioned complete English translations of his corpus (only one translation has appeared also noted in the previous chapter). Thus far, they have organised two major international conferences in 1999 and 2004 designed partly to fulfil the political goal of 'dialogue among civilisations'; five volumes of proceedings of the first conference have appeared. Another contribution is their journal *Khiradnāma-yi Ṣadrā* [issue 1 came out in 1374 Sh/1995 and built up to the conference in 1999]. The journal in particular has played an important role in presenting in many ways some of the most novel interpretations of Sadrian philosophy and other aspects of thought in the

[327] There is a new critical edition of the latter undertaken by Sayyid Aḥmad Tuysirkānī in *Sabʿ rasāʾil* (Tehran 1381 Sh/2002), 241–83.

Safavid period and often juxtaposed them to fruitful comparisons with other philosophical systems.

But the major editor and publisher of philosophical texts from the Safavid period has become the cultural organisation based in central Tehran, *Mīrāth-i Maktūb* (the Written Heritage Organisation). They have attempted to fill the lacunae of the *Anthologie*, publishing texts pre-Dāmād and preparing reliable critical editions. There are a number of other publishers producing editions of relevant texts, not least the publication section of the Ministry of Culture and Islamic Guidance (*Vizārat-i farhang va irshād-i islāmī*). The best way to keep current with the industry is to consult research journals. These organs provide useful information about manuscripts, editions in progress, critical reviews of new publications and other assessments about manuscripts and the production of editions. The main players are the following. The most recent journal in this area is the bi-annual *Nāma-yi Bahāristān*, the official publication of the publications department of the Majlis-i Shūrā Library based in Maydān-i Bahāristān in Tehran [issue 1 came out in 1379 Sh/2000]. *Āyīna-yi Mīrāth* is the publication of *Mīrāth-i Maktūb* and is published bi-annually [issue 1 came out in 1375 Sh/1996]. *Āyīna-yi Pazhūhish* is a quarterly journal published by another major religious organisation and press, *Daftar-i Tablīghāt-i Islāmī [Islamic Propagation Office]*, a national body that has major centres in Qum and Tehran [issue 1 came out in 1369 Sh/1990]. *Waqf: Mīrāth-i Jāvīdān* is a quarterly published by the *Sāzmān-i Awqāf va Umūr-i Khayriyya [Oqaf and Charities Organisation]*, an official body and is concerned mainly with historical and architectural heritage but does at times address intellectual history [issue 1 came out in 1372 Sh/1993]. An older organ is *Nashr-i Dānish*, the organ of the *Nashr-i Dānishgāhī-yi Īrān [Iran University Press]*, perhaps the main industry publication which addresses all manner of editions of pre-modern texts, Once we have access to the edited texts we can undertake the task of analysing and assessing the thought expressed in them and in the commentary traditions associated with them.

II Histories of Philosophy

A key genre of texts that assists in the intellectual framing of philosophical texts are histories of philosophies, and doxographies that compile views of past philosophers and often express key ideas about how the author and perhaps the intellectual attitudes of his time saw the philosophical enterprise. The classical works of this genre, especially the *Ṣiwān al-ḥikma* cycle, *al-Milal wa'l-niḥal* of Abu'l-Fatḥ Muḥammad b.

ʿAbd al-Karīm al-Shahrastānī [d. 548/1153] and *Nuzhat al-arwāḥ* of Shams al-Dīn Muḥammad Shahrazūrī [fl. 688/1288], not only provided Safavid thinkers with valuable accounts of philosophical thought in the classical Islamic period but also was a preliminary to pre-Islamic thought Pre-Socratic, Platonic and Aristotelian.[328] They presented a vision of philosophy as a holistic practice, an art of living and stressed the key six definitions of philosophy perpetuated by the Platonic tradition in late Antiquity (the pseudo-Platonic definitions later recounted by al-Kindī in the Islamic classical period).[329] Hellenic thought remained significant in the Safavid period, in particular the famous *Theology of Aristotle (Uthūlūjiyā)* being an adapted paraphrase of sections of *Enneads* IV to VI of Plotinus,[330] and even (neo-)Pythagorean thought in the form of the *Golden Verses (carmina aurea)* attributed to Pythagoras with the commentary of Iamblichus.[331] The former retained an especial appeal and was available in at least two Arabic recensions, one prepared with notes by Ghiyāth al-Dīn Manṣūr Dashtakī,[332] and also a Persian translation (*taḥrīr*). It is not clear who prepared the translation; it may have been Abuʾl-Khayr Muḥammad Taqī al-Dīn b. Muḥammad al-Fārisī [d. 948/1542], a student of Manṣūr Dashtakī.[333] Certainly it was available as the Persian version is cited by Mīr Dāmād in his *Jadhavāt va mavāqīt* and by a late seventeenth century philosopher ʿAlīqulī b. Qarajghay Khān in his *Iḥyāʾ-yi ḥikmat*.[334]

---

[328] Abū Sulaymān al-Sijistānī [d. 330/941–2], *Muntakhab ṣiwān al-ḥikma*, ed. D. M. Dunlop (The Hague 1979); ed. ʿA-R. Badawī (Tehran 1977); Ẓahīr al-Dīn ʿAlī b. Zayd al-Bayhaqī [d. 565/1169–70], *Tatimmat Ṣiwān al-ḥikma*, ed. T. ʿAjam (Beirut 1994); al-Shahrastānī, *al-Milal waʾl-niḥal*, ed. M. S. al-Kaylānī (2 vols, Cairo 1966); Shahrazūrī, *Nuzhat al-arwāḥ*, ed. S. K. Aḥmad (2 vols, Hyderabad 1976).

[329] Pseudo-Plato, *Definitions*, 414b; cf. H. G. Ingenkamp, *Untersuchungen zu den pseudo-platonischen Definitionem* (Wiesbaden 1967); J. Domanski, *La philosophie, théorie ou manière de vivre?* (Paris 1996), 4–7; Jean Jolivet, 'L'idée de la sagesse et sa function dans la philosophie des 4e et 5e siècles', *Arabic Sciences and Philosophy* 1 (1991), 37–8.

[330] The standard edition of the text remains ʿAbd al-Raḥmān Badawī (Cairo 1947); for a study of the text, see Fritz Zimmermann, 'The Origins of the so-called *Theology of Aristotle*', in J. Kraye et al (eds), *Pseudo-Aristotle in the Middle Ages* (London 1986), 110–240, and Peter Adamson, *The Arabic Plotinus: A Philosophical Study of the Theology of Aristotle* (London 2002).

[331] Iamblichus (attr.), *Neuplatonische Pythagorica in arabischem Gewande: Der Kommentar des Iamblichus zu den Carmina Aurea, ein verloner griechischer Text in arabischer Überlieferung*, ed. Hans Daiber (Amsterdam 1995).

[332] I know of two manuscript copies of this text: MS Princeton Yahuda-Garrett 1029, fol. 112–95, and MS Tehran University Central Library 5392.

[333] *Al-Dharīʿa* I, 120, citing MS Āstān-i Quds-i Raḍavī 1070.

[334] Mīr Dāmād, *Jadhavāt*, ed. ʿAlī Awjabī (Tehran 1380 Sh/2001), 15, 27, 49 *inter alia*; ʿAlī-qulī Khān, *Iḥyāʾ-yi Ḥikmat*, ed. Fāṭima Fanā (Tehran 1377 Sh/1998), II, 95–6 *inter alia*. ʿAlī-qulī Khān is also credited

The most significant history of philosophy for the Safavid period, however, was a contemporary account divided into four sections entitled *Maḥbūb al-qulūb*, written by Quṭb al-Dīn Muḥammad b. ʿAlī Ashkivarī known as Sharīf-i Lāhījī [d. ca. 1095/1684], a student of Mīr Dāmād.[335] As a Shiʿi thinker and philosopher, his intention was to produce an Arabic account of philosophers from the beginning of the art up to his time, to demonstrate the continuity of the transmission of philosophical knowledge from its prophetic (Adam, Seth etc) and Hellenic (Plato, Aristotle, etc) roots through the Islamic traditions of philosophy and mysticism up to the Safavid period. He embellishes his account with a number of Persian verses and it seems that he is locating his work, as indeed were the authors of the *Ṣiwān al-ḥikma* cycle, within the genre of belles-lettres. The work is divided into an introduction that presents a common myth of the origins of philosophy, and three sections (*maqāla*). *Maqāla* I draws heavily upon previous sources and is a presentation of the story of philosophy and philosophers before Islam. *Maqāla* II is the most valuable section and continues the story through Islam up to the time of the author; he includes philosophers and Sufis. *Maqāla* III shifts tack and is a standard history of the Shiʿi Imams. The style of the work and the structure reveals some basic assumptions about the nature of philosophy as it was commonly seen in the Safavid period by its practitioners: true philosophy is based on discursive reason, mystical intuition and divinely-granted wisdom through the channel of prophecy and the imamate. It is thus no surprise to find him mixing his sources: earlier doxographies, Qurʾānic verses, *ḥadīth*, and Arabic and Persian poetry.

But arguably one of the most valuable sources for the history of Islamic philosophical tradition in the Safavid period, for the attitudes to the pre-Safavid traditions and in particular for its use of the neglected thinkers of the school of Shiraz is *al-Asfār al-Arbaʿa* of Mullā Ṣadrā. It is often said that his work is a synthesis of four intellectual traditions: the theology of Shiʿi *kalām*, the philosophy of Avicenna and Avicennism, the illuminationist (*ishrāqī*) philosophy of Shihāb al-Dīn Suhrawardī known as Shaykh al-Ishrāq, and the metaphysical Sufism of Ibn ʿArabī and his

with a Persian commentary on the *Theology* which is extant in MS Āstān-i Quds 1070, cited in *al-Dharīʿa* I:120, IV:225.

[335] Ashkiwarī, *Maḥbūb al-qulūb: al-maqāla al-ūlā*, eds. I. Dībājī and Ḥ. Ṣidqī (Tehran 1378 Sh/1999). The only complete printing of the text is a mistake-ridden Shiraz lithograph of 1317/1899–1900. On him, see Jalāl al-Dīn Urmawī, Introduction to *Tafsīr-i Sharīf-i Lāhījī*, ed. M. I. Āyatī (Tehran 1340 Sh/1961), I, 5–85.

school.[336] In terms of the number of citations from these figures and their texts and they interpretations of their thought in the Safavid period, there can be no doubt that these influences are significant. Furthermore, these figures are fairly well known and their own works have been published and made available which facilitates research. Beyond these, *al-Asfār al-Arbaʿa* is also a valuable source and bears the imprint of some of the major figures of the school of Shiraz and their unpublished works.

1) Jalāl al-Dīn Davānī and his treatises on *Ithbāt al-wājib* and his *marginalia* on *Sharḥ al-Tajrīd*: critique of his essentialism;[337] critique of his view (and the claim that it is an Illuminationist doctrine) that quiddity (*māhiyya*) and not existence is the first thing produced by the One;[338] critique of his rejection of a unitive relationship between body and soul;[339] critique of his method of proving the existence of God that he calls experience of theosis (*dhawq al-taʾalluh*).[340]
2) Ṣadr al-Dīn Muḥammad Dashtakī and his treatises on *Ithbāt al-wājib*: approval of his position on the unitive relationship of the body and the soul;[341] affirms his position on the fundamental reality of existence;[342] defends his proof for the existence of God (*burhān al-Ṣiddīqīn*);[343] and agrees that divine knowledge is not identical with the attributes of seeing and hearing.[344]
3) Ghiyāth al-Dīn Manṣūr Dashtakī and especially his *Kashf al-ḥaqāʾiq al-Muḥammadiyya*, a commentary on *Ithbāt al-wājib* of his father and a defence of it against the critique of Davānī that he wrote in Muḥarram 947/May–June 1540: approves of his view that the divine essence gives meaning to the

[336] Seyyed Hossein Nasr, *Sadr al-Din Shirazi and His Transcendent Theosophy* (Tehran 1977), 55–6; J. W. Morris (tr), *The Wisdom of the Throne* (Princeton 1981), introduction, 22–9.

[337] Beirut edition, I, 60.

[338] Beirut edition, I, 399, 407.

[339] Beirut edition, V, 306, 309.

[340] Beirut edition, VI, 63, 78, 82.

[341] Beirut edition, V, 286–9, 292–4, VIII, 392–3.

[342] Beirut edition, I, 59 [*mā dhahaba ilayhi baʿḍu ahl al-tadqīq*], 315 [*wa salaka baʿḍu l-amājid maslakan daqīqan qarīban min al-taḥqīq*], 321.

[343] Beirut edition, VI, 81–2 [*qarīb al-manhaj min manhaj al-ḥaqq*].

[344] Beirut edition, VI, 423.

concept of existence;[345] and approves of his own proof of the existence of God that merely defends the view of his father.[346]

4) Shams al-Dīn Muḥammad Khafarī and his *Ithbāt al-wājib* and *marginalia* on *Sharḥ al-Tajrīd*: approves of his proof for the existence of God;[347] and approves of his propagation of Avicennian ideas on representational forms.[348]

These are just a few examples. A more thorough reading of the nine volume text will not doubt yield further insights into the reception of philosophical traditions from the late Timurid and early Safavid periods.

III Biographical dictionaries and Bibliographical sources

No student of Islamic thought, not least Islamic Studies can be unaware of this key genre of literature.[349] Biographical dictionaries provide short narratives of the lives of scholars insofar as they are individuals within a network of scholarly transmission and as authors and teachers of texts. Although they can be formulaic, imitating established tropic discourses of the narrative of lives, in many cases they contain invaluable and exclusive material on the biographies of prominent scholars including the licenses that they received and issued for transmission. There are further sub-genre of this type of source: dictionaries specialising in narrators of tradition (*rijāl*), lists of poets and examples of their works (*tadhkira*), classes of religious scholars (*ṭabaqāt*, *tarājim*), dictionaries arranged by city or region, and even autobiographical works that yield important information about networks of scholarship and the sociology of knowledge and its transmission.[350] As with any sources, the accounts of these dictionaries ought

---

345 Beirut edition, VI, 74.

346 Beirut edition, VI, 86 [*huwa sirru abīhi Ghiyāthu aʿāẓami l-sādāt waʾl-ʿulamāʾ al-Manṣūru l-muʾayyad min ʿālami l-malakūt*].

347 Beirut edition, VI, 37 [*baʿḍu l-muḥaqqīn min ahl Fārs*].

348 Beirut edition, VI, 221–7.

349 Ibrahim Hafsi, 'Recherches sur le genre *Tabaqat* dans la littérature arabe', *Arabica* 23 (1976), 227–65, 24 (1977), 1–41, 150–86; T. Khalidi, 'Islamic biographical dictionaries', *Muslim World* 63 (1973), 53–65; idem, *Arabic Historical Thought in the Classical Period* (Cambridge 1994), 204–10; Paul Auchterlonie, *Arabic Biographical Dictionaries: A Summary Guide and Bibliography* (Durham 1987); Chase Robinson, *Islamic Historiography* (Cambridge 2003), 68–74. Perhaps the most thoughtful study is Wadad al-Qadi, 'Biographical dictionaries: inner structure and cultural significance', in G. N. Atiyeh (ed.), *The Book in the Islamic World* (Albany, NY 1995), 93–122.

350 On autobiographies in the pre-modern period, see D. Reynolds (ed.), *Interpreting the Self* (Berkeley, CA 2001).

to be critically scrutinised and used; inconsistencies abound and some sources are more accurate and useful than others.

Two early works of the genre are *Jāmiʿ al-ruwāt wa-izāḥat al-ishtibāhāt ʿan al-ṭuruq waʾl-isnād* of Muḥammad b. ʿAlī Ardabīlī Gharawī [d. 1001/1593],[351] and *Naqd al-rijāl* of Muṣṭafā b. Ḥusayn Ḥusaynī Tafrishī Iṣfahānī [d. ca. 1030/1621],[352] which was completed in 1015/1606.[353] As their titles suggest, they are mainly concerned with the transmission of *ḥadīth* and as such contain entries of scholars from the earliest generations of Shiʿi scholarship until the Safavid period including along the way important figures for our purposes such as Shaykh Bahāʾī and Mīr Dāmād.

A slightly different and rather triumphalist work is the Persian *Majālis al-muʾminīn* compiled by Sayyid Nūr Allāh b. Sharīf al-Dīn Ḥusaynī Marʿashī Tustarī/Shūstarī [d. 1019/1610] popularly known as Qāḍī Nūr Allāh because he served in that capacity in Lahore as an official Mughal judge and *Shahīd-i thālith* (the third martyr) in the Shiʿi tradition because he was killed for his faith on the orders of the Emperor Jahangir.[354] Having studied in his hometown and in Mashhad, he moved to the Mughal court in 992/1584 because of the instability of the Khurāsān frontier with the Uzbeks. Earning the favour of the Emperor Akbar, he was appointed to various positions and became famous as a staunch supporter of the Iranian and Shiʿi notables at court. The Sunni courtier and scholar ʿAbd al-Qādir Badāyūnī [d. 1024/1615] wrote of him in his chronicle *Muntakhab al-tawārīkh*,

> Although he is by confession a Shiʿi, he is distinguished for his impartiality, justice, virtue, modesty, piety, composure and other such qualities as are possessed by noble men. He is famed for his learning, clemency and quick-witted understanding.[355]

---

[351] This was published in 2 volumes in Najaf in 1966, and re-issued in 1982 in Qum by the Library of al-Sayyid al-Najafī al-Marʿashī.

[352] Muʾassasat Āl al-bayt li-iḥyāʾ al-turāth issued a modern edition in 5 volumes from Qum in 1998.

[353] As with most works of this type, a completion (*takmila*) was later added by ʿAbd al-Nabī b. ʿAlī al-Kāẓimī [d. ca. 1256/1841] (2 vols, Najaf 1973).

[354] The most recent edition is *Majālis al-muʾminīn* (2 vols, Tehran 1377 Sh/1998). On him, see RU V, 265–75; S. A. A. Rizvi, *A Socio-intellectual History of the Isnāʿasharī Shīʿīs in India* (New Delhi/Canberra 1986), I, 342–84, II, 1–4; *Rawḍāt*, VIII, 146–8; Sayyid Shihāb al-Dīn Marʿashī Najafī, 'Ḥayāt al-ʿAllāma', in *Iḥqāq al-Ḥaqq wa-izhāq al-bāṭil* (Qum n.d.), I, lāmhā to qāfsīnalif.

[355] Badāyūnī, *Muntakhab al-tawārīkh*, eds. Maulvi Ahmed Ali et al (rpt., Tehran 1379 Sh/2001), III, 93–4.

The text itself was compiled between 990/1582 before setting out for India and 1010/1602 in Lahore. It is divided into an introduction and twelve *majālis* on classes of individuals. The purpose of his work, as indeed of most of his work, was to defend Shiʿism and in the *Majālis*, he claims for Shiʿism a number of famous individuals who either had no strong religious beliefs or were certainly not Shiʿi. Thus one ought to bear in mind when consulting this source that it fits a belle-lettrist audience well but some aspects of it may be of questionable historical value. *Majālis* VI and VII on Sufis and philosophers are particularly significant, especially since the latter contains valuable references to the philosophers of Shiraz about whom so little is known. Because the line between a scholar and poet was usually quite thin, the final two *Majālis* on Arabic and Persian poets is also worth consulting.

A major work that continues the desire to focus on the transmission of *ḥadīth* but contains much more is *Amal al-āmil* compiled between 1096/1685 and 1097/1686 by Muḥammad b. al-Ḥasan al-Ḥurr al-ʿĀmilī [d. 1104/1693], a student of Fayḍ Kāshānī and Majlisī II. Entries are rather short and pithy except for major figures. There is also a short autobiographical account within it.[356] The work is divided into two parts: a section of ʿĀmilī scholars entitled *Amal al-āmil fī ʿulamāʾ Jabal ʿĀmil*, and a section on other scholars entitled *Tadhkirat al-mutabaḥḥirīn fīʾl-ʿulamāʾ al-mutaʾakhkhirīn*. In the introduction, he sets forth his twelve reasons (*fawāʾid*) for compiling the work:[357] these include the need to understand and know who the narrators of traditions are in order to assess their probity, knowing the chains of transmissions as expressed in licenses, and requirement to update the earlier works of this kind such as the classical biographical sources and bibliographies (*fihrist*) of al-Ṭūsī [d. 460/1067] and Muntajab al-Dīn ʿAlī Ibn Bābawayh al-Rāzī [fl. 600/1203–4].[358] As was the custom for such works, a number of continuations (*istidrākāt* – fourteen are known to exist) were written to this text that filled in the lacunae and extended the picture of scholarly networks through to the end of the Safavid period and beyond.[359] The most important of these have also been edited. His student Mīrzā ʿAbd Allāh Tabrīzī Iṣfahānī known as Afandī [d. ca. 1130/1717] wrote glosses on it that rectify some mistakes; the resulting text is either known as *Ishtibāhāt al-Amal* or

---

[356] AA I, 141–54.

[357] AA I, 4–21.

[358] Al-Ṭūsī, *Fihrist* (Qum 1997); Ibn Bābawayh al-Rāzī, *Fihrist*, ed. Sayyid ʿAbd al-ʿAzīz Ṭabāṭabāʾī (Tehran 1984).

[359] S. A. Ḥusaynī, Introduction to AA I, 59–61.

Taʿlīqāt al-Amal.[360] ʿAbd al-Nabī Qazwīnī wrote his *Tatmīm* in Najaf in 1191/1777 and included material on the contemporaries of al-Ḥurr as well as other students of Majlisī II.[361] Finally, in the twentieth century another ʿĀmilī scholar al-Sayyid al-Ḥasan al-Ṣadr [d. 1354/1935] wrote a completion (*takmila*) which remains a popular source of reference for the late Safavid and Qajar periods.[362]

The Shiʿi scholar and litterateur Sayyid ʿAlī-Khān b. Aḥmad Ibn Maʿṣūm Shīrāzī [d. ca. 1118/1707] was a scion of the famous Dashtakī family of Shiraz. His father had been the vizier at the Shiʿi court of Golconda in the Deccan at Hyderabad and he himself grew up in Medina.[363] He compiled two different works. The first is a poetic *tadhkira* entitled *Sulāfat al-ʿaṣr fī maḥāsin al-shuʿarāʾ bi-kulli miṣr*, a study of Arabic poets from different parts of the world. In this work, he sets out to describe the biographies of famous poets divided by their geographical location and provides example of their verses. There are five parts: the first is on poets from the Holy Cities and is a useful source for his own teachers and for Shiʿism in Mecca and Medina; the second concerns Syrian and Egyptian poets; the third is on Yemeni poets; the fourth, of particular use for the study of Safavid Iran, discuss the poets of Iran, Bahrain and Iraq; and the final part introduces some poets of North Africa. Since most of the famous thinkers of the Safavid period fancied themselves as poets both in Arabic and Persian, the likes of Shaykh Bahāʾī, Mīr Dāmād and Mullā Ṣadrā can be found in part four. The entry of Mīr Dāmād, whose pen-name was Ishrāq, is particularly extensive.[364] The second work that he composed is more of a standard biographical dictionary (*ṭabaqāt*) of Shiʿi scholars: *al-Darajāt al-rafīʿa fī ṭabaqāt al-Shīʿa*, a fairly brief survey that focuses on his circle of teacher and famous individuals such as Shaykh Bahāʾī and Mīr Dāmād.[365] It is also unusual in that it tends to focus on scholars of the Safavid period, whilst most other biographical dictionaries, especially the comprehensive ones, tend to start in the classical period.

Mīrzā ʿAbd Allāh b. ʿĪsā Beg Tabrīzī Iṣfahānī known as Afandī [d. ca. 1130/1717] wrote *Riyāḍ al-ʿulamāʾ wa-ḥiyāḍ al-fuḍalāʾ* as an extensive source on the

---

360 The text was edited by Sayyid Aḥmad al-Ḥusaynī (Qum 1410/1989).

361 The text was edited by Sayyid Aḥmad al-Ḥusaynī (Qum 1407/1987). For a study of the text, see R. Jaʿfarīyān, *Maqālāt-i Tārīkhī* (Qum 1417/1997), 149–66.

362 The text was edited by Sayyid Aḥmad Ḥusaynī (Qum in 1406/1986).

363 See Shākir Hādī Shukr, Introduction to *Dīwān* (Beirut 1988), and also to his *Riḥla* [*Ṣalwat al-Gharīb wa-uswat al-arīb*] (Beirut 1988).

364 SA 486–7.

365 Ibn Maʿṣūm, *al-Darajāt al-rafīʿa fī ṭabaqāt al-Shīʿa*, ed. M. Ṣ. Āl Baḥr al-ʿUlūm (Najaf 1382/1962).

scholars of his age.[366] A prominent member of the Majlisī circle, he included a number of licenses, used manuscript sources, cited example of manuscripts and their provenance, and cited some earlier works such as *Amal al-āmil* and *Sulāfat al-ʿaṣr.*[367] An extensive biographical dictionary, divided into two parts, one on Shiʿi scholars and the other on Sunni and non-Twelver figures (this section remains unpublished), it is an essential tool for studying Safavid learned culture. Despite the Akhbārī taste of his time that tended to be rather critical of Mullā Ṣadrā, he is complimentary.

One ought not to neglect non-Shiʿi biographical dictionaries. The main source for Arab biographies of the period is *Khulāṣat al-āthār fī aʿyān al-qarn al-ḥādī ʿashar* compiled by the Syrian scholar Muḥammad al-Amīn b. Faḍl Allāh al-Muḥibbī al-Dimashqī [d. 1111/1699].[368] He is especially useful for discussion of Shiʿi scholars within the Ottoman Empire, especially the ʿĀmilīs, and for those who were resident in the Holy Cities and their visitors. Entries can be found on Astarābādī, and his detractor Nūr al-Dīn ʿAlī al-ʿĀmilī.[369]

Given the significance of the migration of litterateurs and scholars from Safavid Iran to India, one ought to consult some Indian biographical dictionaries.[370] One ought to be careful of foisting modern national categories on culture of the period: the Safavid, Mughal (and other Indian) and Ottoman areas shared many assumptions about the nature of culture and pursuit of knowledge and especially shared a Persianate culture.[371] Thinkers often moved freely between the spheres as would be clear from a study of the Dashtakī family. Although it is rather late, the best

---

366 Ed. S. A. Ḥusaynī (6 vols, Qum 1981). A biography of the compiler written by the late al-Sayyid Shihāb al-Dīn al-Marʿashī al-Najafī [d. 1990] entitled *Zihr al-Riyāḍ fī tarjamat ṣāḥib al-Riyāḍ* prefaces volume 1 of the edition.

367 Rasul Jaʿfariyan, 'The immigrant manuscripts', in A. J. Newman (ed.), *Society and Culture in the Early Modern Middle East: Studies on Iran in the Safavid Period* (Islamic History and Civilization XLVI, Leiden 2003), 352.

368 There is an old Būlāq edition in 4 volumes, (Cairo 1284/1867–8).

369 Al-Muḥibbī, *Khulāṣat al-āthār*, IV, 46–7, III, 132–4.

370 See Masahi Haneda, 'The emigration of Iranian elites to India during the 16th-18th centuries', in M. Szuppe (ed.), *L'Héritage timouride Iran-Asie Centrale-Inde XVe-XVIIIe siècles* (Tashkent/Aix-en-Provence 1997), 129–43; Abolghasem Dadvar, *Iranians in Mughal Politics and Society, 1606–68* (New Delhi 1999) [note that a portion of this work has been plagiarised from Haneda]; Sanjay Subrahmanyam, 'Iranians abroad: Intra-Asian elite migration and early modern state formation', *Journal of Asian Studies* 51 (1992), 340–63; M. Athar Ali, *The Mughal Nobility under Aurangzeb* (Aligarh 1966, rpt, New Delhi 2001); Afzal Husain, *The Nobility under Akbar and Jahangir* (New Delhi 1999); Aḥmad Gulchīn Maʿānī, *Kāravān-i Hind* (2 vols, Mashhad 1369 Sh/1990).

371 Francis Robinson, 'Ottomans-Safavids-Mughals: Shared knowledge and connective systems', *JIS* 8 (1997), 151–84; Muzaffar Alam, 'The pursuit of Persian: language in Mughal Politics', *MAS* 32 (1998), 317–49.

work (albeit not free from criticism and mistakes) is *Nuzhat al-khawāṭir wa-bahjat al-masāmiʿ waʾl-nawāẓir* by the Indian scholar, Sayyid ʿAbd al-Ḥayy b. Fakhr al-Dīn Ḥasanī Lakhnawī [d. 1341/1923], a thinker who was the director of Nadwat al-ʿUlamāʾ in Lucknow from 1915 to 1923.[372] A prominent scholar, his biographical compilation is practically the only major source for the study of thinkers from the Mughal period onwards and is a testament to his critical insight. The decision to write the work in Arabic was significant since he wished to demonstrate to the wider Muslim world the major role that Indian thinkers had played in the formation of Islamic culture.[373] Entries include Sunni and Shiʿi thinkers, native Indian scholars and immigrants in India. A recent study of the influence of Mullā Ṣadrā upon philosophical traditions in the Indian seminaries has made extensive use of this source.[374]

In passing two works merit mentioning because they are unreliable and partial. The gossipy *Qiṣaṣ al-ʿulamāʾ* of the Qajar scholar Muḥammad Tunikābunī adds nothing of value and merely rehearses earlier reliable information embellishing it with outlandish legends.[375] He mentions two in particular with respect to Mullā Ṣadrā that proffer a good story but are without foundation. First, he quotes a dream in which Mullā Ṣadrā complains to his dead teacher Mīr Dāmād about his rough treatment in Isfahan. But we know that he survived his teacher by a mere five years and none of that time seems to have been spent being harassed in Isfahan. Second, he cites an anecdote about the student and his arrogant master. One day Mullā Ṣadrā disputing with another student the relative merits of Mīr Dāmād and previous philosophers; whenever he is asked his opinion, he is told from behind a screen by a hidden Mīr Dāmād that he should always reply that the best philosopher of all time is Mīr Dāmād.

[372] Abuʾl-Ḥasan ʿAlī Nadwī, *Ḥayāt-i ʿAbd al-Ḥayy* (Lucknow 1970); M. Q. Zaman, 'Arabic, the Arab Middle East, and the definition of Muslim identity in twentieth century India', *JRAS* 8 (1998), 59–81, especially 62–3, 74–5; M. I. J. Nadwī and S. T. Khān, *Tārīkh-i Nadwat al-ʿUlamāʾ* (2 vols, Lucknow 1983–4); B. Metcalf, *Islamic Revival in British India: Deoband, 1860–1900* (Princeton 1982), 335–47; Jamal Malik, 'The making of a council: the Nadwat al-ʿUlamā'', *ZDMG* 114 (1994), 60–90. There are numerous printings of this work, mainly issued from Lucknow or Nadwat al-ʿUlamāʾ. The copy that I use is made up of 8 volumes (Karachi 1991).

[373] This was the subject of his contribution: *al-Thaqāfa al-Islāmiyya fīʾl-Hind* (Damascus 1957).

[374] Akbar Thubūt, *Faylasūf-i Shīrāzī dar Hind* (Tehran 1381 Sh/2002). On the curriculum and the study of philosophy in North India, see Jamal Malik, *Islamische Gelehrtenkultur im Nordindien: Entwicklungsgeschichte und Tendenzen am Beispiel von Lucknow* (Islamic History and Civilization vol. XIX, Leiden 1997).

[375] Tehran lithograph 1888.

While arrogance was never a virtue from which Safavid scholars shied away, the setting of the story let alone the contents seem too bizarre and fantastical.

The second text is useful in its proper context of providing a history of Sufism in Iran but is a hopelessly misleading source on many philosophers of the period.[376] This is *Ṭarāʾiq al-ḥaqāʾiq* written by the Niʿmatullāhī Sufi Maʿṣūm-ʿAlī-Shāh Shīrāzī [d. 1344/1926].[377] His repeated attempt to win major Safavid figures for the Sufi cause leads him to claim that Mullā Ṣadrā, Mīr Dāmād and Shaykh Bahāʾī were members of the Nūrbakhshī order. However, there is no corroborating evidence for this and he himself does not cite an actual source.

Finally, in this category, one ought to signal the significance of two poetic *tadhkiras*. Both are an important source for literary and learned society in Isfahan in the seventeenth century, especially the reign of Shah ʿAbbās II. Muḥammad Ṭāhir Naṣrābādī hosted a salon for poets and literati at his coffeehouse in the Lunbān area of Isfahan. His *Tadhkira* (written mainly in 1083/1672–3) contains valuable accounts of poets and Sufis in the generation of the students of Mullā Ṣadrā.[378] A later source is the work of Luṭf-ʿAlī Beg Ādhar [d. 1194/1780] called *Ātashkada-yi Ādhar*, an account of poets of the later Safavid period divided by their place of birth.[379]

I have focused on contemporary Safavid sources on the whole because modern works tend to rely upon them and do not add much to the account. However, I should indicate one bibliographical source that is indispensable for the study of Shiʿi scholarship in general. This is the well-known work *al-Dharīʿa ilā taṣānīf al-Shīʿa* of Āqā Buzurg Ṭihrānī [d. 1391/1970] based on his meticulous research in public and private manuscript collections around the Shiʿi world.[380] The bibliography is an invaluable tool based on his research initiated in Sāmarrāʾ in 1329/1911 and continually revised. The complete work was only published after his death. It largely surpasses the partial list *Kashf al-ḥujub waʾl-astār ʿan asāmī al-kutub waʾl-asfār* compiled by the Indian Shiʿi scholar Sayyid Iʿjāz Ḥusayn Kintūrī [d. 1286/1870],[381]

---

[376] It is used thus by L. Lewisohn, 'An introduction to the history of modern Persian Sufism', *BSOAS* 61 (1998), 437–64, 62 (1999), 36–59.

[377] Ed. M. J. Maḥjūb (3 vols, Tehran 1339 Sh/1960).

[378] *Tadhkira-yi Naṣrābādī*, ed. V. Dastgirdī (Tehran 1317 Sh/1938); a new edition is available now edited by Muḥsin Nājī Naṣrābādī (2 vols, Tehran 1378 Sh/1999).

[379] *Ātashkada-yi Ādhar*, ed. Ḥ. Sādāt Nāṣirī (3 vols, Tehran 1336–40 Sh/1957–61).

[380] E. Kohlberg, 'al-Dharīʿa', *EIr* VII, 35–6.

[381] The work was published in 1912 in Calcutta by the Asiatic Society of Bengal. On him, see Rizvi, *A Socio-intellectual History of the Isnāʿasharī Shīʿīs in India*, II, 170–1; Lakhnawī Kashmīrī, *Nujūm al-samāʾ*, 422; Lakhnawī, *Nuzhat al-khawāṭir*, VII, 66.

and complements the famous bibliography *Kashf al-ẓunūn ʿan asāmī al-kutub wa'l-funūn* of the Ottoman savant Ḥājjī Khalīfa [d. 1067/1657]. The breadth of genres and sources cited is impressive, from traditions and exegesis to philosophy, mysticism and belles-lettres.

IV Jung-majmūʿa-s

Recent research has signalled the importance of studying miscellanies and anthologies usually in codices yet to be published for research in the Safavid period.[382]

We have already seen how these sources can be used to construct intellectual biography. The famous *Jung-i Qazwīn* is a key source on the early career of Mullā Ṣadrā, his intellectual interests and his relationship with his teachers, His correspondence with Mīr Dāmād is extant in *jung* collections and contains not only evidence useful for dating episodes in his life and relationships but also the particular intellectual concerns that he had at the time whether with respect to philosophical traditions or making sense of mystical experiences. Finally, we have also noted the autograph codex which one may classify as a *Jung* or a *majmūʿa* that records his youthful notes on a variety of topics in Sufism, philosophy, exegesis and poetry, and especially which contains a description of his personal library.

Because these sources tend to be only in manuscript in major collections in Iran, Britain and India, they have been neglected. But the vast amount of the material available (once one begins to consult the relevant manuscript catalogues) should make it quite an attractive approach for future research in Safavid studies and intellectual history.

V Historical/Historiographical sources

The study of Safavid historiography has developed considerably in recent years prompted by the edition and publication of the major histories and chronicles of the period.[383] A careful study of these sources reveals the attitudes of the court towards

---

[382] Iraj Afshar, 'Maktūb and majmūʿa: essential sources for Safavid research', in A. J. Newman (ed.), *Society and Culture in the Early Modern Middle East: Studies on Iran in the Safavid Period*, 51–61; M. Sefatgol, 'Majmūʿahhā: important and unknown sources of historiography of Iran', in K. Nobuaki (ed.), *Persian Documents: Social History of Iran and Turan in the Fifteenth-Nineteenth Centuries* (London 2003), 73–83.

[383] See Jean Calmard et al, 'Notes sur des historiographes de l'époque Safavide' *SIr* 16 (1987), 123–35; idem, 'Safavid Persia in Indo-Persian sources and in Timurid-Mughal perception', in M. Alam et al (ed.), *The Making of Indo-Persian Culture* (New Delhi 2000), 351–91; Sholeh A. Quinn, *Historical Writing*

the hierocracy as well as the religious and intellectual disciplines of the scholarly culture. Many of these sources include sections especially devoted to the major scholars, philosophers, mystics and poets of the period. Safavid chronicles followed earlier Timurid precedents, histories that located the local dynasty within a larger world history starting from Adam. The most significant precedent was *Rawḍat al-Ṣafā fī sīrat al-anbiyā' wa'l-mulūk wa'l-khulafā'* of Mīrkhwānd [d. 903/1498] written at the Timurid court of Herat.[384] It is thus not surprising to note that the first Safavid world history in four parts is *Ḥabīb al-siyar* written by his son Khwāndamīr [d. 941/1534–5] and dedicated originally to the Safavid governor of Herat.[385] The structure, rhetoric and literary style of these works were admired and set the standard for later works.

A number of works were written in the early Safavid period, but the work that became a standard for reference was *Aḥsan al-tawārīkh* completed in 985/1577 by a Qizilbash notable Ḥasan Beg Rūmlū.[386] Later works would draw upon it for material on the early Safavids. The structure of these works was annalistic based around the double use of the Muslim hijrī calendar and the Mongol Turkic calendar, and had separate sections on notices on notables, office-holders and scholars.[387] By the time of Shah ʿAbbās I, historical sources became more dynastically focused, stressing the legitimacy of the Safavids as descendents of the Prophet. The most famous work of that period and a critical witness is *Tārīkh-i ʿĀlam-ārā'-yi ʿAbbāsī* completed in 1038/1629 by Iskandar Beg Turkomān, a *munshī* (chancellery secretary

---

during the Reign of Shah ʿAbbas (Salt Lake City, UH 2000); eadem, 'Historiography vi. Safavid', *EIr* XII, 363–7; Jahānbakhsh Thavāqib, *Tārīkh-nigārī-yi ʿaṣr-i Ṣafavī va shinākht-i manābiʿ va ma'ākhidh* (Shiraz 1380 Sh/2001); Manṣūr Ṣifatgul, *Sākhtār-i nihād va andīsha-yi dīnī dar Īrān-i ʿaṣr-i Ṣafavī* (Tehran 1381 Sh/2002). Some useful comparative studies for the earlier period and the contemporary Mughal state in India and Ottoman state in the west are: Marilyn R. Waldman, *Toward a Theory of Historical narrative: A Case Study in Perso-Islamicate Historiography* (Columbus, OH 1980); John E. Woods, 'The rise of Timurid historiography', *JNES* 46 (1987), 81–107; Āftāb Aṣghar, *Tārīkh-navīsī-yi fārsī dar Hind va Pākistān* (Lahore 1364 Sh/1985); M. Athar Ali, 'The use of sources in Mughal historiography', *JRAS* 3rd series 5 (1995), 361–73; Harbans Mukhia, *Historians and Historiography during the Reign of Akbar* (New Delhi 1976); Khaliq A. Nizami, *On History and Historians of Medieval India* (New Delhi 1982); S. Dale, 'India xvi – Indo-Persian Historiography', *EIr* XIII, 53–63; Cornell H. Fleischer, *Bureaucrat and Intellectual in the Ottoman Empire: The Historian Mustafa Ali (1541–1600)* (Princeton 1986); S. Nur Yildiz, 'Historiography xiv – The Ottoman Empire', *EIr* XII, 403–11.

[384] M. Szuppe, 'Historiography v. Timurid period', *EIr* XII, 356–63. The most recent 10 volume edition is by Jamshīd Kīyānfar (Tehran 1380 Sh/2001).

[385] Ed. M. Dabīr-Siyāqī (4 vols, Tehran 1363 Sh/1984).

[386] Ed. ʿAbd al-Ḥusayn Navā'ī (Tehran 1357 Sh/1978).

[387] For problems that this may raise, see R. McChesney, 'A note on Iskandar Beg's chronology', *JNES* 39 (1980), 53–63.

and probably official historian).[388] The bulk of the work including the notices (such as the passage praising Mīr Dāmād) was completed in 1025/1616. The surprising lacuna is that there is no mention of Mullā Ṣadrā. This may indicate that he was not particularly well known in Isfahan during the time of Shah ʿAbbās I and only became famous in the time of Shah Ṣafī or later. If the stories of him being driven out of Isfahan because of his heterodoxy were true, then it is possible that Iskandar Beg would have mentioned it. Another slightly later account that focuses more closely on Isfahan, *Khulāṣat al-siyar* by Muḥammad Maʿṣūm Iṣfahānī completed in 1051/1642 is also silent on him.[389] Given the desire to establish the legitimacy of the dynasty and of official Shiʿism, it is surprising that a supposed case of heterodoxy would be overlooked. Later histories tended to be chronicles of a partial reign and included as ever informative notices on the scholars of the time. Particularly useful in terms of discerning the role of philosophers and Sufis at court of Shah ʿAbbās II, at the time when their role was increasingly under attack is *ʿAbbās-nāma* of Muḥammad Ṭāhir Waḥīd-i Qazwīnī [d. 1110/1698–9].[390]

Since most of these works are court commissioned official histories, one ought to consider them alongside official documents whether in the form of *firmāns* (official court pronouncements) or *munshaʾāt* (chancellery documents).[391] Collections of such documents are usually in manuscript collections but some have been published.[392] Given contacts with the wider Persianate world, it may also be beneficial studying the documents in Ottoman, Uzbek and Indian sources.[393] Since

---

[388] Ed. Īraj Afshār (2 vols, Tehran 1350 Sh/1971). Cf. R. Savory, 'ʿĀlamārā'-ye ʿAbbāsī', *EIr* I, 796.

[389] Ed. Īraj Afshār (Tehran 1368 Sh/1989).

[390] Ed. I. Dihqān (Arak 1330 Sh/1951).

[391] J. Paul, 'Enšāʾ', *EIr* VIII, 455–7; F. Mojtabai, 'Correspondence: ii. Islamic Persia', *EIr* VI, 290–3; idem, 'Inshā-collections as a source on Iranian history', in *Proceedings of the Second European Conference of Iranian Studies* (Rome 1995), 535–50; H. Roemer, 'Inshāʾ', *EI²* III, 1241–4; cf. special issue of *Kitāb-i Māh: tārīkh va jughrāfiyyā* 51–2 (1380 Sh/2002); M. Mohiuddin, *The Chancellery and Persian Epistolography Under the Mughals* (Calcutta 1971).

[392] ʿA-Ḥ. Navāʾī (ed.), *Asnād va mukātabāt-i tārīkhī-yi Īrān (az Tīmūr tā Shāh Ismāʿīl)* (Tehran 1370 Sh/1991); idem (ed.), *Shāh Ismāʿīl: majmūʿa-yi asnād va mukātabāt-i tārīkhī hamrāh bih dāddāsht-hā-yi tafṣīlī* (Tehran 1347 Sh/1968); idem (ed.), *Shāh Ṭahmāsp: majmūʿa-yi asnād va mukātabāt-i tārīkhī hamrāh bih dāddāsht-hā-yi tafṣīlī* (2 vols, Tehran 1350 Sh/1971); idem (ed.), *Shāh ʿAbbās: majmūʿa-yi asnād va mukātabāt-i tārīkhī hamrāh bih dāddāsht-hā-yi tafṣīlī* (2 vols, Tehran 1366 Sh/1987); idem (ed.), *asnād va mukātabāt-i tārīkhī-yi Īrān (az 1038 tā 1105)* (Tehran 1360 Sh/1981).

[393] For the Indian sources, see S. A. I. Tirmizi, *Mughal Documents I: 1526–1627, II: 1628–1659* (2 vols, New Delhi 1989–95); Riazul Islam, *A Calendar of Documents on Indo-Persian Relations, 1500–1750* (Karachi 1979–82); Abuʾl-Faḍl ʿAllāmī, *Mukātabāt [Inshāʾ-yi Abuʾl-Faḍl]* (Lucknow lithograph 1286/1869), ed./tr. Mansura Haider (2 vols, New Delhi 1998–2000). For a guide to the Ottoman sources, see Suraiya Faroqhi, *Approaching Ottoman History* (Cambridge 1999).

scholars and philosophers were members of elite society, they were often used as ambassadors: a good early Safavid example is the philosopher-theologian (and Imam of the Muḥammad-Shāhī line of the Ismāʿīlī Nizārī community) Shah Ṭāhir Ḥusaynī [d. ca. 956/1549], a student of philosopher Shams al-Dīn Khafarī. Shah Ṭāhir acted as an ambassador between the Safavid court and Niẓām-Shāhs in the Deccan.[394] We also known that later in the time of Shah ʿAbbās I, Shaykh Bahāʾī acted as a negotiator in the conflict with the Mushaʿshaʿ after 998/1590.[395]

Local histories are another useful source especially when a thinker is either from a major provincial history or became famous there.[396] The city of Shiraz has for long played a significant role in Iranian history and histories of the city and of Fārs province date from the classical Islamic period. The most useful of these sources for the study of the Safavid period is a later Qajar source the *Fārsnāma-yi Nāṣirī* written by the Qajar courtier and administrator Mīrzā Ḥasan Ḥusaynī Fasāʾī [d. 1316/1898]. The work was designed as a history and geography of the province and was commissioned by Shah Nāṣir al-Dīn (hence the title) in 1296/1879 and completed in 1304/1887. Fasāʾī was a scion of the famous Dashtakī family of the city whose ancestors included the philosophers Ṣadr al-Dīn Muḥammad and Ghiyāth al-Dīn Manṣūr and part of his motivation to write the work was to settle a *waqf* dispute surrounding the property of the Madrasa-yi Manṣūriyya, founded by the family.[397] However, at the time of his writing, Mullā Ṣadrā was more famous than them because his thought was being championed and his works adopted as school texts by teachers like ʿAlī Nūrī in Isfahan and Hādī Sabzavārī in Sabzavār. Like most local histories, Fasāʾī includes sections on famous individuals including a chapter on scholars.[398] The entry on Mullā Ṣadrā is the longest and is appended by a long sentence of honorifics for him, praises that he does not append to the entries on his ancestors, let alone other ʿulema. The work was designed as a history and geography of the province and was

---

[394] F. Daftary, *The Ismāʿīlīs: Their History and Doctrines* (Cambridge 1990), 486–91.

[395] See Newman, 'Towards a reconsideration of the Isfahan school of philosophy', 177–8.

[396] Thavāqib, *Tārīkh-nigārī-yi ʿaṣr-i Ṣafavī*, 91–105 for the relevant Safavid sources.

[397] Ed. M. Rastigār (2 vols, Tehran 1367 Sh/1988). Cf. H. Buisse, 'Fārsnāma-ye Nāṣerī', *EIr* IX, 374–6. This Madrasa was founded in the 15th century and enjoyed the patronage of the Āq-Quyunlū; later in the Safavid period, the teaching of the intellectual disciplines declined at this institution. See Ḥ. Mudarrissī Ṭabāṭabāʾī, *Farmān-hā-yi turkamānān-i Qārā Quyunlū va Āq Quyunlū* (Qum 1352 Sh/1973), 94–106; cf. V. Minorsky, 'A Soyūrghāl of Qāsim b. Jahāngīr Aq-Qoyunlu (903/1498)', *BSOAS* 9 (1938), 952–6. The family was closely associated with the rulers and Ṣadr al-Dīn Muḥammad Dashtakī praised Uzun Ḥasan in his *Gawhar-nāma*; cf. John Woods, *The Aqquyunlu: Clan, Confederation, Empire* (Salt Lake City, UH 1999), 105.

[398] Fasāʾī, *Fārsnāma-yi Nāṣirī*, II, 1136–53.

commissioned by Shah Nāṣir al-Dīn (hence the title) in 1296/1879 and completed in 1304/1887.

VI Ijāzāt

Despite some protestations,[399] it is clear that licences for transmitting texts and attestations of learning remain key witnesses for the intellectual culture and curriculum of Islamic civilisation.[400] A recent example of the judicious use of such a license is the study of ʿAbd Allāh al-Samāhījī [d. 1135/1722] by Sabine Schmitdke.[401] As a text, it is a license granted by an issuer (*mujīz*) on his authority that authorises the licensee (*mujāz*) to do one of three things. First, if the license concerns *riwāya* or transmission, then the licensee may transmit a particular text or body of traditions to further people and take his place within a chain of narration (*isnād*), the main guarantor of reliability in the learned culture of Islam. This type of license is particularly important in this period especially with respect to the revivification of the Shiʿi intellectual and spiritual tradition manifested in the renewed interest in early texts and *ḥadīth*. Second, the license may recognise that a student has memorised a text and has been examined orally on his knowledge of it. This is known as an *ijāzat al-ʿarad* and is fairly rare in the sources of the period. The third type is a license to teach (*ijāzat al-tadrīs*), in particular law, and a recognition of the ability of the student to engage in independent legal reasoning and issues response (*fatāwā*). This presumes an Uṣūlī theory of the law. Often called an *ijāzat al-ijtihād*, it became popular in the sixteenth century, was then contested in the later seventeenth century and returned to fashion in the nineteenth century consistent with the fortunes of the Uṣūlīs.

Although the texts can be formulaic and bombastic with rather baroque *proemia* written in rhyming prose (*sajʿ*), they can contain valuable information: who

[399] Robert Gleave, 'The *ijāza* from Yūsuf al-Baḥrānī (d. 1186/1772) to Sayyid Muḥammad Mahdī Baḥr al-ʿUlūm', *Iran* 32 (1994), 120–1, who suggests that as literary artefacts such texts do not provide useful historical information.

[400] Devin Stewart, 'Ejāza', *EIr* VIII, 273–5; K. M. Shānichī, 'Ijāza', *Dāʾirat al-Maʿārif-i Buzurg-i Islāmī (Tehran)* VI, 596–8; G. Vajda, L. Goldziher and S. Bonebakker, 'Idjāza', *EI²* III, 1020–2; C. Pellat, 'Fahrasa', *EI²* II, 743–4; G. Vajda, *La transmission du savoir en Islam* (London 1983); J. J. Witkam, 'The human element between text and reader', in Y. Dutton (ed.), *The Codicology of Islamic Manuscripts* (London 1995), 131ff; ʿAbd Allāh Fayyāḍ, *al-Ijāzāt al-ʿIlmiyya ʿind al-muslimīn* (Baghdad 1967).

[401] Sabine Schmidtke, 'The ijāza from ʿAbd Allāh b. Ṣāliḥ al-Samāhījī to al-Nāṣir al-Jārūdī al-Qaṭīfī', in F. Daftary and J. Meri (eds), *Culture and memory in Medieval Islam: Essays in Honour of Wilferd Madelung* (London 2003), 64–85.

studied with whom, where, how, when, for how long, who else was involved, how did the education proceed and so forth.

A number of rich and useful sources are available, many of which have been published. *Al-Ijāza al-muṭawwala* is an extensive text written by Muḥammad Taqī Majlisī [d. 1070/1659–60] for his son Muḥammad Bāqir Majlisī [d. 1110/1699], transmitting *ḥadīth* and in particular *al-Ṣaḥīfa al-Sajjādiyya*, a collection of supplications attributed to the fourth Shiʿi Imam that became extensively popular (and popularised) in the Safavid period.[402] Another important document on the transmission of *ḥadīth* is *al-Ijāza al-kabīra* of al-Sayyid ʿAbd Allāh al-Mūsawī al-Jazāʾirī [d. 1173/1759–60], a scholar associated with the Majlisī circle.[403] Perhaps the most valuable published source for a range of licenses is the *kitāb al-ijāzāt* of Majlisī II available in volumes 104–107 of his massive encyclopaedia *Biḥār al-anwār*.[404] This work includes licenses from the classical period all the way up the licenses that Majlisī himself issued to his students. The entry under *ijāza* in the twentieth century Shiʿi bibliography *al-Dharīʿa* indicates a number of manuscripts of these texts.[405] This is useful because most *ijāzāt* remain unpublished. It mentions two collections that remain unpublished: *Takmilat Amal al-āmil* of ʿAbd Allāh Afandī, the author of *Riyāḍ al-ʿulamāʾ*, a text that itself is a valuable source for licenses, and *Mustadrak*

---

[402] Majlisī, *al-Ijāza al-Muṭawwala*, ed. M. Wāʿiẓ-zāda in *Yādnāma-yi Shaykh Ṭūsī* (Mashhad 1971); it is also available at the end of volume 107 in *Biḥār al-anwār*. In his study, al-Sayyid Muḥammad al-Ḥusayn al-Jalālī shows that the vast majority of manuscripts of the text were copied in the Safavid period – see *Dirāsa ḥawl al-Ṣaḥīfa al-Sajjādiyya* (Beirut 2000), 34–45. A number of significant figures in the period wrote commentaries (*shurūḥ, ḥawāshī*) on the text (in chronological order): Shaykh ʿAlī al-Karakī (*al-Dharīʿa* XIII, 353); ʿIzz al-Dīn al-Ḥusayn b. ʿAbd al-Ṣamad al-ʿĀmilī (*al-Dharīʿa* XIII, 351); al-Sayyid al-Ḥusayn b. al-Ḥasan al-Karakī (*al-Dharīʿa* VI, 145); Shaykh Bahāʾī wrote *Ḥadāʾiq al-Ṣāliḥīn* on the whole text but only *al-Ḥadīqa al-Hilāliyya* on the supplication for the new crescent of Ramaḍān has been published (ed. Sayyid ʿAlī Mūsawī Khurāsānī, Qum 1990); Mīr Dāmād; Mullā Khalīl Qazwīnī (*al-Dharīʿa* XIII, 351); Fayḍ Kāshānī; Ḥusayn Khwānsārī wrote a commentary along with a Persian translation (*al-Dharīʿa* XIII, 350); ʿAlī b. Muḥammad al-ʿĀmilī (*al-Dharīʿa* XIII, 353); Majlisī II wrote a commentary entitled *al-Fawāʾid al-ṭarīfa*; al-Ḥurr al-ʿĀmilī (*al-Dharīʿa* XV, 21, published in lithograph in Bombay/Mumbai 1311/1893–4); al-Sayyid Niʿmat Allāh al-Jazāʾirī wrote a commentary entitled *Nūr al-anwār*, which was completed in 1078/1667–8 (*al-Dharīʿa* XIII, 358; Beirut 2000); finally, al-Sayyid ʿAlī-Khān Shīrāzī wrote a theological and mystical commentary entitled *Riyāḍ al-sālikīn fī sharḥ Ṣaḥīfat Sayyid al-Sājidīn* (7 vols, Qum 1409/1988). The last commentary remains the most popular.

[403] Ed. M. S. al-Ḥāʾirī (Qum 1409/1989).

[404] It has also been published separately in an edition by Sayyid Aḥmad Ḥusaynī (Qum 1410/1989).

[405] *Al-Dharīʿa* I, 123–266; also available in the library at http://www.rafed.net.

ijāzāt al-Biḥār by Mīrzā Muḥammad b. Rajab-ʿAlī al-Ṭihrānī al-ʿAskarī [d. 1371/1952], which is supposed to have been in fifteen volumes.[406]

Finally, we ought to note that a work that is often treated as a biographical dictionary, namely *Luʾluʾat al-Baḥrayn fī ijāzāt wa-tarājim rijāl al-ḥadīth* of the Akhbārī scholar Yūsuf b. Aḥmad b. Ibrāhīm al-ʿUṣfūrī al-Baḥrānī [d. 1186/1772] is in fact a license written for his two nephews Khalf b. ʿAbd ʿAlī b. Aḥmad b. Ibrāhīm al-ʿUṣfūrī al-Baḥrānī [d. 1208/1793–4] and Ḥusayn b. Muḥammad b. Aḥmad b. Ibrāhīm al-ʿUṣfūrī al-Baḥrānī [d. 1216/1801–2].[407] Despite its title, it does contain entries on the likes of Mullā Ṣadrā whose primary expertise was not *ḥadīth*. Consistent with an Akhbārī distastes for philosophical and rational speculation, he is harsh about Mullā Ṣadrā and says that his son Ibrāhīm exemplifies the Qurʾānic description of God extracting the living from the dead because the son was so much more fitting as a scholar of the traditions and scriptural disciplines and turned his back on the philosophy of his father.[408]

To conclude this section, I want to present two *ijāzāt* written by Mīr Dāmād and suggest ways in which one may read them for information. I would suggest that one can draw conclusions about the relationship between Mīr Dāmād and Mullā Ṣadrā. The first was issued to al-Sayyid al-Ḥusayn b. Ḥaydar al-Karakī in 1038/1627–8 and is recorded by Majlisī:[409]

> This license was written on the back of *Kitāb al-Istibṣār* [an early *ḥadīth* collection compiled by al-Ṭūsī] belonging to the licensee and in the handwriting of the issuer.

He then quotes the text. After the formal praise of God and blessings upon the Prophets and the Imams, Mīr Dāmād writes that the licensee studied months, day and night with him:

> I authorise him to transmit from me my legal opinions and *responsa* concerning what is permissible and what is forbidden and to act according to

---

[406] *Al-Dharīʿa* I, 127 (no. 608), 129 (no. 614). Schmidtke says that she was informed by Professor Hossein Modarressi (Princeton) that this latter work is now lost – see 'The ijāza from ʿAbd Allāh b. Ṣāliḥ', 79 n.1.

[407] LB 6; cf. M. Salati, 'La *Luʾluʾat al-Baḥrayn fī-l-ijāza li-qurratay al-ʿayn* di Shaykh Yūsuf b. Aḥmad al-Baḥrānī', *Annali Ca' Foscari* 28 (1989), 111–45.

[408] LB 132.

[409] *Biḥār*, CVII, 3–5. There is not much information available on him; see *Aʿyān*, VI, 5.

> them and to permit those morally obliged (*li'l-mukallifīn*) to act according to them,[410] and to transmit my works both intellectual and scriptural and the works of my grandfather [the jurist ʿAlī al-Karakī]. I also authorise him to transmit from me the traditions of our master the Messenger of God and of our masters the Infallibles and the Pure Imams, may the blessings and peace of God be with them, from the works of our companions especially the Four Books (*al-Uṣūl al-arbaʿa*) of the three Abū Jaʿfars [i.e. al-Kulaynī, Ibn Bābawayh and al-Ṭūsī]... that is *al-Kāfī, al-Faqīh, al-Tahdhīb* and *al-Istibṣār*, and what has been glossed on them and commented upon them and written in their margins over time and over the ages. So let him transmit all of that to whom he wishes and whom he loves just as I have to whom I love through these reliable and correct chains of narration that amount to an extensive and long license ...
>
> Written by the poor one most desirous of his Lord the Rich and Praiseworthy Muḥammad b. Muḥammad known as Bāqir al-Dāmād al-Ḥusaynī in the year 1038 of the blessed and holy prophetic migration, praising God, and sending blessings and peace upon his prophet and seeking his forgiveness.

This license is mainly concerned with the transmission of legal learning and traditions. But it does mention intellectual works, that is, works of philosophy and theology and demonstrates how he taught a range of works and was famous of his breadth of learning.[411]

The second license for our purposes is even more interesting. In fact, the licensee is the same individual, his son-in-law Sayyid Niẓām al-Dīn Aḥmad ʿAlawī [d. 1054/1644],[412] but there are two licenses.[413] Both licenses were written in Isfahan and both mention philosophical texts and spiritual teaching. The latter which was written in 1019/1608 is subsumed by the former which is more complete and more eloquent:

---

[410] It is clear that he believes that the believers are divided into *mujtahids* and followers.

[411] For a third type of *ijāza*, i.e. an *ijāzat al-ijtihād* that he issued to Sayyid Muḥammad Bāqir Mashhadī, see *Makātib-i Mīr Dāmād* in *Mīrāth-i Islāmī-yi Īrān IV*, ed. R. Jaʿfarīyān (Qum 1376 Sh/1997), 70.

[412] Henry Corbin, 'Aḥmad ʿAlawī', *EIr* I, 644–6; *Aʿyān*, II, 593; al-Ṭihrānī, *Ṭabaqāt aʿlām al-Shīʿa*, V, 27; RU I, 39; Ṣamad Muwaḥḥid, 'Aḥmad ʿAlawī', *Dāʾirat al-Maʿārif-i Buzurg-i Islāmī (Tehran)* VII, 72–5.

[413] *Biḥār*, CVI, 152–6; *Muṣannafāt-i Mīr Dāmād I*, ed. ʿAbd Allāh Nūrānī (Tehran 1381 Sh/2002), 581–4.

My spiritual son and intelligent companion, the luminous, illuminating *sayyid*, whose knowledge is rare and unique, possessor of a pure pedigree and manifest lineage, clear nobility and brilliant excellence ... has studied with me the intellectual disciplines from the works of our predecessors who mastered the discipline [of philosophy i.e. Avicenna in particular], studying them deeply ... the thirteenth part of *al-Shifāʾ*, which is the divine part, I mean philosophy, the metaphysics. At the moment, he is busy studying the part on the *Categories*, and he is also auditing and studying the first two *namaṭ*s of *al-Ishārāt wa'l-tanbīhāt* of al-Shaykh al-Raʾīs [Avicenna]... and its commentary by the Seal of the investigators [Naṣīr al-Dīn al-Ṭūsī]... [He has studied] from my books *al-Ufuq al-mubīn*, which is the manifesto of Truth ..., *Kitāb al-Īmāḍāt wa'l-tashrīqāt*, which is a heavenly epistle, and *al-Taqdīsāt*, which contains the way of glorification and unicity of the explicit verses [of the Qurʾān]. He has studied these proficiently and thoroughly. Among the scriptural disciplines, [he has studied] the book of purity of *Qawāʿid al-aḥkām* of Jamāl al-Milla waʾl-Dīn al-Ḥillī and its commentary by my grandfather [al-Karakī] ... and a part of *al-Kashshāf* of the learned al-Zamakhsharī, and the *Ḥāshiya Sharīfiyya* [of al-Sharīf al-Jurjānī], and these days he is busy with the *Qawāʿid* of al-Shahīd II. I authorise him to transmit all of this to whom he wishes and he loves provided they preserve them and are careful and fulfil the conditions required by the specialists in the study of narrations.

I urge him first to fear God, fear him in seclusion and in the open as the pious fear of the heart is one of the greatest keys to being bestowed the secret of receiving divine grace and being illuminated by the intelligible and holy lights... [I urge him to] enunciate supplications and litanies of remembrance and to recite the Qurʾān constantly, especially *Sūrat al-Tawḥīd*, whose similitude in the Book is like that of the speaking Qurʾān, the Commander of the Faithful ʿAlī b. Abī Ṭālib, the blessings of God be with him, in the book of existence.

Second, [I urge you] to protect the secrets of the holy world, which are committed to my books and words... and heed the advice that came before in my book *al-Ṣirāṭ al-mustaqīm*, everything is made easy for one who is created for it ...

> Third, [I urge you] to repeatedly remember me through the most righteous supplications and prayers that are answered and are thought to be answered since God is the friend who gives grace and every matter reverts to him.
>
> Written by one most desirous of his Lord the Rich and Praiseworthy Muḥammad b. Muḥammad known as Bāqir al-Dāmād al-Ḥusaynī in Jumāda I of the year 1017 [August-September 1608] of the blessed and holy prophetic migration, praising God, and sending blessings and peace upon his prophet and seeking his forgiveness.

This fascinating text tells us a number of things about the teachings of Mīr Dāmād: the range of subjects and disciplines, rational, spiritual and scriptural, and the teachings that he imparted as a spiritual master. Given that all the texts mentioned in it were in the library of Mullā Ṣadrā, I think it is safe to surmise that he studied them with him and the Sufi language of the master-disciple relationship is strikingly similar to the terms in which he speaks of his teacher.

VII Anthologies

The Safavid period was one of consolidating heritage, of producing large anthologies of traditions and belles-lettres as well as scholarly opinions, response, and anecdotes. This type of source can reveal interesting facets of the intellectual development of the period. An early example is *al-Kashkūl*, the anthology of Shaykh Bahāʾī.[414] In his youth, he allegedly compiled a short literary anthology, a nosebag as he called it, *al-Mikhlāt*.[415] The work published in that name seems to be quite a Sunni work; Stewart suggests that internal evidence indicates that it was written in Mamluk Egypt. The famous bibliographer Āqā Buzurg al-Ṭihrānī argues that the real *al-Mikhlāt* has never been printed and remains in manuscript.[416] Bosworth assesses the printed text as a jejune and moderate work; but since it is not the work of Shaykh Bahāʾī, it cannot

[414] The text has been published many times in Iran and Egypt usually in four volumes. The best study of it is C. E. Bosworth, *Bahāʾ al-Dīn al-ʿĀmilī and His Literary Anthologies* (Journal of Semitic Studies Supplement no. 10, Manchester 1989); cf. the critical notice by Devin Stewart in *SIr* 19 (1990), 275–82.

[415] A recent edition that appeared is by M. ʿAbd al-Karīm al-Nimrī (Beirut 1998). Cf. Bosworth, *Bahāʾ al-Dīn al-ʿĀmilī and His Literary Anthologies*, 16–20.

[416] *Al-Dharīʿa*, II, 42, XX, 232–3.

compare well with *al-Kashkūl*. The later anthology is more systematic, more Shiʿi and contains Persian as well as Arabic sources. It represents the fruits of his travels in the Ottoman Empire, especially in Egypt and his role at the heart of the Safavid court in Isfahan. The text itself was completed in 1002/1593, according to Bosworth, probably while he was in Qazwīn. But as a scrapbook, Stewart suggests that it is difficult to decide on a completion date. If we assume that he was responsible for the final version of the text, setting aside the problem of a lack of a critical edition that can collate different possible recensions, the date suggested by Bosworth cannot be accepted. A number of passages post-date it. To cite two examples: first, he quoted a poem that he composed in Mashhad in Dhuʾl-Qaʿda 1007/May–June 1599;[417] second, he mentioned a poem composed by a Jamāl al-Dīn Muḥammad in Kirmān in 1029/1619–20.[418] Sources cited include poetry both classical and post-classical, scriptural and exegetical material, theological discussions and a strong influence of Sufism. This last is particularly striking and provides strong evidence for his mystical tendencies that complemented his role as a jurist and a scientist. The Beirut printing of 1983 includes a long introduction by the Iraqi Shiʿi scholar Dr. al-Sayyid Muḥammad Baḥr al-ʿUlūm in exile in London in 1983, and a useful list of sources and poets cited compiled by al-Sayyid Muḥammad Mahdī al-Kharsān.[419]

The traditionalist and student of Majlisī, al-Sayyid Niʿmat Allāh al-Jazāʾirī [d. 1112/1701] completed an anthology of theological material entitled *al-Anwār an-Nuʿmāniyya* in 1089/1678.[420] In it, he discussed the positions of a number of his contemporary and predecessors including philosophers. An autobiographical section can also be found which described his trials and tribulations as a student, the curriculum he underwent and the state of seminary education in his time.[421] In the introduction, he explained his reasons for collating the anthology:

> I have tried to compose an unusual work in a wonderful manner that have never been written before ... so that it may be a friend and counsel to the illiterate and a rehearsal and reminder for the scholar, that everyone may

---

[417] *Al-Kashkūl*, ed. M. Ṣ. Nāṣirī (Qum 1958), I, 188.

[418] *Al-Kashkūl*, ed. M. Ṣ. Nāṣirī, I, 375.

[419] *Al-Kashkūl* (Beirut 1983), I, 7–72, 73–90.

[420] It was published in Beirut in 4 volumes in 1984 by the famous Shiʿi press Muʾassasat al-Aʿlamī. On him, see RU V, 253–6; *Rawḍāt*, VIII, 138–46.

[421] Al-Jazāʾirī, *al-Anwār al-nuʿmāniyya*, IV, 302–26. Cf. Devin Stewart, 'The humour of the scholars: the autobiography of Niʿmatullāh al-Jazāʾirī', *IS* 22 (1989), 47–60.

> benefit from it according to the measure of their rank and everyone who wishes to emerge from the darkness may be illuminated by it.[422]

Hence, he divided the text into lights (*anwār*). He subscribed to a number of opinions associated with philosophers and Sufis. For example, he presented a section on the nature of the imaginal realm, the intermediary world between the higher divine realm of intelligibles and the lower sensory world that we inhabit by citing passages from *al-Futūḥāt al-Makkiyya* of Ibn ʿArabī and *Ḥikmat al-Ishrāq* of Suhrawardī.[423] Elsewhere, he included encounters with Sufis, both affiliated to orders and qalandars, and provided short notices on some of the scholars of his time.[424] Later, within the context of further biographical notices, he included a charming and, he would think instructive, short discursis on the etiquette of pedagogy.[425] Another major theme upon which he touched is love, discussed in the terms of love mysticism as well as Neoplatonic notion of love as the prime binding force and motivator in the cosmos.[426] A patient study of the miscellany would reveal further aspects worthy of investigation.

A prominent jurist and descendent of al-Shahīd II, ʿAlī b. Muḥammad al-ʿĀmilī [d. 1103/1692] wrote *al-Durr al-manthūr min al-maʾthūr wa-ghayr al-maʾthūr* with the intention of collating a discussion of a number of legal issues and their relationship to traditions.[427] Consistent with his attack on *al-Fawāʾid al-Madaniyya*, this work can also been seen as a strong offensive against the growing tendency towards Akhbārī sympathies among the Iranian ʿulema. Although the work was probably written in the Safavid realm, and he himself had been the recipient of the patronage of Shah ʿAbbās II, he tried to insist that he upheld the family tradition of keeping aloof from the Safavid rulers.[428] Along with the rehearsal of opinions and engagement with ideas in jurisprudence, he included information on the transmission of legal and theological ideas as well as chains of narration for *ḥadīth*. He defended rationalist positions on a number of issues such as the preservation of the Prophet from forgetting during prayer (as it was a common traditionalist position to quote

[422] Al-Jazāʾirī, *al-Anwār al-nuʿmāniyya*, I, 2.

[423] Al-Jazāʾirī, *al-Anwār al-nuʿmāniyya*, I, 164–7.

[424] Al-Jazāʾirī, *al-Anwār al-nuʿmāniyya*, II, 283–4.

[425] Al-Jazāʾirī, *al-Anwār al-nuʿmāniyya*, III, 346–50.

[426] Al-Jazāʾirī, *al-Anwār al-nuʿmāniyya*, III, 150–200.

[427] The text was edited in 2 volumes by Sayyid Aḥmad Ḥusaynī and issued in Qum by the library of al-Sayyid al-Najafī al-Marʿashī.

[428] Al-ʿĀmilī, *al-Durr al-manthūr*, II, 211–12, 242; cf. Stewart, 'Migration', 101.

traditions that he has indeed committed such acts of forgetting).[429] Much of the second volume is taken up with long biographical notices on his family beginning with al-Shahīd II.[430] His own autobiography is a useful source for the curriculum of the time.[431] One peculiar passage to note is a pseudo-Avicennian prayer, a poem that he considered to be among the *mujarrabāt* (efficacious prayers known to be answered), yet another indicator of its use as a source for understanding how philosophy and philosophers were perceived in the period.[432]

Perhaps the most important work of this genre is the massive encyclopaedia initiated by Majlisī and entitled *Biḥār al-anwār al-jāmiʿa li-durar akhbār al-aʾimma al-aṭhār.*[433] On the face of it, it is an exhaustive *ḥadīth* collection consistent with the original intention to produce an index for traditions which Majlisī completed in 1070/1659.[434] However, it grew into a much bigger project involving his students al-Sayyid Niʿmat Allāh al-Jazāʾirī [d. 1112/1701] and ʿAbd Allāh Afandī [d. 1130/1717–8] and incorporated notices on historical figures and scholars, licenses (as we have seen), theological debates and opinions and all manner of texts including a version of the story of the Buddha. Majlisī did not live to see its completion, which was probably the work of his students especially in the end his grandson Muḥammad Ḥusayn Khātūnābādī [d. 1151/1739].[435] Although the text achieved fame fairly early on, a complete edition had to wait until the lithograph of 1303–15/1885–98,[436] and in the twentieth century the *muḥaddith* ʿAbbās Qummī [d. 1359/1940] produced an index for it entitled *Ṣafīnat al-Biḥār.*[437] Modern editions of the complete text vary between 104

[429] Al-ʿĀmilī, *al-Durr al-manthūr,* I, 111–20.

[430] Al-ʿĀmilī, *al-Durr al-manthūr,* II, 149ff, 150–77 on him, 238–59 is autobiographical.

[431] Al-ʿĀmilī, *al-Durr al-manthūr,* II, 238–59.

[432] Al-ʿĀmilī, *al-Durr al-manthūr,* II, 95–100.

[433] Etan Kohlberg, 'Beḥār al-anwār', *EIr* IV, 90–3; Karl-Heinz Pampus, *Die theologische Enzyclopädie Biḥār al-anwār des Muḥammad Bāqir al-Majlisī 1037–1110/1627–1699* (Bonn 1970); Ḥasan Ṭārimī, *ʿAllāma Majlisī* (Tehran 1375 Sh/1996) – I had access to the Arabic translation by Raʿd Jabbāra (Tehran 1378 Sh/1999).

[434] Ḥasan Ṭārimī, *ʿAllāma Majlisī,* tr. Raʿd Jabbāra, 220

[435] For a discussion of his students and their role in collating and transmitting the text, see Sayyid Aḥmad Ḥusaynī, *Talāmidha al-ʿAllāma al-Majlisī waʾl-mujāzūn minhu* (Qum 1410/1990).

[436] The lithograph was sponsored by the entrepreneur Muḥammad Ḥasan Amīn al-Żarb [d. 1898]. On his activities as a merchant and philanthropist, see Shireen Mahdavi, *For God, Mammon and Country: a Nineteenth Century Persian Merchant* (Boulder, CO 1999).

[437] The modern uncritical edition that has been produced in Qum between 1414–20/1993–99 is either in four large volumes or eight standard sized volumes. For a discussion of the publication history of the text and the various appendices and indices on it that were produced see Ḥasan Ṭārimī, *ʿAllāma Majlisī,* tr. Raʿd Jabbāra, 217–27, 267–78.

and 110 volumes, depending on censorship and variant pagination and typesetting.[438] The work is divided into twenty-five books (*kitāb*).[439] The introduction discusses his intentions and his 365 sources and his method for analysing and utilising them.[440] Book I, as with most Shiʿi *ḥadīth* collections begins with the book of knowledge (*kitāb al-ʿilm*). Of particular theological interest are books II on the unity of God which includes a rehearsal of arguments for the existence of God and criticisms of philosophical views on the eternity of the cosmos,[441] IV on disputations, and XV on faith and unbelief, which includes a section criticising the views of philosophers (including Mullā Ṣadrā) on resurrection.[442] Hostile to philosophy, Majlisī is consistently critical of forsaking the *ḥadīth* in favour of independent rational argument: he insists that true knowledge must be derived from the 'light-niche of the knowledge of the prophets'.[443] The last book contains the licenses and notices on scholars.

VIII Travel accounts

For some time now, Safavid studies has utilised European travels accounts to shed light upon Safavid history and culture. I shall briefly consider some useful sources. The earliest relevant account is the Venetian Michele Membre and his ambassadorial journey 1539–42 to Tabrīz and the court of Shah Ṭahmāsp.[444]

A number of accounts are contemporary to Mullā Ṣadrā (but they do not mention him explicitly) and discuss meetings with thinkers in Shiraz and Isfahan. For travellers coming up from the Persian Gulf, it was common to stop in Shiraz, where a possible encounter may have taken place. Antonio de Gouvea [d. 1628] was a Portuguese envoy and Augustinian missionary from Goa who was sent as an emissary of Philip III to Shah ʿAbbās I.[445] He visited Iran three times: 1602–3, 1608–9 and 1613. He wrote a journal (*Jornada*) on the first two trips, and then drew together

[438] As with a number of other texts, it is also available online, for example, in the library at http://www.al-shia.com.

[439] See *Biḥār*, I, 79–80 for the summary.

[440] *Biḥār*, I, 1–79.

[441] *Biḥār*, III, 234ff.

[442] *Biḥār*, LVI, 203ff.

[443] *Biḥār*, III, 321, VI, 332, XI, 80 etc. Ironically, Mullā Ṣadrā is also insistent upon the Prophetic roots of true knowledge but it is clear that the means for acquiring this knowledge are different – see *al-Shawāhid al-rubūbiyya*, Mashhad edition, 280.

[444] Michele Membre, *Mission to the Lord Sophy of Persia (1539–42)*, tr. A. H. Morton (London 1993).

[445] R. Mathee, 'De Gouvea', *EIr* XI, 177–9.

accounts for his book on the relations of Iran usually familiar in its French translation *Relations des grandes guerres et victories obtenues par le Roy de Perse* (Rouen, 1646). Although *Relations* is primarily concerned with foreign affairs, it does touch on aspects on cultural and religious practices and has useful accounts of Shiraz and Isfahan. Section I includes a description of religious rituals in particular the commemoration of ʿĀshūrā in Shiraz in 1602 and a later description in section III on the Armenians on new Julfa in Isfahan.

The famous Italian traveller Pietro Della Valle [d. 1652] has left behind one of the most valuable accounts of the lands between Istanbul and Goa in the seventeenth century. His voyages or *Lettere della Persia* (complete ed. Gancia, Brighton, 1843; partial eds. F. Gaeta and L. Lockhart, Rome, 1972) is a particularly valuable source and includes an account of his stay in Isfahan between 1617 and 1621, interrupted in 1618 when he had access to the Shah and went on campaign with him.[446] We know that Della Valle had met Mīr Dāmād and Sayyid Aḥmad ʿAlawī in Isfahan. In Isfahan, he wrote an anti-Muslim polemic which may have been the target of *Kitāb Lawāmiʿ-yi rabbānī fī radd shubhat al-Naṣrānī* written by Sayyid Aḥmad ʿAlawī. Having arrived via the land route through Iraq, he returned by sea travelling down to Shiraz in 1621, so it is not inconceivable that he had meet our philosopher.

At around the same time, between 1619 and 1624, Garcia de Silva y Figueroa [d. 1624] was an ambassador from Philip III to the court at Isfahan.[447] The account of his embassy contains detailed architectural descriptions, not least of the Masjid-i Shah while it was being constructed.

Sir Thomas Herbert [d. 1682] was a member of the embassy of Charles I to the Safavid court between 1626 and 1629.[448] He left two accounts of it: *A Description of the Persian Monarchy* (London, 1634), and *Some Years Travelled in Diverse Parts of Africa and Greater Asia* (London, 1677). Of value is his account of Shiraz and the hospitality of Imāmqulī Khān; it was there that he visited the Madrasa-yi Khān, where Mullā Ṣadrā may have been.

The Schleswig-Holstein missions to Russia and Iran between 1633 and 1639 have yielded one of the most scholarly travel accounts written in German by Adam

[446] On the latter, see John Gurney, 'Pietro della Valle: the limits of perception', *BSOAS* 49 (1986), 103–16; idem, 'Della Valle', *EIr* VII, 251–4.

[447] His account (*Comentarios*) of the embassy was published in Madrid in 2 volumes in 1903–5; cf. M. Bernadini, 'Figueroa', *EIr* IX, 612–3; cf. Carlos Alonso, *Garcia de Silva y Figueroa: Embajador en Persia* (Badajoz 1993); L. Gil, *Garcia de Silva y Figueroa: Epistolario diplomatico* (Caceres 1989).

[448] R. Ferrier. 'Herbert', *EIr* XII, 229–30.

Olearius [d. 1671].[449] It provides evidence that the Safavids has relations with even minor European powers and insights into relations with Russia. But his observations about social life, science and architecture are the most useful aspects for students of intellectual history.

Perhaps one of the most perceptive and useful accounts is the Huguenot Sir John/Jean Chardin [d. 1713] and his *Travels in Persia, 1673–77*.[450] Having linguistic ability in Persian and Turkish and familiarity with the cultural symbols of Safavid Persia, his account is a useful description of the capital Isfahan and its cultural life as well as a critical evaluation of the religious scholarly class. He notes the use of public ritual and Persian as a language of faith to spread Shiʿism. He also discusses the educational system and the standards in philosophy, science and medicine.[451]

One should not confuse this survey for an exhaustive inventory. There are no doubt other types of sources that may be of benefit as well as other historical sources, biographical dictionaries and travel accounts that I have not mentioned. I have only indicated those which I have used for Chapter 1 and also those that I would envisage using if I were studying other thinkers of the period.

---

[449] John Emerson, 'Adam Olearius and the literature of the Schleswig-Holstein missions to Russia and Iran, 1633–39', in J. Calmard (ed.), *Etudes Safavides* (Paris/Tehran 1993), 31–56.

[450] As it is out of copyright, it is usually available in various printings; one recent one is an old reprint with the translation and introduction of Sir Percy Sykes (New York 1988). For the man, see John Emerson, 'Chardin', *EIr* V, 369–77; C. van der Cruysse, *Chardin le Persan* (Paris 1998). For a study of his travels, see R. W. Ferrier, *A Journey to Persia: Jean Chardin's Portrait of a Seventeenth-Century Empire* (London 1996).

[451] Ferrier, *A Journey to Persia*, 97–109, 129–42.

A Brief Guide to Further Reading on Mullā Ṣadrā and the Safavid Period

One should start with the historical background in the relevant chapters in P. Jackson and L. Lockhart (eds), *The Cambridge History of Iran Volume 6: The Timurid and Safavid Periods* (Cambridge 1986). The chapter by Seyyed Hossein Nasr is a useful if rather partial approach to the religious history and scholarship of the Safavid period. The multi-authored *EI²* entry on the Ṣafawids is another, albeit more brief introduction.

Safavid Studies has blossomed in recent times. An initial conference on Isfahan was held at Harvard University in 1974 and later published as a special issue of *Iranian Studies* vol. 7 (1974). That initial impetus was taken up with the establishment of the Safavid Rountable. Four Safavid Roundtable conferences have now taken place and their proceedings are a good indication of avenues of inquiry and research: Paris in 1989 (Jean Calmard ed., *Etudes Safavides* Paris/Tehran 1993); Pembroke College, Cambridge University in 1993 (Charles Melville ed., *Safavid Persia* London 1996); Edinburgh University in 1998 (Andrew Newman ed. *Society and Culture in the Early Modern Middle East: Studies on Iran in the Safavid Period* Leiden 2003); and Bamberg University in 2003 (Bert Fragner ed. *Proceedings*, forthcoming). In recent years, wider linkages have been made connecting Safavid Studies with Mughal and Ottoman Studies. In 1991, the Accademia Nazionale dei Linei organised a conference in Rome on the Shiʿa in the Ottoman Empire (*La Shīʿa nell'Impero Ottomano* Rome 1993) which contains a number of studies on Safavid-Ottoman relations. The University of Utah hosted a colloquium on Safavid Iran in 1998 and a large number of the contributions have been published in a collection (M. Mazzaoui ed. *Safavid Persia and her Neighbours* Salt Lake City, UH 2003). The most recent expression of the comparative and cross-disciplinary meetings was the conference held at the School of Oriental and African Studies in the University of

London in 2002 on Iran and the World in the Safavid Age. No doubt the proceedings will soon be made available.

A few recent monographs are worthy mentioning. Said Amir Arjomand's revised University of Chicago dissertation *The Shadow of God and the Hidden Imam* (Chicago 1984) set the agenda for studies of Safavid society and continues to be influential. In 2000, the University of Utah Press published Sholeh Quinn's revised University of Chicago dissertation *Historical Writing during the Reign of Shah ʿAbbas*, a major contribution to Safavid historiography. Kathryn Babayan's Princeton University dissertation was substantially revised and portions published as *Mystics, Monarchs and Messiahs: Cultural Landscapes of Early Modern Iran* (Cambridge, MA 2002), an ambitious if not always successful cultural history of the Safavid period. She then published along with Susan Babaie, Massumeh Farhad and Ira Baghdiantz-McCabe a wide ranging study of shifts in art, culture, politics and society entitled *Slaves of the Shah: New Elites of Safavid Iran* (London 2004). Rula Abisaab's revised Yale University dissertation has also recently seen the light of day as *Converting Persia: Religion and Politics in Safavid Iran* (London 2004), a study of the impact of the ʿĀmilī immigrants in Persian scholarship, society and politics. We finally have a textbook to supplant Roger Savory (*Iran under the Safavids*, Cambridge 1980): Andrew Newman, *Safavid Iran* (London 2006).

Interest on the Safavids in Iran has seen a number of important editions of texts appearing which have facilitated the production of new monographic syntheses. Aḥmad Tājbakhāsh's *Tārīkh-i Ṣafaviyya* (Shiraz 1372 Sh/1993) is a useful historical survey. Aḥmad Tamīm-dārī has produced a two volume study of Sufism and poetry in the period entitled *ʿIrfān va adab dar ʿaṣr-i Ṣafavī* (Tehran 1373 Sh/1994). Religious history is covered by Maryam Mīr-Aḥmadī in her *Dīn va madhhab dar ʿaṣr-i Ṣafavī* (Tehran 1363 Sh/1984). Mansur Sefatgol's revised Tehran University dissertation on religious institutions and the development of religious thought in the period entitled *Sākhtār-i nihād va andīsha-yi dīnī dar Īrān-i ʿaṣr-i Ṣafavī* (Tehran 1381 Sh/2002) has recently appeared. A most novel contribution is Banafshah Hejazi's study of women and gender in the period entitled *Żaʿīfa: bar-rasī-yi jāygāh-i zan-i Īrānī dar ʿaṣr-i Ṣafavī* (Tehran 1381 Sh/2002).

Introductions to Islamic philosophy and thought remain, however, sparse beyond relevant sections in the works mentioned above. The *Anthologie* of Corbin and Āshtīyānī remains an indispensable source. *En Islam Iranien* (4 vols, Paris 1972) is also still a major achievement of Henry Corbin. His brief history of philosophers of the Safavid period is another useful starting point: *La Philosophie iranienne islamique aux XVIIe et XVIIIe siècles* (Paris 1981). *An Anthology of Philosophy in Persia* (5 vols, London 2006; the first 2 vols, New York/Oxford 1999–2000 were published in an awful state) will fill a major lacuna by providing students with translations of sections of major texts. The short introduction to metaphysics by the late seminarian and philosopher Mehdi Hairi Yazdi, *Haram-i hastī* (Tehran 1981) is a quite brilliant exposition of traditional Islamic philosophy with an eye to the analytical tradition. Numerous introductions by Āshtīyānī to editions that he produced are indicators to intellectual history; on metaphysics in particular, his *Hastī az naẓar-i falsafa va ʿirfān* (Mashhad 1980, rpt, Qum 1998) is traditional but useful.

On Mullā Ṣadrā himself, there are a number of biographies available, most of which are not worth considering. However, two that stand out for different reasons are Sayyid Jalāl al-Dīn Āshtiyānī, *Sharḥ-i ḥāl va ārāʾ-yi falsafī-yi Ṣadr al-Mutaʾallihīn* (Mashhad 1980) because of its engaging and sophisticated presentation of the ideas, and Sayyid Muḥammad Khāminihī, *Mullā Ṣadrā: zindagī, shakhṣiyyat va maktab-i Ṣadr al-mutaʾallihīn* (Tehran 1379 Sh/2000), which is the most sound biographical account. Fictionalised representations of Mullā Ṣadrā seem to be popular, not least with the dramatised series on his life shown on Iranian National Television (IRIB) in autumn 2004, and the appearance of two 'historical novels' on him, one in Persian and the other in Arabic: Nādir Ibrāhīmī, *Mardī dar tabʿīd-i abadī bar asās-i dāstān-i zindagī-yi Mullā Ṣadrā Shīrāzī* (Tehran 1375 Sh/1996), and Jamāl Yūzbakī, *Ghaḍbat al-falāsifa* (Tehran 1999). Given the present taste for a revival of Ibn Rushd among Arab thinkers (in opposition to the 'obscurantist Iranian thought of the East' condemned by Muḥammad ʿĀbid al-Jābirī in his series of works entitled *Naqd al-ʿaql al-ʿArabī*), it is interesting to see a Maghribī, Driss Hani (Idrīs Hānī) championing Mullā Ṣadrā in his provocative *Mā baʿd al-Rushdiyya: Mullā Ṣadrā rāʾid al-Ḥikma al-mutaʿāliya* (Beirut 2000). However, the best study of his philosophy albeit with an Avicennian bias remains Fazlur Rahman's *The Philosophy of Mulla Sadra* (Albany 1975). Seyyed Hossein Nasr was one of the first to write about Mullā Ṣadrā in a European language: his *Sadr al-Din al-Shirazi and his Transcendent Theosophy* (Tehran 1977) is still serviceable. Finally, one of the last students of Corbin, Christian Jambet has been working on philosophy in the Safavid period. In 2000, he published a study of the metaphysics of Mullā Ṣadrā entitled *L'acte d'être* (Paris). The encouraging state of play is that a number of younger academics have been working in this area and books on his thought are forthcoming from Cécile Bonmariage, Caner Dagli, David Dakake, Ibrahim Kalin, and Sajjad Rizvi. With the gradual appearance of critical editions of texts, we should soon be in the position to produce a new and far more definitive history of philosophy in the Safavid period.

Index of Qurʾanic Citations

Index of Ḥadīth Citations

Index of Persons, Groups and Places

ʿAbd al-Jalīl al-Qazwīnī Rāzī 38
ʿAbd al-Rafīʿ Ḥaqīqat 33
Abisaab, Rula 178
al-Abharī, Athīr al-Dīn Mufaḍḍal b. ʿUmar [d. 663/1264] 24, 71, 122, 130
Ādhar, Luṭf-ʿAlī Beg [d. 1194/1780] 160
Afandī, Mīrzā ʿAbd Allāh Tabrīzī Iṣfahānī [d. ca. 1130/1717] 156, 157–8, 166, 173
Akbar, Emperor Jalāl al-Dīn Muḥammad [d. 1605] 155
Akhbāriyya 37–41, 47, 165, 166, 172
ʿAlawī, Sayyid Aḥmad al-ʿĀmilī [d. 1054/1644] 32, 45, 48, 147, 168, 175
ʿAlīqulī b. Qarajghay Khān 151
al-ʿĀmilī, ʿAlī b. Hilāl Minshār [d. 1576] 9
al-ʿĀmilī, ʿAlī b. Muḥammad b. al-Ḥasan b. Zayn al-Dīn [d. 1103/1691–2] 38, 118, 172–3
al-ʿĀmilī, ʿIzz al-Dīn al-Ḥusayn b. ʿAbd al-Ṣamad [d. 1576], father of Shaykh Bahāʾī 9, 11
al-ʿĀmilī, Muḥammad b. al-Ḥasan [d. 1030/1621], the grandson of al-Shahīd II 17
al-ʿĀmilī, Nūr al-Dīn ʿAlī [d. 1086/1657–8] 37–8, 39, 158
al-ʿĀmilī, al-Sayyid Muḥammad b. ʿAlī [d. 1009/1600] 40
Āqā Buzurg Ṭihrānī [d. 1970] 160, 170
Āqājānī, Muḥammad Riḍā [d. after 1071/1660–1] 19–20, 147
Ardabīlī, Aḥmad known as al-Muqaddas [d. 1585] 31, 122, 123
Ardabīlī, Kamāl al-Dīn Ḥusayn Ilāhī [d. 950/1543–4] 142
Ardabīlī, Muḥammad b. ʿAlī Gharawī [d. 1001/1593] 155
Ardistānī, Mullā Muḥammad Ṣādiq [d. 1134/1722] 148, 149
Aristotle 122, 127, 130–1, 145
Aristotelianism 1, 151
Arjomand, Said Amir 33, 34
Armenians 174
Ashʿariyya 105, 117, 124
Ashkiwarī, Quṭb al-Dīn Muḥammad b. ʿAlī [=Sharīf-i Lāhījī, d. ca. 1095/1684] 152
Āshtiyānī, Sayyid Jalāl al-Dīn [d. 2005] 137, 144, 145, 179

Astarābād 11
Astarābādī, Mīrzā Muḥammad [d. 1028/1619] 39, 40
Astarābādī, Mullā Muḥammad Amīn b. Muḥammad Sharīf [d. 1033/1623–4 or 1036/1626–7] 37–46, 48
Avicenna [= Ibn Sīnā d. 1037] 1, 7, 11, 24, 67, 75, 105, 122, 123, 124, 128, 130, 131, 147, 148, 169

Babayan, Kathryn 178
Badāyūnī, ʿAbd al-Qādir [d. 1024/1615] 155
Bahmanyār [d. 1066] 11, 131
Baḥr al-ʿUlūm, al-Sayyid Muḥammad 171
al-Baḥrānī, al-Sayyid Mājid b. Hāshim al-Ṣādiqī [d. 1028/1619] 17
al-Baḥrānī, Yūsuf [d. 1186/1772] 22, 33, 167
Baghdad 10, 38, 118
al-Balāghī, Muḥammad ʿAlī b. Muḥammad al-Najafī [d. 1000/1591] 48
Baʿlbakk 9
Barakat, Muḥammad 116, 141
Basra 28–9
al-Bayḍāwī, Nāṣir al-Dīn Abuʾl-Khayr ʿAbd Allāh b. ʿUmar [d. 685/1286] 118, 119
Bayezid II [d. 918/1512] 122
Bīdābādī, Muḥammad [d. 1198/1783] 53, 149
al-Bīrjandī, ʿAbd ʿAlī b. Muḥammad [d. 934/1527] 128, 133
Browne, Edward 1
Bukhārī, Mīrak Muḥammad b. Mubārakshāh [d. ca. 880/1440] 69–70
al-Bukhārī, ʿUbayd Allāh b. Masʿūd al-Maḥbūbī [d. 747/1347] 121

Chardin, Sir John/Jean [d. 1713] 176
Charles I [King of England and Scotland, d. 1649] 175
Cooper, John 34
Corbin, Henry [d. 1978] 2, 5, 14, 23, 35, 65, 110, 113, 137–8, 140, 144, 178

Dabīrān Kātibī Qazwīnī, Najm al-Dīn ʿAlī b. ʿUmar [d. 675/1276] 24, 115, 131
Dashtakī, Mīr Ghiyāth al-Dīn Manṣūr [d. 1542] 7, 11, 96, 122, 124, 129, 140, 141, 151, 153, 164
Dashtakī, Mīr Niẓām al-Dīn Aḥmad [d. 1015/1606] 97, 111, 112, 113, 114, 115, 140
Dashtakī, Mīr Ṣadr al-Dīn Muḥammad [d. 1497] 41, 96, 111, 113, 115, 122, 140, 141, 153, 164
Davānī, Jalāl al-Dīn Muḥammad [d. 1502] 41, 95, 96, 97, 115, 120–1, 122, 123, 124, 127, 128, 129, 132, 141, 153

al-Fārābī, Abū Naṣr [d. 339/950] 124, 133

Fārisī, Abu'l-Khayr Muḥammad Taqī al-Dīn b. Muḥammad [d. 948/1542] 151
Fārs 5, 164
Fasā'ī, Mīrzā Ḥasan Ḥusaynī [d. 1316/1898] 164
Figueroa, Garcia de Silva y [d. 1624] 175

Ghazālī, Abū Ḥāmid Muḥammad [d. 505/1111] 35, 88, 125, 131, 132
Gīlānī, Mullā Naẓar ʿAlī [fl. 1193/1779] 149
Gīlānī, Mullā Shamsā [d. 1080/1669–70] 102, 147
Goa 176
Golconda 39, 157
de Gouvea, Antonio [d. 1628] 174

Ḥājjī Khalīfa [d. 1067/1657] 161
Ḥasan Beg Rūmlū 162
Ḥanābila 42, 43
Ḥashwiyya 38, 42
Herat 9, 162
Herbert, Sir Thomas [d. 1682] 23, 175
al-Ḥillī, Fakhr al-Dīn Muḥammad b. al-Ḥasan [d. 771/1370] 132
al-Ḥillī, Najm al-Dīn Abu'l-Qāsim Jaʿfar b. al-Ḥasan [d. 676/1277] 119, 127
Horten, Max 137
al-Ḥurr al-ʿĀmilī, Muḥammad b. al-Ḥasan [d. 1104/1693] 156
Ḥusaynī, Shah Ṭāhir [d. ca. 956/1549] 164
Hyderabad 157

Iamblichus 151
Ibn Abī Jumhūr al-Aḥsā'ī [d. 906/1501] 2
Ibn ʿArabī [d. 638/1240] 20, 24, 33, 62, 99, 111, 129, 132, 152, 172
Ibn Bābawayh, Muntajab al-Dīn ʿAlī al-Rāzī [fl. 600/1203–4] 156
Ibn al-Fāriḍ, Abu'l-Qāsim ʿUmar [d. 632/1235] 131
Ibn Ḥājib [d. 646/1248] 120, 127, 130
Ibn al-Muṭahhar known as al-ʿAllāma al-Ḥillī [d. 726/1325] 38, 39, 45, 119, 120, 121, 122, 126, 131, 133, 134, 169
Ibn al-Nafīs al-Dimashqī [d. 687/1288] 125, 126
Ibn Turka Iṣfahānī [d. ca. 835/1432] 2
al-Ījī, Aḍud al-Dīn [d. 756/1355] 111, 120, 121, 132
Illuminationists [*Ishrāqiyyūn*, 'Platonists'] 7–8, 139–40
Imam ʿAlī b. Abī Ṭālib [first Imam, d. 661] 11, 29, 35, 129, 169
Imam al-Riḍā, ʿAlī b. Mūsā [eighth Imam, d. 817] 10
Imam Zayn al-ʿĀbidīn, ʿAlī b. al-Ḥusayn [fourth Imam, d. 712] 133, 166
Injū, Abū Isḥāq 6

Isfahan 9, 10, 11, 14, 16, 17, 21, 31, 33, 34, 35, 138, 139, 148, 160, 164, 168, 174, 175, 176
Iṣfahānī, Muḥammad Maʿṣūm [fl. 1642] 163
al-Iṣfahānī, Shams al-Dīn Maḥmūd b. ʿAbd al-Raḥmān [d. 749/1349] 121
Iskandar Beg Turkomān [fl. 1629] 162
Istanbul 175
Izutsu, Toshihiko [d. 1993] 137

Jābirī, Mīrzā Salmān [d. 1583] 6
Jaghmīnī, Maḥmūd b. ʿUmar [d. 744/1344] 128
al-Jāribirdī, Aḥmad b. al-Ḥasan [d. 746/1345] 127
al-Jazāʾirī, al-Sayyid ʿAbd Allāh al-Mūsawī [d. 1173/1759–60] 166
al-Jazāʾirī, al-Sayyid Niʿmat Allāh [d. 1112/1701] 171–2, 173

Kahak 14, 15, 16, 31, 35
Kamarihī, Sayyid ʿAlī-Naqī [d. 1060/1650] 35
Karakī, ʿAbd al-ʿĀlī b. ʿAlī [d. 993/1585] 9, 11
al-Karakī, Mīr Ḥabīb Allāh 17
al-Karakī, al-Shaykh ʿAlī [d. 940/1534] 11, 135, 168, 169
al-Karakī, al-Sayyid al-Ḥusayn b. Ḥasan [d. 1592–3] 9, 10, 11, 122
al-Karakī al-Sayyid al-Ḥusayn b. Ḥaydar 167
Karbalāʾ 11
Kāshān 9, 12, 15, 21, 22
Kāshānī, ʿAbd al-Razzāq [d. 736/1336] 98, 129
Kāshānī, Afḍal al-Dīn [d. 1214] 94, 123
Kāshānī, Muḥsin Fayḍ [d. 1680] 15, 16–17, 21, 24, 29, 32, 41, 111, 147, 148, 156
Kāshānī, Āqā Muẓaffar Ḥusayn 145
Kāẓimiyya 10
Khafarī, Shams al-Dīn Muḥammad [d. 942/1535 or 957/1550] 114, 125, 128, 130, 131–3, 142, 147, 154, 164
Khājavī, Muḥammad 5, 53, 76–8
Khājūʾī, Mullā Ismāʿīl Māzandarānī [d. 1173/1760] 149
Khāminihī, Sayyid Muḥammad 24, 42, 52, 149
Khān, Allahvirdī [d. 1613] 23
Khān, Imāmqulī [d. 1633] 22–3, 175
Khātūnābādī, Muḥammad Ḥusayn [d. 1151/1739] 173
al-Kharsān, al-Sayyid Muḥammad Mahdī 171
al-Khaṭīb al-Qazwīnī [d. 739/1338] 121
Khayr al-Nisāʾ Begum [=Mahd-i ʿUlyā, d. 1579] 6
Khusrawshāhī, ʿAbd al-Ḥamīd [d. 1254] 103
Khwāndamīr [d. 941/1534–5] 162

Khwānsārī, Ḥusayn [d. 1098/1686–7] 147
Khwānsārī, Jamāl al-Dīn [d. 1125/1713] 33
Kintūrī, Sayyid Iʿjāz Ḥusayn [d. 1286/1870] 160
Kirmān 171
al-Kirmānī, Burhān al-Dīn Nafīs b. ʿIwaḍ [d. 853/1449] 126
al-Kīshī, Shams al-Dīn Muḥammad [d. 695/1296] 118
Kulaynī, Abū Jaʿfar Muḥammad b. Yaʿqūb [d. 329/941] 47, 73, 168

Lāhījī, ʿAbd al-Razzāq Fayyāḍ [d. 1072/1661–2] 16–9, 21, 34, 146
Lāhījī, al-Ḥasan b. ʿAbd al-Razzāq [d. 1709] 21, 148
Lahore 155, 156
Lakhnawī, Sayyid ʿAbd al-Ḥayy b. Fakhr al-Dīn Ḥasanī [d. 1341/1923] 159
Leaman, Oliver 139
Lucknow 158, 159

Madrasa-yi Fayḍiyya 17
Madrasa-yi Khān 2, 22, 23, 27, 175
Madrasa-yi Maʿṣūma 18
Madrasa-yi Manṣūriyya 164
Majlisī II, Muḥammad Bāqir [d. 1110/1699] 13, 22, 33, 50, 156, 166, 167, 173–4
Majlisī I, Muḥammad Taqī [d. 1070/1659–60] 22, 49, 166
Mashhad 9, 10, 11, 20, 145, 146, 171
Maʿṣūm-ʿAlī-Shāh Shīrāzī [d. 1926] 14, 160
Maʿṣūma [d. 1061/1651], wife of Mullā Ṣadrā 21
Maʿṣūma, daughter of Mullā Ṣadrā 21
Maybudī, Mīr Ḥusayn [d. 910/1504] 70, 122, 129
Māzandarānī, Muḥammad Ṣāliḥ [d. 1081/1670] 49
Mecca 14, 19, 20, 28, 37, 41, 157
Medina 17, 20, 42, 157
Membre, Michele 174
Mīr Dāmād [Muḥammad Bāqir Astarābādī, d. 1631] 8, 10, 11–3, 15, 17, 20, 26, 32, 34, 48, 68, 76, 116, 121, 126–8, 138, 139, 140, 145, 147, 151, 152, 155, 157, 159, 160, 161, 167, 168, 175
Mīr Findiriskī [d. 1641] 14, 145, 146, 147
Mīrkhwānd [d. 903/1498] 161
Mīrzā Ṭālib Khān [d. 1044/1634] 17
Modarressi, Hossein 38
Mohaghegh, Mehdi 137
Muḥammad ʿAlam al-Hudā [d. 1115/1703–4], son of Fayḍ and grandson of Mullā Ṣadrā 29–30
Mughals 158, 159

Muḥammad Quṭb-Shāh [d. 1035/1626] 39
Muḥammad Shāh Taqī al-Dīn Nassāba [d. 1019/1610] 40
al-Muḥibbī, Muḥammad al-Amīn b. Faḍl Allāh al-Dimashqī [d. 1111/1699] 158
Mushaʿshaʿ 164
Murtaḍā-qulī Khān 17

Nadwat al-ʿUlamāʾ 159
Najaf 11, 29, 30, 34, 40, 156
Narāqī, Mullā Muḥammad Mahdī [d. 1209/1794–5] 149
al-Nasafī, Abuʾl-Barakāt ʿAbd Allāh b. Aḥmad [d. 710/1310] 118
Nasr, Seyyed Hossein 2, 4, 110, 137–8, 139, 177
Naṣrābādī, Muḥammad Ṭāhir Naṣrābādī 160
Nayrīzī, Maḥmūd b. Muḥammad 142
Nayrīzī, Quṭb al-Dīn Muḥammad, son-in-law of Mullā Ṣadrā 21
Neoplatonism 1, 2, 3, 8, 129, 139, 172
Newman, Andrew 138, 178
Nūrbakhshī order 13, 160
Nūrī, Mullā ʿAlī [d. 1246/1831] 52, 149, 164
Nūrī, Mīrzā Ḥusayn 33

Olearius, Adam [d. 1671] 175–6
Ottoman Empire 120, 121, 132, 158, 160, 163, 170, 177

Peripatetics [*mashshāʾiyyūn*, ‘Aristotelians’] 7, 11
Philip III [Habsburg King of Spain, d. 1621] 174, 175
Pīrzāda, Muḥammad Rafīʿ [late 17th century] 148
Plato 92, 151
Platonism 130, 139
Plotinus [d. 270] 3, 130, 151
Porphyry [d. 309] 3, 105
Pythagoras 151

al-Qaffāl, Abū Bakr Muḥammad b. ʿAlī al-Shāshī [d. 365/976] 86
Qawāmī, Ibrāhīm b. Yaḥyā, father of Mullā Ṣadrā 5–6
Qazwīn 8, 9, 10, 11, 13, 14, 170
Qazwīnī, ʿAbd al-Nabī [fl. 1191/1777] 22, 157
Qazwīnī, Mullā Khalīl b. Ghāzī [d. 1089/1678] 49
Qazwīnī, Sayyid Abuʾl-Ḥasan Rafīʿī [d. 1976] 28
Qum 14, 15, 16, 17, 21, 22, 23, 29, 31, 33, 35, 150
Qummī, ʿAbbās [d. 1359/1940] 173
Qummī, Muḥammad Ṭāhir [d. 1098/1686] 31

Qummī, Qāḍī Sa'īd [d. 1107/1696] 31, 34, 139, 144, 148
al-Qūshjī, 'Alā' al-Dīn 'Alī b. Muḥammad [d. 879/1474] 114, 121

Rahman, Fazlur 179
Rayy 38
al-Rāzī, Fakhr al-Dīn [d. 606/1210] 126, 128
Rāzī, Mīrzā Żiyā' al-Dīn Muḥammad 12, 21
Rāzī, Mullā 'Abd al-Raḥīm b. Muḥammad Yūnus Damāvandī [d. before 1170/1757] 148
Rāzī, Qawām al-Dīn Muḥammad [late 17th century] 148

Sabzavār 11, 164
Sabzavārī, Muḥammad Bāqir [d. 1090/1679] 33, 148
Sabzavārī, Mullā Hādī [d. 1289/1873] 52, 53, 63, 138, 149, 164
al-Ṣadr, al-Sayyid al-Ḥasan [d. 1354/1935] 157
al-Sakkākī [d. 626/1229] 121, 132
al-Samāhījī, 'Abd Allāh [d. 1135/1722] 165
Sāmarrā' 160
Sammākī, Mīr Fakhr al-Dīn Muḥammad b. Ḥusayn Astarābādī [fl. 980/1572] 11, 121, 140, 141, 142
Savory, Roger 6
Schmidtke, Sabine 165
Shah 'Abbās I [d. 1629] 2, 8, 10, 11, 16, 34, 162, 163, 164, 174
Shah 'Abbās II [d. 1667] 16, 17, 34, 146, 147, 160, 172
Shah Ismā'īl II [d. 985/1577] 132
Shah Muḥammad Khudābanda [d. 1587] 5–6
Shah Nāṣir al-Dīn Qājār [d. 1896] 165
Shah Ṣafī [d. 1642] 11, 17, 34, 35, 163
Shah Ṭahmāsp [d. 1576] 6, 11, 174
Shahid II [=Zayn al-Dīn b. 'Alī al-'Āmilī, exec. 1558] 9, 17, 22, 39, 120, 122, 124, 169
Shahrastānī, Abu'l-Fatḥ Muḥammad b. 'Abd al-Karīm [d. 548/1153] 151
Shahrazūrī, Shams al-Dīn Muḥammad [fl. 688/1288] 151
al-Sharīf al-Jurjānī [d. 816/1413] 121, 127, 131, 169
Shaykh Bahā'ī [Bahā' al-Dīn Muḥammad b. al-Ḥusayn al-'Āmilī, d. 1621] 8–10, 13, 16, 24, 28, 34, 41, 116, 127, 135, 137, 155, 157, 160, 164, 170
Shaykh al-Mufīd [d. 413/1022] 38
al-Shaykh al-Ṣadūq, Ibn Bābawayh al-Qummī [d. 381/991] 120, 134, 168
Shaykhiyya 138
Shiraz 2, 5, 7–8, 10, 11, 12, 13, 14, 16, 17, 21, 22, 24, 31, 33, 35, 40, 41, 116, 152, 153, 156, 157, 164, 174, 175

Shīrāzī, Ibrāhīm b. Ṣadr al-Dīn Muḥammad [d. 1660–1], son of Mullā Ṣadrā 5–6, 14, 15, 21, 167
Shīrāzī, Jamāl al-Dīn Maḥmūd [fl. 1550] 122
Shīrāzī, Mīr Makhdūm [d. 995/1586] 132
Shīrāzī, Mīrzā-jān Ḥabīb Allāh Bāghnawī [d. 994/1586] 142
Shīrāzī, Muḥammad Riḍā, son of Mullā Ṣadrā 22
Shīrāzī, Niẓām al-Dīn Aḥmad [d. 1074/1664], son of Mullā Ṣadrā 22
Shīrāzī, Quṭb al-Dīn Maḥmūd b. Masʿūd [d. 710/1311] 75, 116, 126
Shīrāzī, Sayyid ʿAlī-Khān b. Aḥmad Ibn Maʿṣūm [d. ca. 1118/1707] 157
Shīrāzī, Shāh Fatḥ Allāh [d. 997/1589] 40
Shūstarī, Sayyid Nūr Allāh b. Sharīf al-Dīn Ḥusaynī Marʿashī Tustarī [=Qāḍī Nūr Allāh , d. 1019/1610] 155–6
al-Siyūrī, Miqdād b. ʿAbd Allāh [d. 826/1423] 120
Skinner, Quentin 3
Stewart, Devin 39–40, 118, 119, 170
Sufis 21, 24, 31, 32, 36, 49, 152, 170
Suhrawardī order 124
al-Suhrawardī, Abū Ḥafṣ ʿUmar [d. 632/1234] 125
Suhrawardī, Shihāb al-Dīn Yaḥyā [d. 586/1191] 8, 11, 24, 66, 75, 113, 124, 130, 131, 132, 138, 152, 172
Sulṭān Ḥamza [d. 1586] 6
Sulṭān al-ʿulamāʾ, Sayyid Ḥusayn b. Rafīʿ al-Dīn Marʿashī [d. 1064/1654] 34
Sulṭān Yaʿqūb [d. 896/1490] 121

Ṭabāṭabāʾī, Sayyid Bahāʾ al-Dīn Muḥammad [=Fāḍil-i Hindī, d. 1137/1725] 148
Ṭabāṭabāʾī, Sayyid Muḥammad Ḥusayn [d. 1981] 5, 52
Ṭabāṭabāʾī, Sayyid Muḥammad Rafīʿ al-Dīn b. Ḥaydar known as Mullā Rafīʿā Nāʾinī [d. 1083/1672–3] 49
al-Ṭabrisī, Abū ʿAlī al-Faḍl b. al-Ḥasan [d. 548/1154] 118, 135
Tabrīz 17, 174
Tabrīzī, Rajab ʿAlī [d. 1080/1669–70] 146, 147
Tafrishī, Mullā Murād [d. 1051/1641–2] 24
Tafrishī, Muṣṭafā b. Ḥusayn Ḥusaynī Iṣfahānī [d. ca. 1030/1621] 155
al-Taftazānī, Saʿd al-Dīn Masʿūd b. ʿUmar [d. 792/1389] 24, 120, 121, 129
Taḥtānī, Quṭb al-Dīn Muḥammad Rāzī [d. 765/1365] 128, 132, 133
Ṭāliqānī, Mullā Muḥammad Naʿīmā [d. after 1151/1738] 148
Tehran 145, 147, 149, 150
Ṭihrānī, Mīrzā Muḥammad b. Rajab-ʿAlī ʿAskarī [d. 1371/1952] 167
Tunikābunī, Ḥusayn [d. 1105/1693–4] 19–20, 147
Tunikābunī, Muḥammad [d. ca. 1892] 33, 159
al-Ṭūsī, Muḥammad b. al-Ḥasan [d. 460/1067] 118, 134, 156, 168

Ṭūsī, Naṣīr al-Dīn [d. 672/1274] 11, 18, 19, 24, 103, 114, 121, 122, 127, 128, 129, 130, 132–3, 147, 169

Umm Kulthūm, daughter of Mullā Ṣadrā 21
al-Urmawī, Sirāj al-Dīn Maḥmūd b. Abī Bakr [d. 682/1283] 131
Uṣūliyya 37–8, 42, 43, 47, 165
Uzbeks 155, 163

della Valle, Pietro [d. 1652] 175

Waḥīd-i Qazwīnī, Muḥammad Ṭāhir [d. 1110/1698–9] 163
White, Hayden 3

Yazdī, Mullā ʿAbd Allāh [d. 981/1573] 9, 130

al-Zamakhsharī, Abuʾl-Qāsim Jār Allāh Maḥmūd b. ʿUmar [d. 538/1144] 117, 132, 169
al-Zarīrātī, Taqī al-Dīn ʿAbd Allāh [d. 729/1329] 118
al-Zubārī, al-Sharīf Jalāl al-Dīn Abū Manṣūr Muḥammad Ḥusaynī [d. 539/1145] 118
Zubayda, daughter of Mullā Ṣadrā 21
Zunūzī, ʿAlī [d. 1889–90] 6, 52, 53